BASIC TEACHINGS OF
THE GREAT PHILOSOPHERS

BASIC TEACHINGS OF
THE GREAT PHILOSOPHERS

A Survey of Their Basic Ideas

S. E. FROST, JR., Ph.D.

REVISED EDITION

ANCHOR BOOKS
DOUBLEDAY
NEW YORK LONDON TORONTO SYDNEY AUCKLAND

An Anchor Book
PUBLISHED BY DOUBLEDAY
a division of Bantam Doubleday Dell Publishing Group, Inc.
1540 Broadway, New York, New York 10036

Anchor Books, Doubleday, and the portrayal of an anchor
are trademarks of Doubleday, a division of Bantam Doubleday
Dell Publishing Group, Inc.

Basic Teachings of the Great Philosophers
was originally published in hardcover by
Doubleday in 1942. The revised edition was originally
published in paperback by Dolphin Books in 1962.
The Anchor Books edition is published by arrangement with Doubleday.

Library of Congress Cataloging-in-Publication Data
Frost, S. E., 1899–
Basic teachings of the great philosophers:
a survey of their basic ideas / S. E. Frost. —
Rev. ed., 1st Anchor Books ed.
p. cm.
Reprint. Originally published: Garden City, N.Y.:
Doubleday, 1962.
1. Philosophy—Introductions. I. Title.
BD21.F73 1989 89-48158
100—dc20 CIP
ISBN 0-385-03007-X

25 27 29 30 28 26 24

CONTENTS

BASIC TEACHINGS OF
THE GREAT PHILOSOPHERS

INTRODUCTION

Everyone, whether he be plowman or banker, clerk or captain, citizen or ruler, is, in a real sense, a philosopher. Being human, having a highly developed brain and nervous system, he must think; and thinking is the pathway to philosophy.

The world in which we live will not let us rest. It keeps prodding us, challenging us with problems to be solved, demanding that we act wisely or be destroyed by the forces which inhabit our world. In this way experiences are born—hungers and satisfactions, pains and pleasures, sights, feelings, sounds, and a host of others.

But we cannot rest contented with a mass of unrelated experiences scattered at random throughout life. We must take our experiences and weave them into some kind of a pattern, a whole which is more or less satisfying. This pattern, this whole, is our philosophy.

Your philosophy, then, is the meaning which the world has for you. It is your answer to the question, "Why?" Having fitted your experiences into a whole, having related them to each other, you say of the world, "This is *the* way things fit together. This is *the* world as I understand it. This is *my* philosophy."

Your philosophy and the philosophy of those whose names appear in books of Philosophy differ only in that the latter use more experiences in weaving their patterns, those patterns which satisfy them, and are more careful and thorough in fitting their experiences into a pattern. Theirs is a more complete, more all-inclusive pattern, more logical, more consistent, more accurate.

What are the great philosophic problems which puzzle all of us, and which the great philosophers throughout the ages have sought to answer? We find that there are ten major problems which have always challenged thinking men and women.

The first of these problems is: *What is the nature of the universe?* Did this universe come into being through an act of divine creation or is it the result of a gradual process of growth? Of what substance or substances is the universe created? How does the universe change?

The second problem is: *What is man's place in the universe?* Is the human individual the crowning achievement of a growing and creating universe, or is he a mere speck of dust in unlimited space? Does the universe care for you and me, or are we of no more concern than a grain of sand on a vast beach? Can we mould the universe to our liking, or will it eventually destroy us?

The third great problem is: *What is good and what is evil?* How are we to know the good from the evil? Has some divine power set standards of good and evil for all times, or are good and evil matters of the local culture? Is good in the very nature of things, or is it something which we can decide for ourselves? How can we distinguish good from evil?

A fourth problem is: *What is the nature of God?* Is God a being very much like man who governs the universe, or is He a spirit which pervades everything? Is God all-powerful, all-good, and all-just, or is He just another individual who has little more power or insight than you and I?

A fifth problem is related to the question of *Fate versus free will?* Are we free individuals who can make our choices and determine our actions without let or hindrance, or are we determined by a fate over which we have no control? Can we determine tomorrow in any significant sense, or is it all determined for us from the beginning of time?

The sixth problem is concerned with the *Soul and immortality*. What is the soul about which we have heard so much? Is it of such a nature that it lives after the death of the body, or does it die with the body? Is there a future life in which good is rewarded and evil punished, or does death mark the end of everything?

A seventh problem consists of man's questions about *Man and the state*. Is the state a human creation which has been brought into being to serve man, or is it something that has divine origin? Are the rulers of states given their power by those they rule or by God? Does man have a right to rebel against his rulers and create a new kind of state? What is the best form of state and what is the worst?

The eighth problem is that of *Man and education*. What is education? Why do we have a system of education and why do we send our children to school? Who shall control education, the people or the state? Is education designed to make free men or to make men who will serve blindly an all-powerful state?

The ninth problem has to do with *Mind and matter*. Which is superior, mind or matter? Is matter a creation of mind, or is mind merely another kind of matter? Can mind be superior and free from matter, or is it so tied up with matter that it is doomed? Is matter the source of all evil in the universe? How can mind remain pure and at the same time inhabit a body?

And the tenth problem is concerned with *Ideas and thinking*. Where do we get our ideas? Are they inherent in the very nature of our minds, or do they come to us from outside the mind? What are the laws of thinking? How can we be sure that our thinking is correct? Is thinking significant in the universe or is it a mere sham?

This book brings together the answers which the great philosophers of all times have offered to the problems which you and I think about today. They have toiled to form an answer that seems to them satisfactory. We have brought it to you.

Our method is to bring together what each philosopher has written on each of these problems as briefly and concisely as possible. This is done so that you, busy as you are, do not have to read long discourses on philosophy to discover that which will help you in your thinking. By reading any one of the chapters in this book, you can get a clear picture of what the philosophers down through the ages have said about one of your real problems.

Although each chapter is a unit to itself and can be read without reference to the other chapters, it is advisable for the reader to begin with the first chapter and go through the book. This will give you a wide view of the great philosophers and will help you to see each problem or group of problems in relation to the other problems and groups of problems in the book.

Following these ten chapters arranged according to philosophical problems, we include a new chapter dealing with *Some Recent Approaches to Philosophy*. The views of the men discussed in this eleventh chapter apply to many of the problems which are the topics of earlier chapters and should be considered in relation to them. But most readers will prefer to have these newer approaches grouped together at this one point in the book, as a survey of important aspects of recent philosophical thought.

At the end of the book you will find Biographical Notes concerning the philosophers whom you meet in the pages of the book. This section should be used as a quick reference when you want to know the exact dates during which the philosopher lived or other pertinent facts about him.

Chapter I
THE NATURE OF THE UNIVERSE

THALES PYTHAGORAS HERACLITUS
PARMENIDES PLATO ARISTOTLE
AUGUSTINE AQUINAS BACON HOBBES
DESCARTES SPINOZA LOCKE KANT HEGEL
MILL DEWEY BERGSON SANTAYANA

*The world in which you and I live was here long be-
fore us. How did it come to be? Was it created, or
has it existed forever? Who or what made it, and how
was it made? Are the trees, stars, men and women
really "there," or are they mere creations of our minds
or of the mind of God? How came this universe to be,
and what is it made of?*

There is no one of us who has not wondered how the
universe came into being. This world, with its flowers,
rivers, rocks, sky, stars, sun, and moon, all did not come
about by mere chance, we reason. All that we see around
us, and all that we know of, must have become what it is
today by some process. If we could understand this process, we would understand the nature of the universe.

The earliest people that we have any records of had
theories of the beginning and nature of things. They wove
these ideas into their religion and the priests and religious
men explained them to the young men, who in turn passed
them on to their children. In the first book of the Bible,
Genesis, is one of these theories. Here we are told that God

created the world out of nothing in six days. He made light and darkness, the sun, moon, and stars, the earth and the waters, and finally made all living things, including man. Then, when all was completed and man along with woman was placed in a beautiful garden, God came to the world and walked in the garden, contented with his handiwork.

The Views of the Early Greek Philosophers

The earliest philosophers, the Greeks, were greatly interested in this problem of the nature of the universe. Indeed, it was the first problem they attacked. Just as children break open their toys to discover how they are made, so these philosophers of the childhood of the human race sought to break apart the universe in their minds, and to penetrate the mystery of the making of all things found in it. "What is the 'stuff' from which all things come?" they asked themselves. "How does it happen that there are many things in the universe?"

THALES, who lived in Miletus in Ancient Greece (about 600 B.C.), was the first to propose a solution of this problem. He told his neighbors that water was the original "stuff." He saw water turning into a solid, ice, when it was frozen, and into air, steam, when heated. Therefore, he reasoned that everything, from the hardest rock to the lightest air, originally came from water and in the end returned to water.

A little later another citizen of Miletus, ANAXIMANDER, wrote that the original "stuff" of which everything in the universe was made was not, as Thales had suggested, water, but was a living mass which filled all space. He called this mass "the infinite." In the beginning, he told his fellows, this mass, this "infinite," was whole, not broken into pieces. But it contained "motion." This "motion" caused it to begin to move up and down, back and forth, and around. Slowly pieces were broken off from the mass so that eventually all the things which we now have in the universe came into being. As the motion continued, he believed, these innumerable pieces would be brought back together and the mass, the "infinite," would assume its original unbroken unity.

Anaximander wrote a very detailed account of how he believed the world, the sun, the stars, air, animals, fishes, and man developed out of this original mass.

A third resident of Miletus, ANAXIMINES, was not satisfied with the accounts which had been given by these two thinkers who had preceded him. He suggested that the original "stuff" of which all else in the universe was made was air. He realized that men and animals breathe air and are able to live, and reasoned that the air turned into flesh, bone, and blood. Therefore, he went on to reason that air could become wind, clouds, water, earth, and stone.

These three philosophers of Miletus were interested in discovering the original "stuff" of which all else in the universe was made. They were followed by a group of philosophers who, although they were interested in the same problem, were more interested in finding out in what ways the many things in the universe were related. These were the *Pythagoreans*, a group or school founded by *Pythagoras*.

PYTHAGORAS and the Pythagoreans were impressed by the fact that many things in the universe were related in ways that could be stated by numbers. For example, the tone of a wire or piece of gut is related to its length in a manner that can be expressed in numbers. So, they reasoned, number must be this "stuff" for which philosophers were looking. To them numbers became things, entities, and they taught that the whole universe was built of numbers. They believed that since the harmonious octave reached over eight notes, eight was friendship. A point, they held, was one, and a line two. And on they went to develop a most complicated system of numbers in their effort to show how everything was actually made of numbers.

All the philosophers whom we have mentioned so far took it for granted that things change. They saw change all about them and did not recognize it as a problem. Water changed into ice or into steam, air became wind, numbers became things, motion was in everything producing these changes. For them this fact just was; and why be concerned about it?

But as philosophers continued to work with this problem of the nature of the universe, they began to recognize that change was itself a problem. What is it? How does it come about? Is there really change, or do we just imagine that things change? These questions began to rear their heads and demand an answer.

This fact of change so impressed HERACLITUS, a son of a noble family of Ephesus, that he concluded that fire was the original "stuff" of which all else in the universe was made. Fire, he believed, was forever changing, never still, never the same. Since everything is constantly changing, since change is the fundamental characteristic of the universe, the forever-changing fire must be the material of the universe. "You could not," he wrote, "step twice into the same river, for other and yet other waters are ever flowing on." There is nothing permanent, stable. Change is all that is.

We may think that we see things that do not change, Heraclitus taught, but we are fooled. If we could really see what is happening, if we had eyes powerful enough to see exactly what is happening, we would realize that even the most stable thing in the universe is actually changing all the time. The universe, then, is ruled by "strife." The moment a thing is made, strife begins to break it up. All things are changing all the time, and there is nothing permanent.

While Heraclitus was preaching the doctrine that change is the essence of all things, there were Greek philosophers living in Elea who taught that change is impossible. Nothing, they said, can possibly change. If we think we see change, we are fooled; for it cannot be. XENOPHANES, the earliest of these Eleatics, believed that the universe was a solid mass which was forever unchangeable, unmovable. The parts might change, but the whole could never change. PARMENIDES, another member of this school at Elea, taught that all change is inconceivable. If there were such a thing as change, he reasoned, something would have to come from nothing, and that was impossible. What we see with our eyes is not true but an illusion. The universe is unchangeable and unmovable. ZENO, a third member of this school, sought to prove that anyone who attempted to prove the existence of change would contradict himself.

These arguments of Heraclitus and of the Eleatics were so interesting to philosophers that some set about to see if the positions of both sides could be reconciled in some way. They felt that this "riddle of permanence and change" had to be solved, and they turned their attention to the task.

EMPEDOCLES agreed with the Eleatics when he said that in the strict sense there can be no change, but he also agreed with Heraclitus in holding that there is "mingling and separation." The universe, said he, is composed of four elements or "roots of things": earth, air, fire, and water. There are millions and millions of very tiny particles of each element. These combine in various ways to form the many things in the universe. As things decay or change, the elements separate. Then they may come together or mingle again in another thing. The elements never change. They are permanent. Thus, actually there is no change, but merely a mingling and separating of elements. This mingling and separating is caused, he believed, by Love and Hate. Love brings the elements together to form things. Hate breaks them apart.

Empedocles' solution of the problem of change and permanence interested ANAXAGORAS but did not satisfy him. After much study, he reached the conclusion that there must be more than four elements. Indeed, he became convinced that there were untold millions of elements or substances. Each of these was in untold millions of tiny pieces. Flesh was a result of millions of flesh elements coming together in one place. Bone was the result of millions of bone elements combining. So with everything in the universe. Numbers of elements come together and the thing is formed. No element can be changed into another. Therefore there is in reality no change. But as these elements combine, separate, and recombine, we have change. These elements combine and separate, not because of anything in them, but because of the rotation of the heavenly bodies. As a whirling motion was first produced in the original mass of elements lying quiet, they began to combine and the many things in the universe were formed.

All of this thinking paved the way for another important group of early Greek thinkers, the *Atomists*. The most noted members of this group were LEUCIPPUS and DEMOCRITUS. These men agreed with their predecessors that change was a result of the mingling and separating of tiny units. But they disagreed with them as to the nature of these elements. All the thinkers before the Atomists had taught that the elements differed in quality. There were flesh elements, bone elements, hair elements, and so on. The flesh elements were different from the bone or hair elements. The Atomists taught that all units, or atoms, are alike as far as quality is concerned. Some have hooks, others eyes, and still others grooves, humps, or depressions. As these atoms unite in different ways and in different numbers, things are formed. Each atom has motion inside it, so that it moves about of its own accord and attaches itself to other atoms.

Change, then, for the Atomists was a matter of the mingling and separating of atoms. The atoms never changed, but were eternal, minutely small, and all alike. Real change of an atom was impossible. The only change possible was as atoms grouped themselves together to form a thing or separated from each other.

Thus the early Greeks, working with the problem of the nature of the universe for about 250 years, reached the conclusion that everything in the universe was composed by the uniting in various ways and in various numbers of tiny atoms which were all alike.

Plato's Theory of the Universe

None of these early theories satisfied PLATO, one of the greatest thinkers of all times. For Plato, the world which we see, touch, and experience through our other senses is not real, but is a copy world. In it we find things changing, coming and going, and in great abundance. It is a world of many mistakes, deformities, evils. It exists and we experience it every day. But it is not real.

There is, however, a real world in which are to be found the true things of which all that we experience are mere copies. He called this the world of "ideas." Here is to be found the ideal tree of which all trees which we see are copies, the ideal house, and ideas of all other objects in the universe. These are perfect, do not change in any way, never fade or die, but remain forever.

These "ideas" or "forms" (Plato uses both words to describe them) were never created, but have existed from the very beginning in just the perfect state in which they will always exist. They are independent of all things, and are not influenced by the changes which take place in the world which we experience through our senses. These objects which we experience are reflections of these "eternal patterns."

All "ideas" are arranged in the "ideal world" in order; the "highest idea," the idea of perfect goodness, being at the top.

But there is another principle in the universe, that of "matter." This is all that "ideas" are not. It may be thought of as the raw material upon which the "ideas" are impressed. Let us think, for example, of the work of a sculptor. He has an idea of a figure which he wishes to reproduce in marble, let us say. Now, this idea is independent of all the marble in the universe. But the marble is necessary for its realization so that others may experience it through their senses. Therefore, the sculptor takes a slab of marble and creates a statue. The marble, as raw material, has the idea impressed upon it. The sculptor may make many statues without affecting his idea in the least.

In this way Plato thought that the world was created. Nature,—all that we experience through our senses,—owes its existence to the influence of the world of ideas upon matter. It is not the "real" world, but an impression of the "real" world upon matter. Thus, all the mistakes, all the changes, all the imperfections of the world of our senses are due to matter and not to the ideas.

In one of Plato's famous Dialogues, the *Timaeus*, he tells us how the world of our senses was created. There was an "architect," the "Demiurge," who brought the ideal world and matter together just as a sculptor might bring his idea and marble together to produce a statue. This "Demiurge" had perfect ideas of everything, and he had a great mass of matter. Plato never tells us where either the "Demiurge," ideas, or matter came from originally. They were just there when things began. As the "Demiurge" brought an idea in touch with some matter, a thing was created. Indeed, a great many things were created from one idea. There is one perfect idea of an oak tree, but there are millions of oak trees. So with everything else in the universe,—it is a combination of a perfect idea and matter. And the idea is not at all influenced by this. It remains perfect and unchanged forever.

Plato has been called an Idealist because he thought that the real world was this world of ideas. Some students of his philosophy say that it would be truer to call him an "Idea-ist" since he was interested in ideas. But, whatever we choose to call him,—Idealist or Idea-ist,—we recognize that he believed the universe to consist of a realm of perfect and unchanging ideas and matter. The world of ideas was, for him, the true, the real, world. That which we experience through our senses was, for him, a copy world, an "unreal world" in this sense. It was a world of objects produced by impressing a perfect idea upon matter. All of its imperfections came from the fact that it was impossible to impress the idea perfectly upon matter; matter is imperfect and thus distorts the idea to some extent, twists it out of shape.

Aristotle's Conception of the Universe

Democritus and the Atomists, as we have seen, explained the universe in terms of moving identical atoms. Plato explained it in terms of perfect ideas which somehow were impressed upon matter. ARISTOTLE, who stands with

Plato among the world's very greatest philosophers, attempted to arrive at a theory of the universe which would mediate between that of the Atomists and of Plato.

Aristotle was willing to admit that matter does exist. And as a pupil of Plato, he believed that ideas existed. But, he wanted to bring these together in a way that would be more satisfying than the solution suggested by Plato. His problem was, then—How can perfect, changeless, eternal ideas be impressed upon lifeless matter? And his answer was that ideas, or "forms" as he called them, are not outside of and above things, are not "transcendent," but are *in* things. He taught that form and matter are always and eternally together. Therefore, the world which we experience through our senses is not, as Plato taught, a mere copy of the real world, but *is the real world*. Here form and matter are one, and neither can be experienced separately. Only by thinking can we separate the two; actually we always find them together.

Let us take an acorn as an example. An acorn is a unity of form and matter. We recognize the form "acorn," which is characteristic of all acorns. Wherever we see an acorn, we discover this form. But our example is a particular acorn. Never do we have the form "acorn" divorced from a particular acorn. But, in addition to form, our example has matter. The form "acorn" seeks to realize itself in matter, and the result is the acorn which we have. The more perfect the acorn, the more perfectly the form is realized.

But the acorn may become an oak tree. Thus this acorn which we hold in our hands is matter, and the form which it seeks to realize is the oak tree. As the acorn is planted and as it grows, it is striving to realize the form of the oak tree; it is seeking to become an oak tree. In the same way, the oak tree may become oak boards which are used to build tables, chairs, or other pieces of furniture. Here the oak tree is matter, and the particular piece of furniture is the form which the oak tree seeks to realize.

In every case,—the acorn, the oak tree, the piece of furniture,—we have matter and form. At every stage the object which exists is both the realization of a form and also matter for the realization of another form. Thus, forms never change, but are eternally the same. The form "acorn" is always the same and never becomes the form "oak tree." But matter takes on different forms as it changes. First it took on the form of an acorn, then the form of an oak tree, and then the form of a piece of furniture. And the process goes on indefinitely as change takes place. Matter is always taking on, striving to realize, forms.

Wherever we look in nature, in the universe, Aristotle taught, we find both matter and form. For him there can be no matter divorced from form, nor can there be any form divorced from matter. And both matter and form are eternal, never being created or destroyed. Thus the entire universe can be explained, he believed, as the process in which matter constantly seeks to realize different forms, to become what it can become.

If we wish to understand the universe, then, we may think of it in terms of a sculptor producing a statue. But, while in the case of Plato the sculptor is independent, free from his marble, in the case of Aristotle he is dependent on his marble. His idea of a perfect statue is actually in the marble, a form which the marble seeks to realize.

Therefore, Aristotle taught that every object in the universe had four causes. The first corresponds to the idea of the statue which the artist has before he begins work, the form which is to be realized. This he called the "formal cause." Then there is the marble with which the artist is to work, the matter. This is the "material cause." The third cause is that by which the statue is made, the tools employed to make the statue. This he called the "efficient cause" or "moving cause." The fourth cause is the purpose or end for which the statue is made, that for the sake of which the work is done. This he termed the "final cause."

For Aristotle, all these causes are operating in the thing as it develops, changes, grows, becomes. We must not think of an artist separated from his marble, but rather of an artist as a part of his marble. A better illustration may be that of a man seeking to become, let us say, a doctor.

He seeks to change himself into something else. His idea of "doctor" is the "formal cause"; his body with all its characteristics is the "material cause"; that which he does to change himself is the "efficient cause"; and the reason he makes this change from what he is originally to a doctor is the "final cause." Here the man is within that which is changed and he is what is created.

For Aristotle all motion is to be explained as the union of form and matter. When matter offers resistance to form we have deformities, mistakes, evils. However, matter is also a help to form in that it seeks to realize form, to become something.

It is clear from what we have already said that Aristotle's world is not a purely mechanical something. It is not a mere mass of units or atoms moving about and forming objects, as the Atomists taught. Rather, it is characterized by purposes which matter seeks to realize. There is striving in this universe, a seeking to become. We call such a world "teleological," not a world of mere chance but one of purpose.

If the acorn seeks to become an oak tree and the oak tree seeks to become a piece of furniture, where does the process stop? Is everything seeking to become something else, and is there no end to the chain? Aristotle believed that there was an end. This he thought of as the first cause or the "unmoved mover." It is pure form without any matter. It does not cause anything else, but just is. It is not in matter and does not seek to impress itself upon matter. We cannot experience it, but we can think it.

Thus, at one extreme we may think of pure matter without any form, formless matter. And at the other extreme we may think of pure form, matterless form. But we cannot experience either. The universe which we experience, the world of chairs, stars, earth, men, and all other things, is a world in which matter and form are united. And each object is the realization of a form and is the matter for the realization of still another form. In this way Aristotle attempted to solve the problem of the universe.

The Views of the Epicureans, Stoics, and Skeptics

With the coming of EPICURUS and the *Epicureans*, many thinkers devoted their attention largely to the problem of how to live a good life. However, even these philosophers recognized that one could not be good unless he understood the world in which he had to live this life. Thus they struggled with the problem of the nature of the universe.

Epicurus based his solution largely on the theory of Democritus and the Atomists which we have already studied. He taught that the real things in the universe are bodies which we experience through the senses. These bodies are made up of small units or atoms which differ in size, weight, and shape. As they come together in various ways, the bodies which we see are formed. Then, as they separate, these bodies disappear and we experience them no longer.

The universe, Epicurus taught, came to be by mere chance. Atoms have the power to swerve from a straight line. Thus, in the beginning, all atoms were falling straight down in space. Being able to swerve, some went one way and some another, deviating from the straight line. In this way all the bodies of the universe have been formed and are being formed.

The atoms cannot be destroyed or divided into smaller units. They have existed just as they now are from the beginning and will continue to exist in the same way forever.

The *Stoics*, a school of Greek thinkers founded by ZENO during the fourth century before Christ, were as interested as were the Epicureans in the problem of the good life, or "ethics" as it is called. But they too developed an explanation of the nature of the universe which is important.

These philosophers agreed with Aristotle that the universe is composed of two principles: form or "force" and matter. Force moves and acts, while matter is acted upon. These two principles are not separated from each other, as Plato taught, but are united in every object. Further, both force and matter are, for the Stoics, bodies. The bodies which are force are very fine-grained, while those which are matter are coarse and formless. Thus, everything in the universe is a body, is corporeal.

All the forces in the universe form a force which is in everything, a sort of fire which is the active soul of the universe. The Stoics thought of this world soul as fire because they believed that heat produced everything and moved everything. Heat, for them, is the giver of life. Consequently, fire is the basic principle of the universe.

This fire, or world soul, is related to everything in the universe just as the soul of a man is related to his body. Indeed, the world is merely the body of the world soul.

From the original fire, the Stoics taught, air, water, earth, and all else in the universe arise. These four elements, fire, air, water, and earth (which were also the four elements of Empedocles), combine in many ways to form the things of the universe. And through every object in the universe the divine principle flows, making it alive.

The Stoics were not willing, as were the Epicureans, to think of the universe as something that just happened by chance. Nor were they willing to go along with the Epicureans to the extent of holding that the universe is purely mechanical. Their principle of force was alive, and the universe which came into being was also alive. For them the universe was a perfect sphere or ball floating in empty space, a ball held together and made alive by its soul.

From the time of Thales to that of the Stoics, thinkers had been busy attempting to account for the universe, to explain how it was made, to develop a theory of the nature of things. Each one wove a different theory and offered evidence to prove that he was right.

This diversity of theories and explanations struck a group of Greek thinkers as proof of the fact that man is unable to know what the universe is or how it came into being. This group is known as the *Skeptics*, and its founder was PYRRHO. Its members felt that all attempts to explain the nature of the universe were futile, a waste of time, for, they argued, man cannot know the nature of things. All we see is the world around us. Our senses give conflicting evidence. Different men have different reports to make. We have no way of telling whose report is correct, whose is true to the real nature of the world. Therefore, the Skeptics were willing to give up the search, to say, "We do not know, and no man can know." They recommended that men be practical, accept what they experience through the senses, follow custom. Their answer to the problem of the nature of the universe was one of despair, and they abandoned all further attempts to work with the problem.

The Universe According to the Greco-Religious Thinkers

At about this time, toward the close of the pre-Christian era, men were turning to religions and seeking comfort in them. They were confused, tired mentally, and lost among the many conflicting theories which had been developed in the past. The time was ripe, then, for merging the many religious doctrines and beliefs with one or more of the Greek philosophies which had come down to that day in a more or less garbled form.

PHILO, a Jew living in Alexandria in Egypt, was the leader of the attempt to merge Judaism, the religion of the ancient Jews, with Greek philosophies. For him there was God who was so pure and far above everything in this world that he could not possibly come into contact with it. Thus, to account for the universe, Philo taught that there were many powers, or spirits, which radiated from God as light might radiate from a lamp. One of these powers, which he called the "Logos," was the creator of the world. This Logos, he taught, worked with matter and out of it created everything in the universe. In this way, God, through the Logos, created the universe. Further, everything in the universe is a copy of an idea in the mind of God. This reminds us of Plato's belief that the world which we experience through our senses is a copy of ideas in the ideal world. And, indeed, Philo was attempting here to reconcile Plato's philosophy with the Jewish religion.

Other religious-minded thinkers attempted to do the same thing, reconciling their religious beliefs with Greek philosophy. One of the most noted was PLOTINUS, who was born in Egypt in the third century of the Christian era and taught in Rome. His theory was very much like that of Philo. Out of a pure God flow beings, or emanations, as a stream might flow from an inexhaustible source, or as light flows from the sun without affecting the sun. The further the light is from its source, the dimmer it becomes. At the far extreme is darkness or matter.

Between God and matter Plotinus taught that there existed mind, soul. The soul acts upon matter and the universe is created. Matter, then, is the substance and soul is the form of all things.

In the thinking of all these men we see clearly the theories of Plato, Aristotle, and others. The world is, in each case, a combination of an idea or form and matter. As the two come together in different ways, different objects are created.

The Position of the Early Christian Thinkers

This attempt to account for the universe, which is a theater of change and imperfection, and at the same time teach that God is perfect and unchanging was continued by the Christians. Those men who sought to reconcile Christianity with Greek philosophy were known as *Apologists*. They taught that the universe contains traces of something different from pure matter and thus points to a God who is eternal, unchanging, and good. This God is the First Cause of everything in the universe, the creator of the universe. For them the "ideas" of Plato and the forms of Aristotle become God. God is the eternal and abiding principle in all change, the eternal pattern which never changes. He is the unity of all forms, all ideas. Through divine emanations he has created the world; and everything in the world, in so far as it is a part of God, strives to be more like God, to return to Him. The Creator fashioned the world from matter which He created out of nothing. The pattern of the world is in His mind.

One of the greatest thinkers among these early Christian philosophers, one who worked out the theory of the Apologists most completely, was AUGUSTINE, who became Saint Augustine. God, he taught, created matter out of nothing and then created everything in the universe. The forms which he impressed upon matter were in God's mind from the beginning of time, and even before, for God existed before there was any time. Indeed, God created time and space also. Thus everything that is or ever shall be is a creation of God and must follow His laws and will. Here again we see the influence of the Greeks in the belief that the universe is the result of the coming together of matter and form.

But the Christian thinkers went further than the Greeks in that they attempted to account for the existence of matter. You will remember that the Greeks simply accepted matter as well as the ideas or forms as existing from the beginning. The Christians put the ideas or forms in God's mind and went on to say that God created matter out of nothing. After He had created matter, He had something upon which to impress ideas or forms.

Further, these Christian philosophers taught that the ideas or forms, being in the mind of God, were divine. Therefore, in so far as things are ideas or forms impressed on matter, they seek God, try to return to Him. But matter holds them back. Matter, which God has created, is the principle which makes it necessary for things to struggle in their attempt to become divine.

Augustine lived during the fourth century of the Christian era. He saw the great Roman Empire, which had been established by the Caesars, falling to pieces, and watched the barbarians from the north gradually moving down into the empire and even toward Rome. He lived near the beginning of that period in history known as the Dark Ages, a period when these ignorant, crude barbarians swarmed over the Roman Empire and destroyed the civilization which had been building since the early days of the Greeks.

The Positions of the Medieval Christian Thinkers

After Augustine for centuries few men had time for thinking about the universe and its nature. Philosophy was gradually neglected, and those who did endeavor to think merely repeated the philosophies of those who had gone before them,—Plato, Aristotle, the Epicureans, the Stoics, and others. Most of the books written during this period were "remarkable only for their meagerness of original thought." Indeed, by the time of the seventh century the cloud of ignorance had so settled over Western Europe that this century and the next, the eighth, have been referred to as "perhaps the darkest period of our Western European civilization."

By the middle of the ninth century some men were beginning to think again. By this time the Christian church was in complete control of Western Europe. It dominated everything,—the state, men's lives, and all education and thought. Those who did attempt to think had to confine their thinking to the beliefs which the church accepted. Thus, all thinking was limited to church doctrines. In most cases men merely attempted to show that the beliefs of the church were true, reasonable.

So, when JOHN SCOTUS ERIGENA wrote during the ninth century, he tried to show that the orthodox theory of the creation of everything in the universe was reasonable. He taught that God created the world out of nothing or "out of himself, the causeless first cause." Before God created the world, he had a complete pattern of the world in his mind. Then, as a light is radiated from its source so the world was radiated from God. Consequently, the universe and God are one, but God is more than the universe. God is in his creation and his creation is in him.

Since God is one and is not divided, Erigena taught, so the universe is a unity. We may see differences, many individual objects, but they are all one. They are all God. We call this belief "pantheism." This universe is "an expression of the thought of God" and therefore cannot exist apart from him. Being God, everything in the universe strives to return to the unity of God.

From Plato to Erigena philosophers had been, as we have seen, explaining the universe as the union of ideas or forms and matter. In every instance the idea or form is thought of as a real thing existing before it was impressed upon matter. Plato thought of ideas as existing before things and in an ideal world. Aristotle taught that forms existed in things but were distinct from matter. The Christians taught that ideas or forms existed in the mind of God and moulded matter into things of the universe.

All these philosophers have been called "realists" since they taught that ideas or forms are real things existing independently of whether or not they ever come in contact with matter. In each instance the idea or form could exist without matter.

But there arose a thinker who dared to fling himself in the teeth of all this tradition and to declare that these ideas or forms, these "universals" as they were called, were mere names and had no reality. His name was ROSCELIN, or sometimes called Roscellinus. He taught that the only real things are the individual objects in the universe. Each individual man exists, but the universal "mankind" does not exist at all. It is merely a name for a collection of men.

You can see easily that Roscelin and the great philosophic tradition were directly opposed to each other. The result was a long and bitter dispute between the Realists, or those who believed that universals were real, and the "Nominalists," who taught that universals were mere names and had no real existence. This dispute was very important since it was a fight over the question as to whether the things of nature, the objects of the universe, are real or merely copies of real things. It was an attempt to answer the question: What is real, the world which we can experience with our senses or the world which we think with our minds?

ANSELM, the Archbishop of Canterbury during a good bit of the eleventh century, was on the side of the Realists. He believed that these "reals," ideas or forms, existed independently of any individual object. Mankind, for him, was a real thing which existed over and above any one man. He, along with PETER ABELARD, BERNARD OF CHARTRES, and other members of the School of Chartres, taught that universals or general concepts were ideas or forms having a separate existence and, in some way, the things which mould matter into individual objects which we see and experience through our senses. They were all in the tradition of the Realists.

These philosophers who attempted to reconcile the beliefs of the Christian church and the ideas which had come down to them from the Greeks,—the philosophies of Plato, Aristotle, and others,—were known as "Schoolmen," and the philosophies which they developed were in general called "Scholasticism." In every case the philosopher was a loyal member of the Christian church and believed the doctrines of the church without serious question. But most of them wanted to show that these doctrines were reasonable and could be justified by the mind of man.

The greatest of these Schoolmen, and the one who worked out the relationship between Christian beliefs and forms of Greek philosophy, was THOMAS AQUINAS. Saint Thomas Aquinas, as he was later called, was born near Naples and lived during the thirteenth century. His great ambition was to show that the universe was reasonable. But he was one of the Realists, and endeavored to show that universals were real. These universals, he argued, exist in particular objects, in things, in such a way as to make them what they are. The real thing about a tree, for example, is not its bark, its leaves, its height, and the like. These are qualities in which each tree differs from other trees. That which makes a tree a tree is its "treeness," and this is a universal. This universal exists in each particular tree.

But, agreeing with the Christian tradition, he held that all universals existed in the mind of God.

To explain the world which we experience through our senses, Saint Thomas followed Aristotle in introducing matter as that upon which universals work. Nature, for him, was a union of universals and matter. It is matter which makes one tree different from another. All trees contain the universal "treeness," but they differ, they are elms, oaks, spruces, tall, short, green, red, and the like, because of the different amounts of matter which each contains. All the universe, then, is a result of the coming together of matter and universals, and the many things in the universe differ in the amount of matter which they contain.

For Saint Thomas, God created the world out of nothing. He was the cause of both matter and the universals. Further, God is continually creating the world as he brings universals and matter together to produce new objects. Thus, all creation did not happen at one time, but creation is going on all the time and all about us.

The Schoolmen, as we have seen, were attempting to show that the beliefs of the church and the best thought of the philosophers were in agreement. In this they opened the door to those who would take a different position, who would argue that the two were in no real harmony. As soon as men began to study Christian beliefs and the philosophy of Aristotle, for example, and put them side by side, there were some who believed they saw contradictions. Thus they felt forced to choose sides. In such instances most of the loyal Christians sided with the church. But there were those who were not sure that the church was always right. Gradually they began to question the beliefs of the church and to look about for other material which might help them. In this way there arose a group of thinkers who accepted the beliefs of the church only if they could be justified by reason. Those beliefs which they could not justify, they discarded as false. With the coming of these men the period known as Scholasticism began to fade and a new period to dawn.

JOHN DUNS SCOTUS, a monk of the order of Saint Francis, attempted to stem this tide of questioning and to maintain the doctrines and beliefs of the Church at all cost. He taught, along with Saint Thomas and others, that universals existed before things in God's mind, as forms or ideas in the divine mind. When things came into being, ideas or universals existed in them, making them what they are. Further, when things are not present, universals exist in our minds as concepts or ideas which apply to all things of the same kind,—all trees, for example.

For Scotus the individual object, the tree which you see, is different from all other trees because of its "individuality," not because of the amount of matter which it contains, as St. Thomas had argued. Man, argued Scotus, is different from an animal because there has been added specific differences,—humanity. Both man and animals have life. When humanity is added to life we have man. Now Socrates is a man, like all other men in many respects. He is alive and he is distinguished from animals in that he has humanity. But Socrates is different from all other men. This difference is due, Scotus argued, to his individual character or individual difference. So, all things differ from all others because of their individuality.

And everything in the universe is a result of the union of form and matter. Matter is common to all things. God alone is pure spirit without matter, God is form not touched by matter. All else is both matter and form combined.

Although there was some opposition, the Realists were in command of philosophy throughout a good bit of Scholasticism. Near the beginning of the Scholastic movement, Roscelin, as we have seen, questioned the theory that universals are real existences. Now, many years later, there arose a concerted movement to deny the reality of universals. The leader of this movement was WILLIAM OF OCCAM, an English thinker of the thirteenth century.

William taught that particular objects and things were the only realities. This world which we see and experience is real. Ideas, concepts, universals are mere thoughts in the mind, abstractions which the mind makes. They have no other reality. It was this position which was called "Nominalism."

The universe, for the Nominalists, is composed of individual objects, each a thing in itself. We can see how these objects differ and in what ways they are alike, and can draw conclusions about them. But these conclusions are mere ideas in the mind.

Thus, there developed two great theories about the nature of the universe. One, following the tradition which was begun by Plato and Aristotle, held that forms, ideas, universals, were real things existing either apart from objects or in them and in some way determining what they are. This tradition taught that the real things of the universe are not the individual objects of our experience, but the universals, the forms which determine likenesses; the tree which you see is not real, but the universal "tree" of which all trees are copies is the real thing. The other theory of the nature of the universe taught that the real things in the universe are the individual objects which we experience, and that universals are mere thoughts in the mind.

The first tradition has been that in which religion has flourished. The second tradition is the basis for all modern science.

MEISTER ECKHART, a German mystic of the thirteenth century, held that God is the home of eternal ideas just as the artist is the home of ideas which may later become works of art. The world which we experience, this world of creatures and things, is a copy of the ideas which are in God. This world God created out of nothing. He, of course, is in the realist tradition but with an emphasis upon mysticism (which is the belief that God is all and man can find salvation only as he loses himself in God).

When the Christian church became interested in making its beliefs reasonable, it turned to the philosophy of Plato. Here the doctrine of a world of ideas distinct from the world of things fitted nicely into the Christian belief in a God who created the world out of nothing and remained distinct from the world. Ideas and matter were distinct in both Plato's philosophy and in the doctrines of the Christian church. The great Schoolmen, who sought to make religion reasonable, made much use of Plato.

But, as we have seen, there were thinkers who were not satisfied. They leaned toward Aristotle in holding that the form of an object is in some way in the object and not distinct from it. Matter and form are combined to form things which we experience. They did attempt to fit God into the picture, but were never wholly successful. Forms, they held, were in things and also in the mind of God. But how could they be in both places? This they never could answer clearly.

Thus, there arose philosophers who became interested

in things and in their study. Some denied that the beliefs of the church could be made reasonable. They held that there were two kinds of truth,—that of the church and that of philosophy. One may deny the other, but we should believe both. We should accept the doctrines of the church by faith and the doctrines of philosophy by reason. This was, of course, a denial of the attempt of the Schoolmen to reconcile the doctrines of the church and philosophy.

As Aristotle became more prominent in the thinking of Schoolmen, heresies began to develop. Philosophers came forward to propose that ideas or forms were not existent, and that the only real things are objects, individuals. Thus Nominalism grew out of an increasing interest in Aristotle, but came eventually to deny Aristotle's doctrine of forms. In this way Aristotle lead to the disintegration of Scholasticism and the growing concern of thinkers with the world of experience. The world was ready for an entirely new approach to the problem of the nature of the universe.

The Views of the Forerunners of the Renaissance

But the thinkers who tended toward a new approach moved slowly. After all, they were children of their times and the influence of the church was strong upon them. Thus, the early philosophers of this movement exhibited a strange mixture of the old and the new.

Nicholas of Cusa taught that the universe is God divided into small bits. If we think of the universe as a whole, all of it put together, we find that it is God. But each part is a part of God and God is in each thing.

Ludovico Vives, a Spaniard of this period—the sixteenth century—taught that we should stop trying to learn about the world by reading what others·in the past had written and should go out and study nature, observe the world about us, and make experiments to discover how it is made. He was typical of those philosophers who wanted to turn away from the theories of the past and study the universe as it is experienced. In this way, they believed, man could learn the real nature of the universe.

As philosophers became more interested in the study of

nature they sought to understand it and gain power over it. Of course, they did not have our modern instruments or our modern knowledge. They stood on the threshold of the modern world. Thus, they sought short cuts to these goals. The result was a form of magic, a belief that the secrets of the universe could be understood if one had the right secret word to utter or the correct magical act to perform. Thus there arose Alchemy, an attempt to make gold out of baser metals, Astrology, a belief that the movements of the stars determined man's life and all of nature, and many other strange doctrines.

PARACELSUS, for example, taught that man possessed two bodies and a soul. The visible body comes from the earth, the invisible body comes from the stars, and the soul comes from God. He believed that there were three basic substances: sal (the principle of all solids), mercury (the principle of all liquids), and sulphur (the combustible). Each of these elements is ruled by spirits. To control nature one must control these spirits. All nature is the home of strange spirits which must be handled by magic acts and words.

Other philosophers followed in this line, seeking to account for the universe as the home of many spirits. But, gradually there arose thinkers who threw off this mass of superstition and began to look at the world as a place where forces met and opposed each other. BERNARDINO TELESIO taught that the universe is made up of matter and force. Matter is created by God and remains constant all the time. Heat is a force which expands matter, and cold is a force which contracts matter. Thus, all objects in the universe are, for him, a result of either expansion or contraction of matter.

In time men were able to move beyond the strange magical theories of their predecessors and study nature as the result of moving bodies. As they did this, they saw how bodies moved in certain definite ways. This observation lead to the statement of certain laws of the universe.

GALILEO was influenced by the theories of Democritus, and believed that all change in the universe is due to the movement of parts or atoms. He developed his thinking along mathematical lines and attempted to show that the entire universe was mathematical. His work, along with that of Kepler, established the belief that the sun and not the earth is the center of the universe. This is known as the Copernican or heliocentric theory of the universe. With the coming of Sir Isaac Newton, this theory was proved beyond the shadow of a doubt, so that today we recognize that the sun is the center of our universe and all the planets move about it in very definite ways.

Giordano Bruno, writing in the spirit of the new age, conceived the universe as composed of numerous uncaused and wholly imperishable parts which he called "monads." These parts unite to form bodies and things in various ways. Further, the universe is the result of the union of form and matter, much as Aristotle had held. Change results from matter taking on new form. Particular objects, therefore, may change. But this is only change of parts; the whole, the universe, remains constant.

Tommaso Campanella, another early philosopher of this new age, held that nature is a revelation of God. The world is the result of emanations from God. God produced angels, ideas, spirits, immortal human souls, space, and bodies. Thus, the universe is a result of God's creative activity.

The Universe According to the Philosophers of the Renaissance

Francis Bacon lived during the sixteenth and early part of the seventeenth centuries. Although he did not construct a theory of the universe, as "trumpeter of his time" he laid the foundation for a modern theory. Bacon completely separated religion and philosophy. He argued that the doctrines of religion could not be proved by thinking and that men should give up the attempt; that to try was a great waste of time and energy.

Having relegated the doctrines of religion to a realm all their own, Bacon set about to develop a method of thinking which he believed would give mankind true knowledge about his universe. This method we speak of as "induction." By careful study of the likenesses and differences among things, man could discover the laws, causes, or "forms" of objects in the universe. In this way he would come to understand the universe.

For Bacon, nothing exists in the universe save individual bodies. These act according to fixed laws which, if understood, serve as the keys to unlock the mysteries of the universe and the levers by which to control this universe. In this Bacon had turned wholly in the direction of modern science and put the ancients and the Schoolmen to his back. He was marching forward toward the world which we understand today, a world of things and laws. Although he did not offer a complete theory of the nature of the universe, he pointed the way which others might take in developing such a theory.

With THOMAS HOBBES philosophy has entered upon the new and modern era. Hobbes breaks completely with the past, with Greek philosophy and with the Schoolmen. Being a student of mathematics, Hobbes set about to think of the world in terms comparable to mathematics. As a result, his philosophy is wholly materialistic—concerned with the material.

Hobbes assumes dogmatically, without trying to prove it, that the world is a world of bodies in motion. These bodies are in space and have certain characteristics or "accidents" such as motion, rest, color, hardness, and the like. Motion is the continuous giving up of one space by a body and the assuming of another. When one body affects another, it either generates an accident in the affected body or destroys an accident. For example, let us imagine a body at rest. Hobbes would say that this body had the accident of rest. Now, suppose another body so affects this one that it is no longer at rest, but is in motion. In this case the second body has destroyed the accident of rest and generated or created the accident of motion. This is what we call the law of cause and effect, one accident perishes and another is generated.

All objects are in motion, according to Hobbes. This motion was given to them by God at the creation. As bodies move about, they influence each other so that accidents are destroyed or created.

Everything in the universe, even God, is a body (is corporeal) and is moving. Thus, with bodies and motion, Hobbes conceives the entire universe. This is why his philosophy is spoken of as materialistic.

Descartes' Conception of the Universe

RENÉ DESCARTES was also a mathematician. His study of this subject and his respect for its certainty made him seek to build a philosophy which would be as certain as mathematics. He decided very early in his career that everything in nature must be explained mechanically, without the aid of forms, ideas, universals. Thus, his whole philosophy is machine-like, mechanistic.

At the base of everything in the universe, of all bodies, is substance, he wrote. Substance is that which exists by itself and independently of anything else. There are, he believed, two kinds of substance, mind and body. These exist independently of each other, but both depend upon God who is the only absolute substance.

The substance that is body has the attribute of extension—that is, it has length, breadth, and thickness. This body substance expresses itself in many modes, many individual objects in the universe. Therefore, every thing in the universe is a mode of the substance which is body. And each thing stems back to God, the absolute substance.

Further, in the universe there is no empty space or vacuum. Bodies fill all space. And bodies can be divided infinitely, into smaller and smaller particles.

Everything that goes on in the universe, according to Descartes, is in some way a modification of extension. Extension may be divided into an infinite number of particles which may be united into different forms of matter.

Motion causes bodies to pass from one place to another. Motion, then, is a mode of movable things. All that happens in the universe is the transference of motion from one part of space to another. But the motion in the universe is constant. At the beginning God gave the world a certain definite amount of motion. Thus motion remains the same in the universe; it cannot be destroyed. If one object slows up, another must move faster.

Further, according to Descartes, all change in the world must take place according to laws. Indeed, all the laws of nature are, in the philosophy of Descartes, laws of motion.

The universe, then, is composed of bodies created by God and endowed with motion. These bodies move about according to fixed and purely mechanical laws. As we learn these laws, we can understand the universe and come to control it. This is a purely mechanical theory of organic nature. It contains no forms or ideas, no universals.

Mind, which we shall discuss in more detail in a later chapter, is for Descartes also a substance. Its attribute is thinking, and it expresses itself in many modes. Although body and mind are both substances, and both stem from God, they are independent. To maintain this complete independence, Descartes gave himself the most difficult problem of showing how mind can influence body or body influence mind. His solution of this problem will be discussed when we come to the study of mind and matter.

The great merit of Descartes' philosophy was, however, this extreme separation of body and mind. We may speak of his thought as emphasizing the "dualism" of mind and matter; that is, stressing the "two-fold" nature of the universe. By making these two substances entirely independent, he left nature free for the mechanical explanations of natural science. The scientists could busy themselves with a study of nature without having to worry about mind. Science could develop along purely mechanical lines without having to make room for purposes, goals, and other characteristics of mind or spirit. It could busy itself with the discovery of the laws by which all bodies act and move. Indeed, in this way modern science was made possible.

This dualism of Descartes brought to the fore the problem of how we can know anything about the material world. How can mind, which is absolutely distinct from matter, know a material world? How can we answer any of the questions about the nature of the universe? ARNOLD GUELINCX, a successor of Descartes, teaches that God alone has knowledge of things, and all that we can know is ourselves. NICOLAS MALEBRANCHE, another thinker of the period following Descartes, agreed with Guelincx that we cannot know anything about the universe. However, we do have ideas about the world, we think we see it, and experience it in many ways. And we act accordingly. But all we have are ideas which God has put in us. "If God," he writes, "had destroyed the created world, and would continue to affect me as he now affects me, I should continue to see what I now see." Thus, the universe which we experience is a universe of ideas. Whether or not there is a material world "out there," we cannot know.

Consequently, by making a sharp distinction between the material and the mental, Descartes opened the door to complete skepticism as regards the existence of a universe outside of the human mind. And many thinkers entered this door and denied the existence of such a world. If mind and matter are distinct, then neither can influence the other, and mind cannot know matter, the world of things.

Spinoza's Theory of the Universe

Descartes, as we have seen, taught that the universe is made up of two kinds of substance, mind and body. This dualism did not satisfy BENEDICT SPINOZA. Spinoza taught that there is only one substance, one basic "stuff" which constitutes the entire universe. This he called God. For Spinoza, everything in the universe is God, and all the individual things are actually one great whole.

We may think of the basic substance as, for example, a great metal shield, with different designs on each side. If we look at it from one side we see a definite design, but if we look at it from the other side we see a wholly different design. So with substance. If it is seen in one way it is body. If seen from another position it is mind. Spinoza called the one extension and the other mind.

Thus, every object in the universe,—star, tree, man, animal, water, wind, stone,—is a part of God, is God. Every object is also both extension and mind. There is no body without mind and no mind without body.

Substance, the underlying "stuff" of the universe, is absolutely independent of everything, for it is everything. It is infinite, self-caused, and self-determined. It has no limits, was made by itself, and is determined by nothing but itself. This God, or Nature, is the world. This unifying conception is known as "pantheism." So thorough is Spinoza in holding this position that he has been referred to as "God-intoxicated."

This substance, God, expresses itself in an infinite number of attributes, but man can grasp only two,—extension and thought. God, or Nature, is both body and mind. Further, these attributes are absolutely independent of each other. Body does not affect mind nor does mind affect body. But both are manifestations of one and the same universal reality, God.

These attributes appear to man in specific ways or "modes." There are many bodies and many ideas. The particular body, a tree, is a mode of extension which is an attribute of God. My particular thought at this moment is a mode of mind which is an attribute of God.

All the bodies in the universe and all the ideas grouped together form a totality which is God or substance. This constitutes the "face of the whole universe." The individual objects or ideas may change, but the whole, the "face of the whole universe," does not change.

Further, all the bodies in the universe form a chain of causes. The tree you see was caused by something else, which in turn was caused by something else, and so on. Thus this particular tree owes its existence to some other physical object. It is not necessary that God create this tree; but, having it present, he is the underlying substance of it. If, for example, we have a triangle, we know immediately that certain things must be true of it. It has certain properties, and all triangles will have these properties. However, we cannot tell from the concept of a triangle the number, size, and shape of different triangles.

In the same way, from substance we can state the properties of bodies, but we cannot state the properties of the different objects in the universe.

For Spinoza, then, the entire universe is one substance, which he called God or Nature. This substance has at least two attributes,—extension and mind. And there are many modes of each attribute. Thus, God is the universe and the universe is God. But bodies are independent of mind and mind is independent of body. However, when something happens in body, it also happens in mind. This is called "psycho-physical parallelism"; that is, body and mind are always parallel, for they are two aspects of one and the same substance.

The Positions of Locke, Berkeley, and Hume

JOHN LOCKE, admirer of Descartes but thinker who gave to the modern world a new interpretation of man, began his thinking with the question: How does man know? His conclusion, after a long and painstaking investigation, was that all knowledge comes from sense impressions. This point of view made it necessary for him to account for the universe as the source of these impressions.

Is there a real world which corresponds to our ideas? If there is such a world, how can we, having only ideas, prove its existence? Locke's answer was to the effect that there is such a world. Our senses, he said, tell us of this world. We do experience this world and are justified in saying that it exists. Though we may not be able to say much about the source of our sensations, we are able to say that the sensations are caused. Thus, the real world is the cause of our sensations. This much we can say. For example, we have an idea of white. This idea is not born in us, but is caused. From this we can reason that the real world contains something which causes in us an idea of white.

However, even of this we cannot be absolutely certain. Our knowledge of this world is probable. We can be more certain of the existence in the universe of ourselves and of

God. But all else is only probable. Therefore, Locke argued, we can never have a perfect natural science.

At this point Locke follows fairly closely the position of Descartes, which we have outlined. The world, he holds, is composed of substances. These are the bases, the supports, of all qualities. We experience, for example, white. This quality just does not float around in space, but is the whiteness of something. This something is a substance.

Further, there are two kinds of substances, bodies and souls. Bodies have the attributes of extension, solidity, and impenetrability. They fill space, are solid, and cannot be penetrated. Souls are spiritual substances, are immaterial.

Souls, minds, and bodies act upon each other. The body can cause happenings in the soul, and what happens to the soul may affect the body. For example, bodies act upon the mind so that we have experiences of color, sound, touch, and the like. Despite his belief in interaction, Locke's theory of the universe is dualistic. There are minds and there are bodies. While both are substances, they are different kinds of substances.

Here it is evident that, with some changes, Locke follows in the footsteps of Descartes in holding that bodies and mind are two kinds of substances, or bearers of qualities. The universe is made up of these substances. However, we can know only the ideas which these substances produce in us through sensations.

If, however, the basis of knowledge is sensation and reflection upon sensations, how can we know that a world of bodies distinct from our ideas of bodies exists? GEORGE BERKELEY asked this question. John Locke had taught that, actually, all we can know are our ideas, and had presupposed a world which causes our sensations. But Berkeley recognized immediately that he could not prove the existence of such a world on the basis of his philosophy. Further, Berkeley, being a deeply religious man and seeing so much atheism or disbelief in God in the world, was convinced that atheism would be abolished if one could disprove belief in matter.

Consequently, Berkeley carried Locke's philosophy to its

logical conclusion as he saw it, and taught that there can be no universe of material objects. All we can prove, he argued, is that we have ideas.

But what about the source of these ideas? Do we create our own ideas? Berkeley answered, "No." The cause of sensations, and thus the cause of all ideas, is God. We cannot perceive God but can perceive the effects of his work, ideas.

Berkeley held consistently, as he believed, to the position that nothing in the universe existed unless it was perceived. I am sitting in my room. I look about and see chairs, a table, books, and other objects. These are not real in the sense that they are material objects. They are ideas in my mind. But, if I leave the room, do these objects vanish? Do I carry them out of the room in my mind? Berkeley taught that they might still exist in some other mind. If other people are in the room, they may exist in their minds. If there are no other people in the room, they may still exist in the mind of God. But, all the time, they are ideas and not material objects.

The material universe, which Descartes, Spinoza, and Locke had taught existed, was denied by Berkeley. For him, all that exists are ideas in the mind. If they are not in my mind, they may be in your mind or in God's mind. Of course, they seem to be material, but actually they are not. Berkeley was simply following the ideas of Locke to their logical conclusion, to a denial of the existence of a material universe.

DAVID HUME, a Scot of the eighteenth century, felt that Berkeley had not gone far enough. Not only must we abandon the idea of substance, he taught, but we must also abandon the idea of a God in whose mind all ideas exist. Hume could find no good argument for the existence of God.

Then, all that we have is a succession of ideas. These are caused by impressions. Hume agreed with Berkeley that only those things exist which are perceived. My table exists only when it is perceived. I may perceive it, my friend may perceive it, or God may perceive it. Thus, "to

be is to be perceived." However, we cannot prove that
God exists. Therefore, if I am in a room alone and perceive a table, the table exists as I perceive it. When I
leave the room, the table no longer exists.

There is, then, in Hume's view, no substance. All that
we have is a succession, a stream of ideas, one following
the other. We cannot prove the cause of these ideas. It is
foolish to say that there is a substance "out there" in space
causing our ideas. No one can prove this. Whenever we
look, we find ideas following each other,—ideas of chairs,
tables, people, trees, stars, and the like. Thus we have no
evidence of the existence of a world of nature or of God.

Hume carried Locke's theory to its logical and final conclusion in skepticism. Locke had taught that we have ideas
which are caused by an outer world. Hume admitted the
existence of ideas, but showed that, if this is all we have,
we are shut up in our own minds and cannot prove the
existence of an outside world. All we can be sure of is a
parade of individual ideas, one following the other. Their
cause, their connection, even the place where they are
parading is unknown. We have come in Hume to a dead-
end street.

It is natural that man would not remain satisfied with
the skepticism of Hume. THOMAS REID, another Scot, led
the opposition. He taught that Hume had reached an impossible position. Common sense tells us that a real world
exists as the cause of our sensations and ideas. We may
speculate all we want, but we will not be contented to deny
what common sense tells us. Therefore, he argues, those
things which we perceive distinctly by our senses exist,
and they exist as we perceive them. There is a world "out
there" corresponding to our ideas. Tables, chairs, and the
like do exist independently of our ideas of them. Common
sense tells us that this is so, and we cannot deny common
sense.

German thought took a different road from that of England or Scotland. It was concerned with the then developing natural sciences, but found itself believing in the values
of Christian beliefs. Consequently, it sought to reconcile

science and these valuable elements in Christian speculation.

Leibnitz' Theory of the Universe

GOTTFRIED WILHELM LEIBNITZ, one of the leaders of German thought in the seventeenth century, became convinced after much careful study and investigation that the essential attribute of the bodies in the universe is force. By force he meant "the tendency of the body to move or continue its motion." The entire universe is, for him, built out of units of force. Each body consists of a number of these units of force, and all nature consists of an infinite number of such units. These units of force Leibnitz called "monads," or force-atoms. Each monad is eternal, it cannot be destroyed or changed.

But monads have different degrees of clearness. The most obscure, vague, cloudy monads form plants. Those less cloudy form animals. The monads which form man are still clearer. And the clearest of all monads is God. The universe is composed of an infinite number of monads extending all the way from the most cloudy monad to God. There is no break in this series. At one extreme is inorganic matter, rocks and the like. And at the other extreme is God.

Each monad contains within itself the entire universe. Thus, since the monad has no "windows," all that it becomes is contained within it from the beginning. Each monad realizes its nature with an inner necessity. Nothing can be in a monad but what has been there from the beginning.

The organic bodies, living beings, contain a "queen monad" or soul which is the guiding principle of all the monads which make up the body. No monad can influence another. God created monads in the beginning so that they operate together in harmony. When one monad does something, it does not influence another monad. But, because the other monad is so created, it acts as though the one had influenced it. Thus all monads act together just as do the various parts of an organism.

Leibnitz' universe, then, is not mechanical, but is dynamic, alive. It is composed of an infinite number of monads of various degrees of clearness. Here we sense the old theory of Democritus, the atomistic theory. But the atoms of Leibnitz are not all alike, nor are they pure mechanical units. They are units of force and differ in clearness. And God is the clearest monad.

By means of this theory, Leibnitz believed that he had reconciled the science of his day with the values of the Christian doctrine. He had a scientific universe in which God was the supreme being or monad.

Kant's Conception of the Universe

German philosophy reached its height in the work of IMMANUEL KANT, one of the great philosophic system-builders of all times. His fundamental problem lay in the question, What is knowledge, and how is it possible? What can we really know, and how? His conclusion was that we can know only our experiences. We have sensations. We see a chair. Because our minds are such as they are, we receive this sensation in a definite way. But we cannot know the cause of the sensation.

On this theory, we cannot know the universe which exists outside of our thinking. Our minds receive sensations and shape them into ideas because they are what they are. What the world is without our minds, it is impossible for us to know.

But, by Reason we can form an Idea of this world, this universe. As we experience the world in our minds, we find that the world has no beginning in time, that bodies in the world cannot be divided infinitely, that everything in the world takes place according to the laws of nature, and that there is no absolutely necessary Being who causes the world to be. We must accept this theory of the world of experience because we cannot experience it otherwise.

However, Reason can construct a world of Idea which has no beginning in time, in which bodies can be divided infinitely, in which there is freedom, and in which there is an absolutely necessary Being, God, who is the cause of everything. Although we cannot know such a universe through experience, we can reason its existence and we can act as though it were real. Indeed, Kant believed that man must act as though this kind of a world existed if he would preserve his moral integrity. For, on the basis of such a world Kant reasoned to the existence of God, freedom, and immortality. Further, he showed that all goodness, all morality, was dependent upon acting as if this kind of a world existed. The Idea of this world, he held, is regulative,—it directs man to certain goals. Believing in the eixstence of such a universe, man strives to be good.

Thus, for Kant, there are two universes: one of experience, the "phenomenal" world, and one of reason, the "noumenal" world. The one is scientific, the other is practical.

Kant taught that the fundamental principle of the practical world is a moral law which may be stated: "Always act so that you can will the maxim or determining principle of your action to become universal law; act so that you can will that everybody shall follow the principle of your action." This he called the "categorical imperative."

If one is to act so that the principle of his action shall become a law for all men, he must be free to act in this way. Therefore, Kant placed freedom at the center of his practical world. We shall discuss Kant's view of the practical world more fully in our chapter on "What Is Good and What Is Evil?"

Fichte, Schelling, and Hegel

JOHANN GOTTLIEB FICHTE took this principle of freedom and made it fundamental to his whole philosophical position. He took the stand that the self, the "ego," is a free, self-determining activity.

The starting-point of Fichte's thinking is this ego or creative, free principle. It is God, and is the creator of all that is. It creates each individual person, you and me and all the individuals in the universe. It also creates the entire world of things.

But, we and all things are not matter, material. There is

no material in the sense of lifeless matter such as the older philosophers taught. Everything in the universe is spirit. The tree and your mind are both the universal, absolute ego or God. Thus, the real world is a world of mind or spirit and not a world of dead matter. Everything is the ego, God. But the ego creates a limit to itself so that it may contend against this limit and grow to perfection. Thus, the world of objects, the so-called "material" world, is produced by the ego to furnish an arena in which it may exercise its freedom.

Freedom would mean nothing if there were not something hindering the exercise of freedom. Therefore, the eternal ego, God, has created the world, the "non-ego," as a limit to itself, a world of opposition in which it can struggle, in which it can become conscious of itself. This is a world of law, a world in which things happen according to set rules.

My reason, your reason, our minds are also creations or parts of this universal ego. We do not create our world of things, but are creations of the same ego which has created this world. Since the universal ego is the universal active reason, the same in all persons, we all see the world alike.

This point of view is called "Idealism." It is based upon the belief that there is no matter in the universe, but everything is mind or spirit, idea. Descartes, Locke, and even Kant had taught that there are two principles in the universe, mind and matter. Fichte denied this recognition of two principles. He eliminated matter, and held that everything in the universe is mind or spirit. The world only seems to be material. If we understand aright, we shall realize that even this is spirit. The universe is mind, spirit, ego, God. Thus, though the universe is a reality outside of individual personal minds, it is not made of a different material, it is not a world of dead things. But, it is "the revelation in human consciousness of the absolute principle." Nature is spirit, mind, and can be nothing else.

Thus, for Fichte, the moral law of Kant implies freedom, freedom implies deliverance from obstacles. There must be obstacles. Therefore, the universal self or ego created out of itself the world of sensible things to serve as its opponent. The world of experience is deduced from the moral law. Because this concept of Kant's influenced Fichte and many other thinkers, we speak of Kant as the father of modern Idealism.

Following in this same idealistic tradition was FRIEDRICH WILHELM JOSEPH SCHELLING, brilliant German philosopher and student of religion. For him, as for Fichte, the ground of all the universe was one all-pervading world spirit or ego. However, he taught that this spirit as found in nature was not conscious of itself, and that it became fully self-conscious only in man.

Thus there is a development in consciousness from nature through man. Nature and thinking are steps or stages in the development of the absolute mind. God is nature and God is mind. The one is God asleep while the other is God fully awake. But, in either, or throughout the whole development, God remains the same.

All the universe, including man, is a whole. The parts, the objects and individuals are all parts of the whole. Thus nature is alive, dynamic, creative. Wherever one may stop to investigate, he will find spirit striving to realize itself fully, to become wholly self-conscious. Inorganic nature, the trees, rocks, earth, and the like, are of the same material as is the human mind. But the former are blind, "unripe," unconscious.

This doctrine is pantheism. The universe is conceived as a living, growing, moving system. God is the universe and the universe is God. In plants and rocks, God is blind, unconscious impulse. Move upward to man and God becomes conscious or seeing, he comes to knowledge of himself.

GEORG WILHELM FRIEDRICH HEGEL attempted to bring the philosophical positions of Kant, Fichte, and Schelling into a whole which would be complete and satisfying. Thus, he taught that the entire universe is an evolution of mind from nature to God.

Everywhere, in the natural world or in the mind of man, we find a process of unfolding. This he called the dialectical process or the principle of contradiction. Everything tends to pass over to its opposite. The seed tends to become a flower. However, nature does not stop with these contradictions, but strives to overcome them, to reconcile them in a whole or unity.

The entire universe is a whole. In it this principle is working, a principle which is rational. Mind is everywhere. Within this whole there is development. And this development proceeds by the dialectical process. First we discover a thing, a "thesis." Then we discover its opposite or contradiction, an "antithesis." These two are at last reconciled in a "synthesis" which becomes another "thesis" and the process starts again.

All the universe is a continuation of this process within the whole. Reality then is a process of evolution, a developing from a less clear to a more clear.

This process is the process of thought. Therefore, the universe is thought and is subject to the laws of thought. As we think, so the universe develops. But this is all a process of a thinking whole. Nature and man are one within this whole. The same processes which are found in man's mind are also found in nature. In nature this movement proceeds unconsciously. The seed grows into a plant, and into a flower. But it is not conscious of its growth. In man the process becomes conscious and man knows that he is developing. This same process is discovered everywhere.

For Hegel, then, the universe is a whole or totality. This whole is a thinking process and it develops as does all thought,—thesis, antithesis, and synthesis. This is Idealism worked out completely and to the last degree.

The Views of the Later German Philosophers

The idealistic philosophy of Hegel certainly could not go unchallenged. It contradicted so much of common sense that it was inevitable that a thinker, or group of thinkers, would arise to present the other side of the picture. JOHANN FRIEDRICH HERBART was such a thinker. He took issue with every phase of Hegel's philosophy and sought to show that the idealistic philosophy was full of impossible theories.

For Herbart the universe consists of a great number of unchangeable principles or substances which he called "reals." Each real is a simple thing, is changeless, absolute, indivisible, not extended in time or in space. In the world of reals there is no change, no growth; it is static.

Our bodies are aggregates of these reals, and each soul is a real. Each real strives to maintain itself against anything that would affect it. In this striving for self-preservation, each real will behave differently in the presence of different reals.

We relate reals together into aggregates and thus create the universe which we experience. For example, I come into relationship with many reals and bring them together into a red apple. Then, by bringing other reals into the situation and rejecting some which I had there first, the apple becomes a peeled apple. Thus, the real world is absolutely static. Nothing happens in it. All happenings are phenomena in consciousness. As consciousness arranges and rearranges reals, things appear, change, and disappear.

The entire universe, then, is, for Herbart, made up of these spaceless, timeless, units which never change, but which exert activity in preserving themselves against other reals. As we arrange and rearrange reals we produce the world of experience.

This theory of the universe is known as "Realism," and its basic idea is that the universe is real and is not a creation of mind. Although experience reveals only phenomena, an appearance must always be the appearance of something. There is a reality which causes the appearance. Kant had called this reality the "thing-in-itself." Hegel had argued that there is no such "thing." Herbart agreed with Kant and sought to describe this real cause of appearances.

ARTHUR SCHOPENHAUER attacked the problem from another angle. He agreed with Kant that the world of experience is a world of phenomena; but he disagreed with him in holding that we can become aware of the thing-in-itself. He noted that when man wants something he sets about to build or create it. I want a table, and I get boards, tools, nails, and build one. Or I work to make the money to buy one.

From this, he argued that will is the cause of all things in the universe. The thing-in-itself, for him, is will, the cause of everything. The universe is a result of will.

In organic and inorganic life the fact is the same. In a rock, will is blind, but it is the creative principle which brings the rock into being. As we move up to man, will becomes conscious. Man may direct his will by intelligence in getting what he wills. The universe, then, is a result of will, a primal will which continues to work regardless of the coming or going of individuals.

RUDOLF HERMANN LOTZE sought to interpret Kant's thing-in-itself in terms of mind. He taught that the physical world is to be understood as purely mechanical, as a matter of physical and chemical laws. But, this is the world of perception. The cause of this world is comparable to soul or mind.

Thus, there are various degrees of reality. In the case of matter mental life is present but clouded. In man this mental life is conscious and clear. The universe, then, is alive and is mind. Here again we encounter Idealism.

The work of Lotze and other Idealists made a profound impression on the thinking of their age. GUSTAV THEODOR FECHNER conceived the universe as similar to human individuals. The material world is the body of the universe. But this body has a soul or a mental life. This mental life is to be found in descending degrees in animals, plants, and lastly in organic matter. God is the soul of the universe, just as the human body has a soul. FRIEDRICH PAULSEN and WILHELM WUNDT followed in the same tradition. Wundt taught that the external world is "the outer husk behind which lies concealed a spiritual creation, a striving and feeling reality resembling that which we experience in ourselves."

By admitting the existence of a material world they met

the objections of those who felt that the Idealists had denied common sense. But, by holding that mind or spirit is the creative spirit in this world, that the world is alive, they believed that they had conserved the values of Idealism. Their philosophies were attempts to meet the demands of the then growing natural sciences while at the same time to escape the crass materialism which threatened philosophy as science became stronger. They believed that the values of mind, spirit, or soul should not be covered up and lost completely in the landslide of modern science.

The Positions of John Stuart Mill and Herbert Spencer

JOHN STUART MILL taught that actually our ideas are all that we can know. We find these ideas following each other in consistent ways and so often that we can be reasonably sure that they will continue to do so. For example, the idea of being burned always follows the idea of sticking one's hand into a fire.

Mill holds that law and order reign in the universe and that there are invariable sequences of events upon which we can depend. Further, he teaches that the law of cause and effect is universal. We find a certain set of ideas being followed in every case by the same idea. This leads us to recognize that the effect is caused by the set of preceding ideas.

But, as is evident, up to this point Mill is discussing phenomena, experiences, ideas. What of the cause of these? Is there an external universe? Mill believes that there is such a universe which is the cause of our sensations. I see a piece of white paper in a room. Then I leave the room and remember that the paper was experienced under certain conditions. I return to the room and again experience the paper. After I have done this several times with the same results, the paper is always experienced upon my return to the room. I generalize that the paper is there in the external world and causes my experience. I form the notion of something permanent, persisting. Thus "the so-called external world is simply the possibility that certain sensations will recur in the same order in which they have occurred."

It is evident that Mill, although he thinks largely in the Idealistic tradition, believes that there is a cause of our sensations, experiences, a "thing-in-itself." There is a universe distinct from our sensations and experiences, the cause of ideas which we have.

But we cannot know with absolute certainty anything about this world. From our experiences of it, we can be reasonably certain about some things in it, and not so sure about others. However, all that we know about it is based on experience, and no one has had every possible experience so as to be able to make a generalization which will be without exception. There is still the possibility that some exception, some new experience, will arise to prove the generalization applicable only to certain sets of conditions and not to others.

HERBERT SPENCER is the great philosopher of evolution. He sought to develop a philosophic theory based on the findings of Darwin and other biologists; build a system of thought which would embody the important ideas of the doctrine of evolution.

He began his philosophy with the recognition that phenomena, things as presented to us, are all that we can know. The cause of these phenomena is unknowable. But there is a cause, an Absolute Being behind all phenomena. Of course, we do make judgments about it. We conceive it as a force or power causing all that we know. Further, we think of it as both mental and physical. It is the cause of our thoughts and of the universe. But, all these ideas are mere symbols, ways which we have invented of thinking of the Absolute. Actually we can know nothing about it. It is the Unknowable. All that we can know are the inner and outer expressions of the Absolute.

And these expressions obey the law of evolution. We see them becoming groups and these groups organizing into wholes. As the groups are organized, various forms of life evolve. The human individual is a result of the formation of groups of atoms into hands, arms, heart, lungs, feet, and

THE NATURE OF THE UNIVERSE

the like, and the organization of all these into a body in which each part does its duty as part of the whole body. The legs walk, the hands grasp, the heart beats, etc.

Thus, Spencer believes in the existence of a world external to our consciousness. This world we infer because it is impossible for us to do otherwise. Because we have impressions, we reason that there must be a cause of these impressions, an external world. But the impressions are not pictures, copies of the external world. As far as we can know, they may be as unlike the external world as letters of a word are unlike the idea which the word means. "H-o-r-s-e"—the letters themselves do not suggest the idea of a horse which the whole word calls before us. Likewise, our impressions and the actual external world may be wholly unlike one another. All that we can say with certainty, Spencer believes, is that there is something beyond consciousness which is the cause of our impressions, the Unknowable, the Absolute.

Josiah Royce, William James, and John Dewey

JOSIAH ROYCE, leader of the Idealistic school of thought in the United States, began his thinking from the nature of man. We are conscious beings and organize our experiences into wholes or a system. Likewise, he teaches, the universe is a conscious Being, a whole. My thinking, your thinking, the thinking of everyone are parts of the whole thinking universe.

I have an idea of a table. I do not create this idea or the table. The table is there. But it is not matter. Rather, the cause of my idea of a table is the idea of a table in the mind of the Absolute. It is, therefore, an idea which causes my idea, but is God's idea. The whole universe, then, is similar to my own ideas. This universe is a self-conscious organism idealized. It is all the ideas of all mankind and the causes of these ideas. The outer world is mental just as is the inner world of my experience.

These thinkers, the Idealists, have attempted to interpret the universe in terms of the thinking individual in order to conserve the values of spiritual life. They have relegated science to a secondary or lower position, but have taken it into account. For them, the laws of science are actually the laws of thinking. But, the real world is not to be limited to the unchanging laws of material things. Above these laws are the laws of man's spirit. By this belief, they escape strict determinism and make possible freedom and morality. If man is subject to the inevitable laws of science, he cannot be free and it is futile to hold him to account for his actions. He cannot be blamed. But freedom and moral responsibility are too valuable to be lost in this way. Consequently, the Idealists hold on to them by arguing that the world is actually spiritual rather than physical. Modern science seems to them to destroy all that makes human life human.

Recent philosophy is characterized by this attempt to take account of the whole realm of modern science with its laws and consistencies and at the same time preserve those things which men have found of value. The Idealists lay emphasis upon these values and think of a universe in which they are dominant.

WILLIAM JAMES, one of the first Pragmatists, found that a "block-universe" in which everything was governed by the laws of science was not satisfying. He wrote, "If everything, man included, is the mere effect of the primitive nebula or the infinite substance, what becomes of moral responsibility, freedom of action, individual effort, and aspiration?" He believed that the test of any theory or belief should be its practical consequences. This is the pragmatic test. And he was certain that only a theory of the universe which took into account moral responsibility, freedom of action, and the like, and made room for them, would have consequences that were good.

The real world, for him, was the world of human experience. Here we find science and human values all included. Beyond this he believed it impossible for a thinker to go. Although he did not doubt the existence of a world outside of experience, a world that caused experiences, he believed that we could not experience it and therefore could know nothing about it.

JOHN DEWEY, one of the leaders of present-day Pragmatism, held that the universe is a changing, growing, developing thing. He concentrates his attention upon experience, which he finds is ever becoming, changing, being enriched. The philosopher, he argues, must cease to spend his time with questions of beginnings, of what lies outside of experience, of a world "out there." It makes no difference for us whether or not there is such a world. For us it is the experiences which we have that are the important things, and the explanation of how they come, grow, change, and influence other experiences. The universe of our experience is uncertain, doubtful, full of surprises, but is also characterized by consistencies upon which we can depend. This is the only world in which Dewey was interested.

The Views of Henri Bergson and George Santayana

HENRI BERGSON, who was the leader of another attempt to conserve values in a world of science, taught that a universe as described by science would not be adequate. It leaves out too much. To know the universe in its fullness, one must live in it and apprehend it by "intuition." A man cannot know a river by merely sitting on its banks; he must jump into it and swim with its current. We must immerse ourselves in the universe to understand it.

The universe for Bergson is a moving, growing, becoming, living thing. Science cuts a slice out of it and tells us that this slice is the universe. For Bergson, the slice by itself is dead, unreal. The true universe is living, rich, containing the slice, but more than the slice. He characterized the universe as a process of "creative evolution," a becoming in which new things appear. The cause of this is the creative nature of the universe. "The whole evolution of life on our planet is an effort of this essentially creative force to arrive, by traversing matter, at something which is only realized in man and which, even in man, is realized only imperfectly." In seeking to organize matter, this creative force has been trapped. In man, creativity is seen to be breaking away from matter and becoming free.

Another modern philosopher who deals with this problem of science and values is GEORGE SANTAYANA. His real universe is the universe of human experience in all its richness and fullness. That there is a substance causing such experience he does not doubt, but rather seeks to justify its existence. He writes that Herbert Spencer was correct in maintaining the existence of such a substance, but believes that it is knowable through experience. We are certain of this world of experience. We find in it the laws of science and all the beauty, truth, and goodness for which we long. It is a real world in any true sense of the term real.

Thus, modern science will not permit us to deny that the real world is as the scientist finds it, a thing upon which we can depend and the laws of which men can discover and act upon with a high degree of certainty. We can trust the universe as explained by the scientists. But philosophers are keenly conscious that this universe of the scientists is not all. They discover in the universe the human mind, human hopes and fears, love and hate, dreams and defeats. Here they find men acting as though they were free and others holding them responsible for their actions. The universe for them is also a place of struggle, planning and realization, willing and creating. It is this that the philosophers will not give up.

Consequently, the universe of modern philosophy is one in which both science and human values are accounted for. Today no thinker can claim recognition unless he has in some way at least accounted for the discoveries of the laboratories and those of the inner man. This whole universe is real, and any other is but a part, and no one must hold that the part, any part, is the whole and the rest unreal. All the universe, the outer and the inner, is real, and the philosopher must find place for it all in his system. This is the problem of modern philosophy, the problem of the nature of the universe as seen by philosophers now writing and teaching.

Chapter II
MAN'S PLACE IN THE UNIVERSE

PROTAGORAS SOCRATES PLATO ARISTOTLE
AUGUSTINE ABELARD AQUINAS
SPINOZA LOCKE LEIBNITZ ROUSSEAU
KANT NIETZSCHE COMTE
SPENCER JAMES DEWEY RUSSELL

*Is man the destined master of the universe, or is he a
"worm of the dust"? What is the relation between
man and the universe? Is man the center of the universe, the goal of all creation, or is he a mere incident of no more significance to the universe than a
speck of dust? Is the universe friendly or unfriendly to
man, or is it merely unconcerned?*

"When I consider thy heavens, the work of thy fingers,
the moon and the stars, which thou hast ordained; what is
man, that thou art mindful of him?" wrote the ancient
Hebrew Psalmist many centuries ago. And his answer revealed a high opinion of the dignity of man. "Thou hast
made him but little lower than God, and crowned him with
glory and honor. Thou makest him to have dominion over
the works of thy hands; thou hast put all things under his
feet."

This is one attitude toward the problem of man's place
in the universe. It is the belief that man is the crowning
creation of the entire creative process, and that he may

rule over everything in the universe. Man is "but little lower than God."

Another belief about man's place in nature is expressed by the Biblical author of "Ecclesiastes." This skeptical individual teaches, "For that which befalleth the sons of men befalleth beasts . . . as the one dieth, so dieth the other . . . man hath no pre-eminence above the beasts. . . . All go unto one place, all are of the dust, and all return to dust."

Here is extreme pessimism about man. He is nothing but dust, a miserable worm with no pre-eminence or power. He suffers, struggles, is beaten down by the forces of the universe which are mighty and powerful. His life is a "way of suffering," a "vale of tears and sorrows."

As the early wise men of Judaism thought about this problem, so thought those of other races and peoples. The Egyptians, Babylonians, Assyrians, Phoenicians, and other early peoples strove to understand man in relation to his universe. And there were among them optimists who placed man above all else in the universe, and pessimists who saw him as nothing more than an insignificant second in time.

Man's Importance According to the Early Greek Philosophers

While the very early Greeks did not deal directly with the problem of man's place in the universe, their theories of the nature of the universe left man, by implication, as a part of this universe. For THALES, for example, man, as everything else in the universe, was made of water. Man, like all else in nature, came to be by a natural process and in due time returns to the original stuff of the universe.

In the thinking of all these early Greeks, nature is supreme, and man is a part of nature. HERACLITUS taught that man is part of the universal fire, he is subject to the law of the universe. He wrote, "This one order of things neither any one of the gods nor of men has made, but it always was, is, and ever shall be, an ever-living fire, kindling according to fixed measure and extinguished according to fixed measure." Here is a definite idea of the absolute supremacy of the universe, of nature. Man, as everything else including the gods, is subject to this universe and can do nothing to change it or to escape.

According to EMPEDOCLES, man, like all other things in the universe, is composed of the elements of the universe: earth, air, fire, and water. All things in the universe are alive and have the power of thought. Man differs from all else in that he has more of this power.

The *Atomists* taught that man was the result of a mingling of atoms just as was a tree, a star, or anything else. The human individual has an abundance of "soul atoms" which he breathes in and out throughout life. When this process ceases, he dies and the soul atoms are scattered.

All the Greek thinkers before the time of the *Sophists* thought of man as a part of the universe, composed of the same elements as everything else in the universe, and subject to the same laws of the universe. In man some of the elements were a little more refined than those in other bodies, but that was all the difference. Man, for them, was a product of the universe, and had to meet the requirements of the universe or be destroyed.

The Sophists took the opposite position as regards man. They thought of man as the center of the universe. "Man," said PROTAGORAS, the most noted of the Sophists, "is the measure of all things." Protagoras, along with the other Sophists, turned from the study of nature to the study of man and his relationships. For them, man was no longer tied to the universe and subject to its inevitable laws. Rather, he was thought of as free, as able to determine his own fate, to mould the universe, or at least that part which was of most importance to him, in such a way that his desires would be satisfied. The Sophists tore man loose from natural law and attempted to make him the master of his fate.

Thus the Sophists opened up the problem of man's place in nature. They became skeptical of man's power to understand this universe and concentrated upon a study of man himself and man's relationship to other men.

The Positions of Socrates, Plato, and Aristotle

SOCRATES agreed with the Sophists in turning his thoughts away from problems of the universe. "He set his face against all discussions of such high matters as the nature of the universe; how the 'cosmos,' as the savants phrase it, came into being; or by what forces the celestial phenomena arise. To trouble one's brain about such matters was, he argued, to play the fool." His interest was in man and man's problems. To know what is right and to live by the right is more important than to know how the universe came into being. Man, for Socrates, is the center, the pivot, of all that is worth thinking about.

PLATO felt that the Sophists had gone to the extreme in making man the center of the universe. He saw value in this point of view, but he realized that it was not complete. He also recognized that the thinkers of early Greece had something to contribute. Therefore, he attempted to find a solution to the problem of man's place in the universe which would satisfy the best in the thought of both the early Greeks and the Sophists.

Man, Plato taught, is truly the measure of all things, because there lie in him certain universal principles, notions, concepts, or ideas which are basic to all knowing. These ideas correspond to reality, the real world. Man, in his thinking, is able to grasp the true nature of things.

The true universe, as we have seen in the previous chapter, is, for Plato, a universe of changeless, pure, eternal ideas. Man can rise to a state in which he can contemplate, can know these ideas. Man can know the "universals."

Further, man is, Plato believed, a creation of the universe. Pure idea is impressed upon matter and the universe which we experience is created. We experience other individuals. We also experience ourselves, our bodies. All these have come into being as ideas have been impressed upon matter. But man is the only creation which can come to know these ideas and to understand the process by which things of nature came into being. In this way Plato emphasizes the unique place of man in the universe. Man is not like the animals, although his creation took place in somewhat the same way as theirs. His "soul" is part of the divine reason which has entered the body and which is capable of knowing the eternally real things of the universe.

When this rational part of man comes into the body, it is hindered, held down, clouded by the body which is matter. Its task is to overcome this disadvantage and rise above the body. The Philosopher, as Plato sees him, does rise above the body and dwells in a realm of mind in which he can know that which is real, ideas.

For ARISTOTLE, likewise, man is a creation in the same way as are all other objects in the universe. In him we find matter and form. But man is to be distinguished from all other objects in nature by the fact that he possesses reason. Like all lower forms of life, plants for example, man has vital functions. Also, like all animals, he has the power to imagine, remember, to experience desire, pain, pleasure, and the like. But unlike either plants or animals, man has the power to think. His reason is creative. This is the spark of the divine in man.

Thus, although the Sophists and both Plato and Aristotle were primarily interested in man, each had to think of man as living in an environment. The Sophists concentrated upon man's social environment and the problems involved. Plato and Aristotle saw man not only as a member of this environment, but also as an individual in a universe. In the case of both philosophers, man is thought of as the highest creation, a being who in some way partakes of that which is divine in the universe. Although man is of nature, a creature in which is to be found matter, he is also of the divine, able to approach the divine because he is of the same nature as the divine. Man has within him that which rises above matter and approaches that which is most ideal in the universe. Thus, man is not lost in the jumble of senseless matter, but can overcome matter and reach out toward the divine.

The Views of the Later Greek Thinkers

To the *Stoic*, man is a part of the universal order. Indeed, in man is to be found the entire universe in miniature. His nature is the same as that of the All. Thus, in man as in the universe, reason should rule and he should subordinate himself to the law of the universe. Each man has a prescribed place in the divine order. He should discover this place and fit himself into it. Thus, man should live according to nature, as the divine reason directs.

It is evident that the Stoic philosophy subordinates man to that which is the universal ideal. Being a unit in the whole and subject to its demands, man is happy when he understands these demands and obeys them gladly.

Man's Importance According to the Early Christian Thinkers

Although all these Greek philosophers recognized the fact that man is both matter and spirit, they emphasized the spirit, and were optimistic in the belief that man could overcome the disadvantages of matter. Christianity had no such optimism. For it, matter loomed large and foreboding and life was a constant struggle to escape its implications. Indeed, for Christianity, God, or the divine, was so pure and matter so far from God that pessimism was the only possible outcome.

Matter, for the Christian thinkers, was the principle of evil. So long as man was in part matter he was evil and needed redemption. When the soul became attached to matter, it fell from divine grace, and the only way back was through some special act of the divine which would negate matter and release man from its clutches.

The *Apologists* taught that the whole world was made by God for man, to serve as an arena in which man might win eternal salvation. Further, man was given a dominant place in the universe. He was the ruler of all. He was put in the world to tend and govern it.

But some men chose to disobey God, and fell into sin. They turned from God to matter. Through divine grace they may regain their lost divinity and live eternally with God.

The creative principle of the universe, God, made man his masterpiece, but made it possible for this masterpiece to destroy itself. Nevertheless, God is thought of as desiring and striving for man's redemption and as having made this possible through Jesus Christ.

This point of view was developed by SAINT AUGUSTINE. For him God is the cause of everything, the universe and man. But man is God's highest creation, a union of body and soul. Man's life on earth is a pilgrimage to God. Indeed, in comparison to what awaits man after death, this life is actually not life but death. Here is the typical Christian contempt for the world and hope for another world beyond the grave.

Augustine believed that the first man, Adam, set the pattern for all future life of men. Adam, he taught, committed sin and thus handed on to all men the effects of this sin. He corrupted the entire human race, so that all men are condemned to sin for all times. Adam's sin, therefore, is hereditary. But God can reform corrupted man by his grace. And God has chosen certain men for salvation and certain others for eternal punishment. This is the doctrine known as "predestination."

Thus man, a creation of the all-ruling power of the universe, created out of nothing, inherits the weaknesses and sins of the first man. He must pay the price for this sin. But the all-ruling power can and does select some men for forgiveness and leaves others to the natural results of Adam's sin. Man is lost forever unless the Creator of the universe chooses to save him.

The Views of the Medieval Christian Thinkers

This general idea was carried over into the period of Christian thought known as Scholasticism, from the ninth to the thirteenth centuries. The first of the great Scholastics, or philosophers of this period, was JOHN SCOTUS ERIGENA. He taught that man is a revelation of the divine principle which created the entire universe and is that universe. But

man is also a living spirit responsible for his fall away
from God. He is a creation of God, but is able to draw
away from God, to sin.

This attempt to exalt God as the creator of the universe
and yet give to man some dignity reached its fullness in the
great dispute regarding the relationship between "universals" and individuals. If the universals are all supreme,
then the individual man can count for little in the universe.
He is but a mere incident, unimportant. The really important things are these universals. Mankind is important, the
particular man is not. God is the most important, and all
else is secondary. Thus, philosophers began to ask, What
part does the individual play in things? Is he a mere pup-
pet on wires pulled here and there by a divine creator? Or
do his actions, his desires, his struggles actually mean
something in the scheme of things?

WILLIAM OF CHAMPEAUX taught that the universal is
completely present in every individual so that each individual differs from another only in accidental properties.

PETER ABELARD held that universals cannot be entities
apart from things but are in some way in things. God is in
his creatures.

This reasoning led, on the part of some philosophers of
this period, to a definite pantheism. They argued that universals are real and that God is the highest universal. Thus
he is the most real thing in the universe and all else is an
expression of his divine essence. Man, then, is God, and
will eventually return to the totality, the whole, from which
he has come.

This Scholastic movement, with its problems and difficulties, reaches its climax in THOMAS AQUINAS. This thinker set
himself the task of showing that the universe as a revelation
of God is rational. He taught that the universals exist in
particular objects as the essence of things. But matter is the
material in which these universals are implanted. Man,
then, is the universal "mankind" and matter.

God created the universe, including man, out of nothing,
according to Aquinas. Man is both matter and spirit, one

person in which are to be found two principles, mind and body. He is dragged down by matter, the body, and must seek redemption from his inherited sin.

Throughout this period of human thinking, the so-called Middle Ages, man is thought of as a creation of the divine, and, in some way, a being in which is a spark of the divine. But man is also of the earth. He is material, and through this material part he inherits the sin of the first man, Adam. Thus man is debased and must seek salvation from the Creator. The universe is both matter and spirit. Man partakes of both. Therefore part of the universe is thought of as pulling man upward toward the divine and another part is pulling him down.

This fact led to the doctrine of "contempt for the world." At the extreme was the belief that everything in this world was evil and that man should attempt to escape from it. Life was thought of as a pilgrimage, a testing period, a time of trial and tribulation. Either by good deeds, prayer and fasting, or by the grace of God man might escape the consequences of his material part and come eventually into the realm of pure spirit.

Thus, for many thinkers of the period there were actually two universes, one of matter and the other of the spirit. The material universe was the cause of man's sin, and actually sought his eternal destruction. It was his enemy. But the spiritual universe sought his salvation and eternal blessedness. This was the abode of all that is good, the home of the divine.

In their attempt to conserve the spiritual values of the universe, Christian philosophers leaned heavily in the direction of complete contempt for the physical, material universe. However, some of these men were not willing to go to this extreme. They saw that such a solution would actually be no solution at all. It was dimly apparent to them that some way had to be found to reconcile the physical and the spiritual in man and in the universe.

During the Middle Ages the Christian Church was the dominant factor in human thinking and living. Its doctrine of man's relationship to the Creator and ruling power of the universe was supreme. Whatever philosophers thought, it was not allowed that they seriously question the doctrine that the Creator was supreme, and that man, one of his creation, was subordinate to his laws and will.

But the thinking mind of man would not rest contented with this situation. There were many philosophers who rebelled against the complete dominance of the Church. Although they did not state directly that man's dignity could not be maintained under such restrictions, their thinking gradually led them to emphasize the power of the human. The whole trend of thought known as Nominalism stressed the belief that man, the individual, was of most importance, and general ideas, universals, reals, were mere ideas in man's mind. WILLIAM OF OCCAM, for example, taught that universals exist only as ideas or thoughts in the human mind and have no other reality.

As Seen by the Forerunners of the Renaissance

This growing stress upon man and his power and dignity was symbolic of a trend in human thought. It was the stirring of a giant who had been asleep and during his sleep had been tied and fettered until he could no longer move. Slowly the giant broke his bonds, stood up, and proclaimed his power to the world. Man dared to assert his ability to control the world, to know its innermost secrets and, by the power of his intellect, to master its ways and turn them to his desires. Of such was the Renaissance of the human spirit. It was an emphasis upon the human in the universe, and, therefore, has been called "Humanism."

In the philosophies of LUDOVICO VIVES, PETRUS RAMUS, PARACELSUS, and BERNARDINO TELESIO this belief in man's power to force the universe to his desiring is evident. These men were among the pioneers of this rebellion against the forces which would crush man down, subordinate him to the universe. Although their ideas were crude, magical, and full of superstitions in which we cannot believe today, they were seeking to free man and place in his hands the tools for his mastery of the universe. What modern scientists have done for us, these men attempted to do for their age. They attempted to study and control nature with the knowledge and understanding which they possessed, and as such were forerunners of modern science.

As more and more investigations were made into the nature of the universe, this understanding and control grew. Copernicus, Galileo, Kepler, and Newton studied the universe and told their fellows how it worked. Of course the Church saw what was happening, and strove earnestly to root out these new forces. But the spirit of man had caught a faint glimpse of the future and would not be denied entrance into this promised land. Never again would man be satisfied to bow in utter subjection to the powers of the universe. He would stand erect and demand the right to challenge the universe and master its secrets. This was indeed a new day for man and the birth of a new conception of man's place in the universe.

The Positions of Bacon and Hobbes

The opening guns of this new period, the period of modern philosophic thought, were fired by those philosophers who emphasized the necessity for a careful and accurate study of the universe. FRANCIS BACON "gave conscious expression to this new scientific spirit." He would have man clear his mind of all the old and untrue ideas of the past and study the universe in an unprejudiced manner. As man observes and brings the fruits of his observations together, he will discover likenesses and differences among events and objects of the universe. In this way he will establish laws or consistencies among happenings upon which he can depend in all subsequent action.

Bacon laid great stress upon the value of accurate understanding of the universe, but he was unwilling to abandon completely the religious ideas of the past. He recognized, as it was inevitable that he should, that sometimes religious ideas and the discoveries of careful observation were contradictory. But he argued that man must believe both. "As we are obliged to obey the divine law, though our wills murmur against it, so we are obliged to believe in the word of God, though our reason is shocked by it."

Bacon was on the fence. He saw the necessity of studying the universe and mastering its secrets. But he could not go over completely to this as a source of knowledge. It was he, however, who laid the groundwork for man's gradual swing to science and away from religion.

THOMAS HOBBES was not troubled about this division. He went over completely to the scientific position and developed a purely materialistic philosophy. Everything in the universe, including man, is, for Hobbes, material in motion. Thus man's task is to understand the laws of motion and thereby to understand the universe. Having gained this understanding of the immutable and eternal laws of nature, man can adjust them to his will.

The Views of Descartes and Spinoza

RENÉ DESCARTES held that everything in nature must be explained mechanically and that anything spiritual must be reconciled with this. His theory began with one absolute substance, God, and two relative substances, mind and matter. In man we find both mind and matter. Although these two are united in man, they do not influence each other. The body operates by purely mechanical laws while mind is spiritual.

Man, then, partakes of the two relative substances of which all else in the universe is made. Man is of the universe, for Descartes. As part of nature, he is mechanical to the extreme, he is a machine which operates by natural laws just as a watch might operate. Mind is distinct from body and is thus eliminated from nature. But man is composed of both.

For SPINOZA, everything in the universe is actually substance or God. The two attributes of God, extension and thought, are found in man. Man is a form of God or the universal substance or reality. Each individual man is a mode of extension, or body, and a mode of thought. Indeed, everything in the universe is both a mode of matter and a mode of mind. But, while in all objects save man these two modes are fairly simple, in man they are complex, composed of many parts. Further, in man, mind is conscious of its own actions, is self-conscious.

But there is no relation between man's mind and his body. Neither can influence the other. Nevertheless both mind and body are so constructed that what happens in one is accompanied by a similar happening in the other. Thus we seem to be affected by what happens in the body.

For Spinoza, then, all the universe is God or substance in the form of both mind and body. Man is a unit in this whole. He is both mind and body.

Man's Place as Seen by Locke, Berkeley, and Hume

A somewhat different conception of man's place in the universe is held by JOHN LOCKE. For him man is a part of the world, but a part which is sensitive to the world round about. Being sensitive, man has ideas about the world which come through the sense organs, through experience. Although man is both mind and body, the mental part is influenced by the body and the body by the mental. There is, then, interaction between the two parts which make up man.

For Locke, besides these two substances of mind and body, there is another spiritual substance, God. God has made the universe out of nothing and has arranged it so that it acts as we find it acting through our experiences.

With Locke, man's reason is established as the ultimate test of everything in the universe. Locke agrees that an outer world exists and that God exists and has created the world. But he attempts to prove all this in such a way that it will be reasonable, that it will satisfy man's mind. Human reason, for him, becomes the final test of revelation. Locke's followers sought to carry this line of reasoning further and seek the true revelations of God in the laws of nature. With them, Christianity becomes a rational religion and loses its mystery.

Thus, the individual man is coming into his own. He is to be the judge of the universe. His reason is the court of last appeal. He must understand before he accepts a thing as true.

GEORGE BERKELEY carries this idea further by eliminating the material universe and making man the seat of everything in the universe. For him there is no universe outside of mind, either the human mind or the mind of God. Existence is that which is perceived, and nothing exists when there is no mind to perceive it. Bodies, the universe, have no existence outside of mind. Thus the theory of a substance outside of mind which causes the ideas in mind must be given up as wholly meaningless. Our sensations come to us not from material objects but from the mind of God.

The complete, logical outcome of this position is developed by DAVID HUME. He makes man, and man alone, the center and whole of the universe. Since all that we can know, he argues, is our own ideas, there can be no material or spiritual substance causing them. The universe, all the universe that we can prove, is our ideas in succession. These ideas arise from unknown causes, and we are not correct in supposing them to be caused. We may believe in a cause of our ideas, or we may believe in the existence of God and a world outside of us, but we cannot prove either by any rational method known to man.

Hume had led men to the point where he must distrust himself. That fervent enthusiasm for mastery of the universe here had cold water thrown upon it. Man had attempted to understand the universe and thereby control it. Philosophers had abandoned gradually the idea of revelation and set up the human mind as the source of all knowledge. They seemed to be making remarkable headway when Locke brought them up quick with his insistence that they stop to examine the powers of the human mind. Berkeley and Hume began where Locke left off and carried the examination further, to what they believed to be the logical conclusion of the position taken. Hume left man standing alone, his universe within his mind, and unable to prove by the method long cherished that there was a universe, a cause of his ideas, or even that he himself existed. Does man stand alone, isolated? Is it necessary that we think of a mere succession of ideas traveling through space as the end-all? This was the problem which Hume left to those thinkers who followed him.

The Views of Leibnitz

While this advance toward isolation was progressing in England, a somewhat different movement was evident in Germany. It stemmed from the work of Spinoza and was developed by the German thinker GOTTFRIED WILHELM LEIBNITZ. It will be remembered that Spinoza had thought of everything in the universe, including man, as both material and spiritual, and that these were attributes of the one substance, God. Leibnitz broke substance up into an infinite number of small bits or monads. His world was built out of these self-contained units, these building blocks of the universe.

Man, for Leibnitz, was a construct of monads, but differed from the inorganic in that he had a central, controlling monad or soul. God had so arranged the universe that every monad acted in harmony with every other monad. Thus, though God was there in the beginning to start the universe going, he was in no way a part of the universe after the start. He could withdraw and let the monads unite and separate according to their nature. Thus, Leibnitz's universe is wholly mechanical. Man, and all nature, is subject to law, order, uniformity.

Here is a mechanical universe driven onward to creation and dissolution by inexorable laws which are of the nature of the universe. Man, as part of this process, is driven along with all the rest of the universe. Although man is, in some way, the goal of the divine creative will and is, therefore, contained in the universe from the beginning, he is part of the natural whole and subject to its pre-established laws.

Although this point of view differed in many respects from that of Locke and his successors, both streams of thought led in the direction of a mechanical interpretation of the universe and of man within it. Descartes had moved in this direction. Man, to him, was a machine. Leibnitz reduced matter to force. Thus, a mechanistic world view gradually became popular throughout the philosophic world. As a result, the dominant point of view in many quarters was to the effect that all nature was governed by law and that everything in the universe was a product of nature. This led, naturally, to great interest in the sciences and intense study of them. Science seemed to offer great hope for man.

The Position of Rousseau

It was JEAN JACQUES ROUSSEAU who shocked the philosophic world and shook its faith in this process. For Rousseau, man was not a machine, part of the mechanical universe. Rather, he was a thing of feeling, sentiment. Science, culture, Rousseau taught, had bound man in chains which were destroying all that was really human. Rousseau proposed to cast off this shell of civilization and free man for the full development of all his capacities. Indeed, Rousseau believed that science had isolated man from nature and that man's salvation lay in an escape from the bonds of science and a return to nature.

Kant's View of Man's Importance

This bold challenging of the trend of the age, this plea for a return to nature in all its richness and fullness, influenced perhaps the greatest of all modern philosophers, IMMANUEL KANT.

Kant undertook the task of restoring man to his dominant place in the universe. This necessitated the answering of questions raised by the philosophers who had preceded him. It was his task to "limit Hume's skepticism on the one hand, and the old dogmatism on the other, and to refute and destroy materialism, fatalism, atheism, as well as sentimentalism and superstition." It was no small undertaking, and one that waited for the coming of a mind of the greatness of Kant's.

Man, Kant taught, is part of the universe of objects and

things. But actually, although he can be certain of the existence of this world apart from himself, he cannot know it. All that he can know is that world which his mind, because of its nature, constructs from the sensations received by contact with this outer universe. Here he is in agreement with the essential positions of Locke, Berkeley, and Hume. Knowledge is confined to ideas.

But this is not all. Man is able to reason and, on the basis of this, he can form ideas of the outer world, of God, freedom, and immortality. Thus man, by virtue of reason, can act as though there is an outer world, as though this world and himself were created by a Creator, as though he is free and possessor of a soul which cannot perish.

Thus, while Kant acknowledges that from the point of view of knowledge, man is caught in the clutches of his own ideas, this is only part of the picture. The other side is that there are factors within man which justify his assuming the existence of all for which Rousseau was fighting and more. Herein the dignity of man in the universe is restored. Kant believed that he had solved the problems left by his predecessors and that he had solved them well. He believed that man could again stand up and face the universe, confident in his power to understand it and control it to his destiny. He was certain that he had restored to man the dignity which the skepticism of Hume had virtually destroyed.

Kant gave to the philosophic world the clue to all that seemed of value to men. He had suggested with strong and appealing arguments that there is a higher kind of truth than that offered by human intelligence, the moral law within us which guarantees the world of values. This clue fascinated Kant's immediate followers. Consequently, they set about to develop it to the fullest and, by so doing, to give man assurance of his power and dignity in the universe.

Fichte, Schelling, Schleiermacher, and Hegel

JOHANN GOTTLIEB FICHTE made the principle of freedom central to his whole philosophy. Man, for him, is fundamentally a free agent, not a mere link in a predetermined chain of material events. Self-determining activity is the supreme characteristic of man. Fichte sought to prove this thesis by a method similar to that of Kant. He argued that, although theoretical reason cannot prove the primacy of freedom, we must accept such a principle as ultimate because only by so doing can we satisfy the demands of our moral nature, give to life value and meaning.

Further, the fundamental principle of the universe for Fichte is a universal, free, self-determining activity. This he called the Absolute ego. It is a reality above all individual beings, a universal active reason which is, likewise, in every individual. Man, then, is part of the universal ego. He partakes of the nature of the universe. He is dominated by this universal life process.

This ego, this universal activity, expresses itself in man and in nature. The tree, the table, the beast, and man are all expressions of this fundamental principle. Man is the highest expression of the creative ego which is the universe.

In making this free, creative principle, this spirit or mind, the fundamental factor of the universe, and in thereby delivering man from the deadly mechanism into the clutches of which earlier philosophers had tended to condemn him, both Kant and Fichte were answering a deep-seated desire of mankind to find in the nature of the universe justification for its deepest yearnings and highest hopes. FRIEDRICH WILHELM JOSEPH SCHELLING was fascinated by the possibilities of this theory. Being of a poetic and artistic temperament, he carried Fichte's conception further and taught that the universe was a work of art created by the great artist of the universe. The universe, including man, is, for Schelling, a living, evolving system, an organism in which each part has its place, just as each color of a work of art fits into the whole to make a masterpiece.

Naturally this point of view fitted into the thought and temperament of the poets, artists, and creative geniuses of the period. Lessing, Herder, and Goethe, only to mention a few, felt that here was philosophic expression of that which was deepest in their natures. Here was the artist's universe, and in it was a place where the artist would feel at home and contented.

FRIEDRICH ERNST DANIEL SCHLEIERMACHER identified God with the universal creative principle of the universe, the source of all life. God is in the world, but is more than the world. Men, individual egos, are self-determining principles, each with his own specific talent and nook in the scheme of things. Each individual is necessary to the whole. If the universe is to realize itself to the fullest, is to create to the limit of its ability, each unit, each ego, must create to its limit. Man is necessary to the complete self-realization of the universe.

The whole Idealistic movement in philosophy, of which both Fichte and Schelling are representatives, interpreted the universe from the point of view of man. GEORG WIL-HELM FRIEDRICH HEGEL employed the same method. A study of man reveals certain facts and factors. As man, so the universe of which man is a part. So reasoned the Idealists.

In man, Hegel found certain logical processes operating. He recognized that the human mind naturally moves from the statement of a fact to a statement of its opposite. For example, war is evil. But, it is evident that good can and has come of war. Thus, war must also be good. Having recognized both these contradictory facts, the human mind moves on to discover some basis for reconciling them. Hegel believed that this was the way in which all thinking takes place. First, we propose a thesis: war is evil. Then, we propose the antithesis: war is good. The final proposition is the synthesis: despite the evils that come from war, there are certain values which men realize in war.

As with the human mind, so with the universal mind, reasoned Hegel. The universe is like man and the processes in the universe are the same processes, on a larger scale of course, which we find in the mind of man. Reality is, for Hegel, a logical process of evolution. It, too, has its thesis, antithesis, and eventual synthesis. Man is the pattern of which the universe is the complete realization. Man is the universe in miniature. Man is a microcosm of the great macrocosm; that is, man is a little universe which is a miniature of the whole universe.

For Hegel, then, it makes no difference where we begin in our studies, the result will be the same. If we begin with man and move out to nature, we find like processes at work. If we study the universe first, and move to man, we shall find an equal similarity.

In the approach of the Idealists we recognize the hand of the Sophists, Socrates, and Plato at least. The interest of these Greek thinkers, as we have seen, was primarily in man. They were not interested in the universe except as it affected man and his relations with his fellows. They began with a study of man. But inevitably they arrived at a theory of the universe. However, in each case, the universe was interpreted in terms of man. Take Plato, for example. He found that the highest in man was idea. He saw man attempting to mould the world to fit his ideas just as the artist moulds clay to give concreteness to an idea. From this he reasoned that the supreme thing in the universe was idea, pure and untouched by matter. But, as man used ideas to mould matter, so the divine creative principle of the universe used ideas to mould the universe.

So, down the ages has come this approach to the universe, the approach through man and his nature. As man, so the universe, they reasoned.

The Views of Later German Thinkers

But there has been another, likewise powerful, tradition in philosophy. The leaders of this tradition, as we have seen, study first the universe, the material universe. Having discovered its laws and nature, they place man in the chain of inevitable causes and effects. If the universe is a machine governed by unchangeable laws, so is man a machine.

JOHANN FRIEDRICH HERBART is representative of this latter approach, as indicated in our first chapter. Both nature and man, he taught, are constituted by the coming and going, the mingling and separating of units which he called "reals." The universe of reals is absolute. In it there is no change, growth, decay. The only change lies in our own habit of relating reals in such a way as to form objects or patterns.

You have undoubtedly seen drawings which, if looked at steadily for a while, seem to change before your very eyes. Actually we know that the drawing does not change, but our eyes relate parts of it in different ways so that the picture seems to change. So, Herbart thought, must we think of the universe and our experiencing of it. It never changes, but we relate the various reals in such diverse ways that the universe seems to change.

Man, likewise, is a result of the organization of reals. His mental life is a fusion, organization of ideas which result from the interaction of reals. And, Herbart believed, all this can be stated in purely mechanical terms. For him, psychology was nothing other than the mechanics of the mind. As Herbart saw the universe operating in terms of dependable laws, he reasoned that man, in all his actions, can be explained in the same terms. Everything in mind follows fixed laws. Man is part of the natural universe, is governed by the same laws, and can be understood and controlled if we know the laws.

ARTHUR SCHOPENHAUER thought in the Idealistic tradition. He interpreted the world, the universe, in terms of the human individual. In man he found the will supreme. Man wishes, wills to do, make, or have something. This will drives him into action and may result in a changed environment. As with man, so the universe. Will is the fundamental principle of the creative universe. All nature is an expression of will. In the stone, will is blind; in man, it is conscious of itself.

Man, then, is a pattern of the universe, a pattern in miniature. Man is the universe greatly reduced.

RUDOLF HERMANN LOTZE is in this same tradition. The universe, for him, must be understood in terms of the human mind since the mind is the only true reality we can know. Mental life is present throughout nature, even to rocks and dirt. The human mind is the highest stage, that upon which mind becomes self-conscious. Man is the truest representation of the universe, the highest creation of the great creative mind which is the universe.

Man as the model of the universe is exploited by FRIED-RICH NIETZSCHE. In man he finds the will to power, and believes that this is dominant. Therefore, he reasons that this will to power is the fundamental factor in the universe. But, this universal will to power takes on, for Nietzsche, a sinister appearance. The universe cares nothing for man, his dreams and hopes.

Since the will of man drives him on regardless of the consequences to others, so the will of the universe drives on despite its consequences to us. It crushes man in the storm and destroys him in the flood. It cares not for his existence and knows nothing of his plans or struggles. The universe is not friendly to man. Life is terrible. There is no way out. We struggle to realize our wills only to be crushed in the end, to be devoured by death.

The optimism of the Idealists has been turned against them by Nietzsche. They believed that the universe should be interpreted in terms of man if his values were to be preserved. Thus, as mind was the essence of man for them, they reasoned that the essence of the universe was mind, and that such a mind would be friendly to man's values. Nietzsche uses the same method, but finds the essence of man to be a will to power. When he translates this into universal terms, when he makes the will to power the essence of the universe, he reaches the pessimistic conclusion that the universe cares nothing for man and his values.

Man's Place According to Comte

A most radical attempt to interpret the universe in terms of man is to be found in the movement of philosophic endeavor known as "Positivism." The early leader of this movement was AUGUSTE COMTE. He took the position that the only source of knowledge was observation and experience. From this we get only uniform relations between phenomena. As far as inner essences are concerned, we can know nothing.

Consequently, we cannot know the inner essence of the

universe or of man. As man looks at the universe, he finds it operating in certain ways. This is all he knows, and all that he needs to know. Thus, the universe and man's place in it are interpreted in terms of what man can see and experience.

Man finds people getting in draughts, catching cold, and suffering. In so far draughts are enemies of man. But he also finds that by regulating draughts he can keep a fire burning with which he can heat his house or cook his food. In so far draughts are friendly to man. All that man needs to know, and indeed all that he can know are these relationships. Whether there is a basic unity behind these phenomena, man can never know and, in fact, he does not need to know since the fact would not change his life one bit. He would still stay out of certain draughts and use others to regulate his fire.

Man, for Comte, is in the universe, is affected by its parts in various ways and is able to affect the universe in many other ways. As man finds regularities in the relationships between parts of the universe and between himself and these parts, he is able to foresee consequences of his actions and happenings among the parts, and to govern his actions, to a degree at least, in the light of these relationships.

The Positions of Mill and Spencer

JOHN STUART MILL contributed to this position by showing how men may discover regularities within the universe. His logical method of induction was a guide to assurance. We see many events in which there are similarities. We study these and discover consistencies. Experience is evidence that we can depend upon these consistencies. Therefore, we take the position that a certain situation will be followed by a certain phenomenon. We can act on this, Mill believed, with a high degree of assurance that we will not be wrong.

As Mill found order, uniformity, inevitable sequence in the world which we experience, he reasoned that these same factors are to be found within man, since man is part of the universe. But, in man we find that the factors which must be taken into consideration are so numerous that it is impossible for us to predict with any high degree of certainty. Man is a very complex being. Every action of man is the result of a vast number of factors. Thus, although the same fundamental principles apply both in the universe and in man, recognition of them is easier in the universe since here the factors are simpler.

For example, it is possible for an astronomer, on the basis of observation and experience, to predict with absolute accuracy the appearance of a comet many hundreds of years from now. But, to predict whether a newborn baby will be a doctor, lawyer, beggar, or thief, is practically impossible. In the one case the factors involved are fairly simple, in the other they are highly complex. But, and this is the significant thing for our present study, Mill believed that, should it be possible for one to know all the factors and their proper weight, man would find equal certainty, uniformity, and inevitableness in both cases. Indeed, in his treatment of social and political problems, he attempted to show that certain uniformities do exist and can be experienced.

Although HERBERT SPENCER took the position that man can know only his experiences, he was certain that these experiences must have a cause, that there must be a universe outside of our experiences to cause us to experience as we do. Although he called this the "Unknowable," he interpreted it in terms of what he found in man.

Since, he reasoned, man has the subjective feeling of activity, muscular strain, force, the Unknowable is of the same nature. It is activity, force. Thus the fundamental principle of the universe is also the fundamental principle of man. Man is of the universe.

As this force is creative and active according to definite laws of development, so we find man a result of this creative development. Man is a result of the evolutionary processes which are to be found in the universe. And, further, as man develops, he follows these evolutionary processes. The law of evolution, then, is the universal law of things. It is the law of the development of the universe, the law which accounts for the coming of man, and the law which is in man and by which he develops.

Just as, Spencer reasoned, all things in the universe are results of the adaptation of the unit to the environment, so all that is in man is a result of a similar adaptation. Consciousness, for example, has resulted from the necessity to adapt to the environment. Man is what he is because his universe, his environment, makes certain consistent and definite demands upon him. Thus, the law which is fundamental to the universe is also fundamental to man. Man is part, a stage, of the on-going process which is evolution.

The Views of James, Dewey, and Russell

The Positivistic point of view, as developed by Comte, is evident in the thought of WILLIAM JAMES. He, too, places man at the center of the universe. For him, whatever is experienced is real. For him, reality is pure experience. Therefore, on the basis of our experience we construct a theory of the universe. But this theory is determined by what we experience. It is egocentric; that is, centered in man's ego.

For James, whatever satisfies man is true; and whatever does not satisfy him is false. Man finds certain consistencies in his experience. These, he reasons, are true of the universe. We act upon them, and the results which we anticipate follow. They are true. The universe, then, is the universe of human experience. We interpret it in terms of our experience, and all the ideas we have of it result from our experience.

Likewise, JOHN DEWEY thinks of man as the measure of the universe. The universe is that which man experiences. To try to go beyond this to absolute origins and finalities is foolishness. Man cannot get beyond his experiences.

Reality, in the thinking of Dewey, is growing, changing, developing according to laws which are the laws of human experience. Man is part of this process. Man is in the universe, a creation of the evolutionary process which we find everywhere. In him the universe comes to self-consciousness.

As in man we find uncertainty, doubt, and a degree of certainty, so in the universe. Man's experience is the measure of the universe, the only possible measure which we can have, for no man can get outside of his experience.

BERTRAND RUSSELL expresses the same general position in his little book, *A Free Man's Worship*. However, his conclusion, though similar in consequences to that of Nietzsche, is not arrived at by the same method. Russell sees the universe as a great mathematical machine. It is governed by scientific laws which are inexorable, unchanging. Man is part of this system, a very small and insignificant part.

Thus, for Russell, man is caught in the onrolling of the great universal machine. Its laws are inevitable, and its mills grind on regardless of what is thrown into the hopper. Man rises for a moment, thinks that he amounts to something, but his time of exaltation is short. After a brief life, he drops out of the scheme of things, and the universe moves on uncaring and unknowing. In the eternity of a machine universe, one individual with his values amounts to nothing.

Mankind, says Russell, is like a group of shipwrecked sailors on a raft in a vast sea at night. There is darkness all around. One by one they fall off the raft into the waters and disappear. When the last man has fallen off, the sea will roll on and the holes made in the water by their bodies will be covered over. Nature cares not for man.

Thus, throughout the history of human thought man has endeavored to understand the universe as related to himself. Some philosophers have arisen to tell him that the universe is like him and is his friend; that in the universe are forces which are concerned with his welfare. Indeed, the philosophic God is very often a being whose concern is for man. But there are those other philosophers who find the universe, and man included, a vast system of laws and consistencies in which human values have little or no place. Man lives his little day and is forgotten.

At the extremes we have both the religious and the scientific positions. Religious philosophies have attempted fairly consistently to construct a universe that is friendly to man and his values. They recognize the factors which seem to belie this position: death, sin, suffering, hopes unrealized. But they strive to fit these into a whole so that they lose their sting. God and heaven are often offered as the final solution of the problem.

Scientific philosophies, on the other hand, take the universe as they find it in the laboratory or under strict scientific investigation. They find only laws and inevitable consistencies, a great machine rolling on, a machine that can be depended upon to act in certain ways but which is unconcerned with human values.

And there are those philosophers who try to reconcile both extremes. The Pragmatists are of this group, as are many others. But it too often happens that the mediator simply brings the two extremes together in an inconsistent mixture.

Still the question haunts philosophy: Is the universe man's friend or man's enemy?

Chapter III

WHAT IS GOOD AND WHAT IS EVIL?

HERACLITUS   DEMOCRITUS   SOCRATES   PLATO
ARISTOTLE   AQUINAS   ABELARD
HOBBES   SPINOZA   LOCKE   LEIBNITZ
KANT   FICHTE   SCHOPENHAUER
MILL   BENTHAM   SPENCER   DEWEY

*What is the measure of good and evil in the world?
How can we know whether or not an act is good or
bad? Is there in the very nature of the universe a code
of laws which determines good and bad? Or, is goodness and badness a matter of the relation of an act to
other acts?*

Open the book of the story of mankind anywhere and
you will find the question being asked over and over again:
What is good and what is evil? This has been, without
doubt, one of the most persistent problems of philosophers
throughout the ages. Answers have been given in abundance, answers which appeared to the particular philosopher giving the particular answer to solve the problem
for all times, but in a very few years the problem has arisen
again in the thinking of others.

Is there an absolute, ultimate, and unquestioned measure
of good and evil, one that was established at the beginning
of time and that will stand until time is no more? A great
number of people have believed in such a measure, and
there have been thinkers who have attempted to state it in

a code of commandments or basic principles of conduct for all times. The Ten Commandments of the ancient Hebrews is an example of this trend in human thinking. Here is a code of conduct which is believed by many to have been handed down from the seat of divine authority and which has authority at all times and in all places.

At the other extreme are thinkers who have believed that both good and evil are relative to the conditions of the time and place, and that an act which is good in one place and time will be evil in another. For example, a maniac is chasing a man with intent to kill him. The man passes me and turns to the right and disappears. Then the maniac comes up and asks which way his intended victim went. I say that he turned left, and thereby save the life of an innocent man. This untruth is good, they argue in an attempt to prove that truth is not always good.

Between these two extremes are many theories of good and evil. Philosophers desiring to prove the absolute goodness of God have difficulty at times explaining the existence in the universe of death, suffering, and ill will. How can an all-good God create a world in which there are these apparent evils, they ask? And they have offered many ingenious arguments to reconcile a good God and an evil world.

And so, throughout the history of man's thought we discover the problem of good and evil (which we speak of as "ethics" or "the ethical problem") persistently challenging each philosopher.

Good and Evil According to the Early Greek Philosophers

HERACLITUS, the Greek philosopher of change, believed that good and evil were two notes in a harmony. He found many things changing into their opposites. Ice, which is hard, changes into water, which is soft. This led him to believe that the combination of opposites resulted in a whole in which there is harmony. Just as in music harmony results from the combination of low and high notes, so in the universe harmony results from the combination of opposites, good and evil.

We, he taught, see only the opposites, the good and the evil. But God sees the harmony, so that for him all things are fair and just in that they are parts of a great universal harmony. Thus, the good life for man is that life lived in harmony with the universal reason, the law which pervades all things. Man should seek to understand this harmony in the universe and to fit into it so that his actions are in accord with the principle governing the whole universe.

The early Greek philosophers, interested primarily as we have seen in the problem of the nature of the universe, taught that there were all-pervasive laws controlling the entire universe. Therefore, goodness for them was to be found in harmony with these laws. Further, they were so enchanted by this idea of law that even evil did not bother them much. Evil, for them, was but a phase, a note in the universal harmony and, thus, was not really evil but was another kind of good, a necessary part of the good whole.

As philosophers turned from their interest in the universe to a new interest in man, they began to ask most seriously the question: What kind of a life is good for man to live? How can one so regulate his life among his fellows that it is good?

DEMOCRITUS, the leading figure of the Greek Atomists, taught that the goal of life is happiness. At all times man should seek happiness. For him, happiness was an inner condition or state of tranquillity which depended upon harmony of the soul. He taught that one should not depend for happiness upon things of the world since these come and go and a lack of them causes unhappiness. Rather, happiness should be a state of the inner man, a balance of life, an attitude which combines reflection and reason.

Goodness, for him, was not only a matter of action, but depended upon man's inner desire. The good man is not one who does good, but one who wants to do good at all times. "You can tell the man who rings true from the man who rings false," he said, "not by his deeds alone, but also by his desires." Such goodness brings happiness, the goal of life.

With the coming of the *Sophists* thinking on this problem of good and evil entered a period of confusion. If, as Protagoras held, "Man is the measure of all things," then man is the measure of good and evil. And, by man, the Sophists meant the individual man, you, me, your neighbor. Each one has the right to determine for himself what is good and what is evil. The end of this practice is, of course, chaos. What I consider evil, you may consider good. The Sophists let the matter rest here.

As a result, each man had his own code of good and bad. He defied others to prove him wrong or to justify their condemnation of him. Many representative Sophists, such as EUTHYDEMUS, THRASYMACHUS, and CALLICLES, taught that morality was mere convention, habit. That actually there are no moral laws, no all-inclusive principles of right and wrong. These men sought to justify the principle that each man should live as he desired, get what he wanted by any means possible, and frame his own code of good and evil.

The result of this position was moral anarchy, pure individualism, and the ultimate in selfishness. Nevertheless, a closer study of this position reveals a tendency which is rich in possibilities. The Sophists were making their appeal to the independent human mind. They were rebelling against arbitrary authority in matters of morals and were arguing that the human mind must think for itself and in thinking discover a code of right and wrong. The Sophists were champions of the individual and his independence. True, they went to the extreme and lost the forest by concentrating attention upon the trees. Nevertheless, they had hold of a thing which is very precious to modern man, freedom to think and to arrive at conclusions about the good and the evil. The Sophists challenged moral theory to justify itself before the bar of human reason.

The Ethical Views of Socrates, Plato, and Aristotle

SOCRATES was stimulated by the Sophists but was unwilling to go all the way with them. He, too, was most interested in the problems related to living a good life. Thus a great deal of his teaching dealt with the meaning of right and wrong.

It was Socrates' firm belief that there must be a basic principle of right and wrong, a measure which would apply far beyond the beliefs of any one individual. Thus, he asked time and again: What is *the* good? What is the highest good by which all else in the universe is measured? And his answer was that knowledge is the highest good.

If one knows what is right, he argued, he will do it. "No man," he said, "is voluntarily bad." When one knows that a thing is good he will choose to do that thing. Therefore the most important endeavor of man is to discover what is good. Socrates spent his life trying to help men discover what is good. Thus, for him, a life which is always inquiring and trying to discover what is good is the best kind of life, the only life worth living.

PLATO took up the problem of good and evil where Socrates left it. For him, goodness is tied up with his theory of the nature of the universe. The world of sense, he taught, is unreal, fleeting, changing. This is evil. The real world of pure, unchanging ideas is the world of good. Man can know this real world only through his reason. Therefore, reason is the highest good for man. The end or goal of life is release of the soul from the body so that it can contemplate the true world of ideas.

But man may live a just life even though he is held down by the body and remains in a world of changing shadows of real things. This can be done, Plato believed, so long as the rational part of man rules his every action. Plato thought of man as consisting of three parts. The appetites are concerned with bodily functions and desires. The will, or spiritual part of man, is concerned with action, courage, bravery. And the reason is concerned with the highest and best in man. A man is living a good life when reason rules the will and the appetites, and when, as a result, he is wise, brave, and temperate.

Thus, a life of reason is the highest good for man, a life noted for wisdom, courage, and self-control. And, Plato taught, this kind of life will be the happy life. Happiness and goodness go together. However, one should not seek pleasure as the end of life. Pleasure comes when one has attained the good life, a life in which the highest, reason, rules the lower, will and appetites.

ARISTOTLE pointed out that every action of man has some end in view and that these ends seem to be an endless chain. One acts in order to get something, but this something is obtained in order to get something else, and so on. What, he asked, is the highest good, the good for which all else is done? He reached an answer to this question by pointing out that the aim of everything in the universe is to realize itself to the fullest. Each thing is different from all others. It has certain talents, abilities. Thus, it is good when it has realized these talents and abilities to the fullest. Thus, self-realization is for Aristotle the highest good, the goal of all else that is done.

Now, the distinguishing feature of man is his reason. No other entity in the universe possesses reason. Man alone has this characteristic, ability. Therefore, the highest good of man is the complete realization of his reason. This, Aristotle believed, brings happiness. Pleasure accompanies the full realization of man's reason; it is a natural result of such realization.

But, as Plato also taught, reason is only a part of man. He also has feelings, desires, appetites. Therefore, a good life is one in which all these factors are realized in perfect harmony, in which reason rules and the feelings and desires obey. The goal of human life is a rational attitude toward the feelings and desires.

What is this rational attitude? Aristotle taught that it consisted of the "golden mean." For example, courage is to be thought of as a mean between cowardice and foolhardiness. The good man is one who lives a life according to this golden mean, who does not go to extremes in action but balances one extreme over against another.

Thus, the good life for Aristotle is one in which man realizes to the fullest the supreme part of his nature, reason. Such a man will be noble, just, honest, considerate, and will give evidence of all the other virtues of life. And he will do these things because he desires to do them from the depths of his own being. He is not forced to act in this way by some authority outside of himself, but is driven to good actions by his own nature. As Aristotle wrote, "Virtue is a disposition, or habit, involving deliberate purpose or choice, consisting in a mean that is relative to ourselves, the mean being determined by reason, or as a prudent man would determine it."

Good and Evil According to the Epicureans and Stoics

What was for Plato and Aristotle a part of a whole philosophic system became for later philosophers the dominant problem. Both Plato and Aristotle thought of the good life as a natural and logical result of their entire philosophic theories. The *Epicureans*, however, made this problem central to their thinking. EPICURUS taught that the goal of all human activity is pleasure, that happiness is the supreme good for all. But, he cautioned, man should be careful when choosing pleasures. Some immediate pleasures eventually result in pain and suffering. Here is an excellent meal and it is a pleasure to eat it. I eat and eat far beyond reason. I enjoy it all immensely. But later I suffer with indigestion, gout, and other discomforts. Therefore, we need to be able to see way ahead to the consequences of all the pleasures which we enjoy. This will often mean that we will avoid certain immediate pleasures because their eventual consequences are bad.

Further, for Epicurus, mental pleasures are better than physical pleasures, and it is wise to choose pleasures of the intellectual life.

Experience shows, he pointed out, that we obtain pleasure by satisfying desires or by being free from desires. Therefore, we should seek to get rid of desires by satisfying them completely. This brings freedom from pain, the pain of desire, and is therefore good.

The *Stoics* taught that man's highest good lay in acting in harmony with the universe. Man, for them, is part of the universe, with a definite function to perform for the complete development of the whole universe. As the ruling power in the universe is reason, so reason should rule each man in his individual actions.

Further, man should submit to the rule of the laws of the universe; he should live according to nature. The good man is one who lives so that he fits into the scheme of nature, obeys its laws, and is determined in all he does by reason which is part of the universal reason.

Thus man must know the laws of the universe. If he knows the good, knows his place in the scheme of things, knows what is expected of him by nature, he will be good. And the result of such living is happiness. Happiness is not to be sought after nor is it to be gained by itself. We do good, live a virtuous life, and happiness inevitably follows.

The early Greek thinkers conceived goodness as a harmony within the universe. Evil for them was only imaginary, the result of a failure to see that apparent evil was actually part of a whole which is good, a discord which is harmony when heard in relation with the rest of the music. The later Greeks were interested primarily in man's relation with his fellows. Thus, goodness to them was a matter of the good life. The Stoics sought to reconcile these two positions, but leaned more in the direction of the early Greeks.

The Position of the Greco-Religious Thinkers

With the rise of the definitely religious movement in philosophy a sharp distinction was made between the principles of good and evil. This is easily traceable to the Babylonian, Assyrian, and other religious traditions from which the religion of the Western world received much. These early religions drew a sharp line between light and darkness, life and death, good and evil. Indeed, in many instances they conceived of special gods ruling each realm. Although some of the Greek thinkers relegated evil to matter, they were not as definite about the distinction as were the more religious thinkers.

PHILO, for example, thought of God as perfect purity, in no way whatsoever in contact with matter. God was the source of all good, and matter the source of all evil. Like-

wise, the spiritual part of man, his mind or soul, is the seat
of good; and his body, which is thought of as matter, is
the seat of evil. Consequently, when the soul is incorporated in the body it suffers a fall from divine perfection
and becomes predisposed to evil. Thus, the goal of man is
freedom from the body and all its sin, and return to God
and perfect goodness. The position of PLOTINUS was very
similar. Matter is the source of evil and God the source of
good.

The Ethical Views of the Early Christian Thinkers

Thus a definite dualism is to be seen throughout the
Western religious tradition, a dualism borrowed in substance from the religions of the early East. Christianity
accepted this dualism and made it basic to its treatment of
the whole problem of sin and redemption.

The *Apologists* taught that God had created man good,
but he turned from God to the flesh, the body. By this,
sin came into the world. The Christian interpretation of the
story of Adam, the first man, is a picture in symbolic terms
of the coming of sin, a sin which was then transmitted to
all men as original sin. Because man is man, a descendant
of the first man, he is harassed by evil and must seek salvation through the divine grace of God.

SAINT AUGUSTINE found that the presence of evil in the
universe gave him no end of trouble. God, for him, was all
good, all perfection. And God created the universe out of
nothing. If this be true, how could a good God, all powerful, create a universe in which there was evil? How account
for evil in a world created by an all-good God?

To solve this problem, Augustine taught that everything
in the universe is good. Even that which appears to be
evil to us is actually good in that it fits into the whole
pattern of the universe. Shadows, dark spots, are necessary
to the beauty of a painting. If seen by themselves, broken
away from the whole picture, they appear bad. But when
seen in the picture they make possible the beauty of the
whole.

Evil, then, is relative for Augustine, and is actually an

absence of good just as darkness is absence of light. The evil which we find in the universe is put there by God to make the whole universe good.

Further, for Augustine, the goal of all mankind is complete union with God and escape from the world. Man should turn his back on the pleasures of this world which are thin and pale, and direct his attention wholly to God who is perfect goodness. This union with God is to be attained through love of God as opposed to love of the world.

The Views of the Medieval Christian Thinkers

The position of Augustine is also held very largely by the philosophers of Scholasticism. Believing in an all-good God who created everything, they had to explain apparent evil as actually a part of the good whole and thus actually good.

ABELARD added a new note when he taught that the rightness or wrongness of an act does not lie in the act itself but in the intention of the actor. If one steals from another, the act itself is neutral. If the thief intended it as something good, it was thereby good. "God," he wrote, "considers not what is done, but in what spirit it is done; and the merit or praise of the agent lies not in the deed, but in the intention."

If one acts in terms of what he thinks is right, if he believes he is doing good and seeks to do good, he may err, but he does not sin. Goodness, morality, then becomes a matter of conscience. The truly sinful man is one who acts with a desire to do wrong. He is sinful because he shows in his action a deliberate contempt for God.

The greatest of the Scholastics was THOMAS AQUINAS. In his theory of good and evil we find the philosophy of Aristotle joined with the basic principles of Christianity. God made everything, including man, for a purpose, and the highest good of all things is the realization of this purpose. As one realizes the purpose for which he was created, he reveals God's goodness. Therefore, the highest good is the realization of oneself as God has ordained.

Further, the highest form of action is the contemplation of God. This may be done through reason or faith, but it reaches its height in what Aquinas called "intuition," a coming to God which can be completed only in the world to come, in heaven.

Aquinas follows Augustine, also, in holding that the goodness or badness of a particular action depends upon the aim or purpose of the actor. An act may have good consequences, but it is not good unless the actor intended it to have these consequences and knew that they would result. However, Aquinas does not hold with Augustine that an evil act may be good if the actor intended it to be so. Intention will not make a bad act good, but it is the only thing that will make a good act truly good.

The Christian doctrine of "contempt for the world" is prominent in Aquinas' teaching. The best way to attain goodness is to abandon worldly goods and seek the life of God. Thus, the life of the saint in a monastery devoting himself entirely to service to God is ideal.

Evil, for Aquinas, is privation, a lack of the good. All things, created by a good God, aim at goodness. When they fail, evil results.

The mystic teachings of MEISTER ECKHART emphasize the unity of God and the individuality of man. Since God is the pure unity of the world, the universe, any individuality must be a breaking away from God and therefore evil. Consequently, the good life is one which strives to return to the divine unity and become one with God. "Whoever would see God," he writes, "must be dead to himself and buried in God, in the unrevealed desert Godhead, to become again what he was before he was."

The good life for Eckhart, then, is not one of deeds but one of being. We do not attain goodness by striving to do good. We reach that which is perfect goodness by losing ourselves in the unity of God.

Christianity, and the whole Western religious movement, emphasized the great gulf between God and all that is less than God. Goodness is created by God and is to be found in adjustment to God's plan or purpose. Evil is in some way attached to matter, the body, or the world. But God, being the sole Creator of the universe, would not create evil. Therefore, evil must not actually be evil, but must be part of the great good. Not all the Christian philosophers held to this explanation consistently. They were confronted with the fact of human degradation, actions which were evil in intention or in consequences, by deliberate acts on the part of many which caused evil. Consequently, they had to tie this up with the body, the sinful will of man which was in some way inherited from Adam, or the perversity of matter.

Christianity has never been able to solve the problem of evil and sin. Eastern religions were more realistic in this matter. They did not make their gods the creators of the whole universe. Rather they had at least two gods, one the god of goodness and the other the god of evil. In traditional Christianity we find these two beings functioning. God is thought of as the source of all good, and the Devil is the evil principle. But, to the question "Did God create the Devil?" there is no answer. A dualism of good and evil works well until the attempt is made to account for the creation of the universe; but that presents difficulties which have not been solved.

Hobbes, Spinoza, Locke, and Leibnitz

Modern philosophy wrestles with the same problem, but has introduced many new elements in its attempt either to meet the original difficulty or to put the whole matter on a different level.

THOMAS HOBBES was concerned, as we have seen, with interpreting the entire universe on a materialistic basis. Motion was, for him, the fundamental factor in the universe. Thus, good and evil were for him matters of motion. When motion is successful it generates pleasure, and when it is unsuccessful pain results.

That which pleases a man is good, and that which causes pain or discomfort is evil. Thus, good and evil are, as Hobbes sees it, relative to the particular man. That which pleases one man may not please another. Consequently, there can be no absolute good or evil. Both depend upon the nature of the individual at the time, and as he changes good things may become evil and evil things good.

The relation of a philosopher's general view to his attitude toward the question of good and evil is well illustrated by DESCARTES. For him, God is perfect, and incapable of causing us to err. But we do fall into error and suffer from our mistakes. This is explained on the theory that the power which God has given man to distinguish the true from the false is not complete. Thus, man is often guilty of making judgments when he does not have enough understanding to judge accurately. In such cases he may choose that which is wrong, evil, rather than the good. For Descartes, error lies not in God's action but in ours. We make up our minds and act before we have sufficient evidence.

The theory of SPINOZA is much in the same vein. Error is lack of knowledge. Action without knowledge will produce results which are not desired, and pain will follow.

As he studied the individual, Spinoza came to the conclusion that the fundamental striving of everyone is to preserve himself. This striving is good. Thus, anything which tends to block this striving is bad, and everything which helps man to reach the goal of his striving is good.

But man's striving must be rational. Merely to strive is not enough; he must strive intelligently, realizing what he is doing and its consequences. The highest happiness of man lies in the perfect understanding of what he is doing, his striving. As we come to understand our own strivings we recognize that, since we are modes of God, our striving is in truth the striving of God, for we are God. The highest good of man is this complete realization. In it he sees that by loving himself he actually loves God. Spinoza calls this the "intellectual love of God."

The basic philosophic theory of JOHN LOCKE gives rise to his theory of good and evil. Just as all our ideas come from the outside and are written on the mind as one might write on a blank sheet of paper, so our conceptions of what is good and what is evil are produced. The fact is, many people have the same experiences and come to the same conclusions. They agree that certain things are good and others are bad. Further, our parents have impressed upon us ideas of right and wrong from the first days of our lives. Later we come to believe that they are innate, inborn. For Locke, human conscience is nothing more than these ideas which we have had so long that they seem to be given by some divine power.

Further, Locke taught that pleasure and pain are native to man. Nature has made it so that we enjoy happiness and seek to avoid pain. Therefore, those things which bring happiness are called good, and those which bring pain are called evil.

But it is not always true that the same act will bring happiness to everyone. Consequently there are laws which we must obey under penalty of being unhappy if we refuse to obey. Locke believed that three groups of laws existed. Divine laws are those set by God to determine duty and sin. If we break these laws we suffer greatly. Then, there are civil laws established by the group as a constituted civil unit. These determine crime and innocence. Disobedience is punishable by the group making the laws. The third group of laws are those of opinion or reputation. These are by far the greatest in number and are enforced by the mere fact that men cherish their reputations and do not desire the condemnation of their companions and friends.

But, we learn what is good and bad by experience, by the experience of pain if we do evil and pleasure if we do good. Thus, Locke was in the ethical tradition of Hobbes and others who made morality largely a matter of enlightened self-interest: that is, one is good because being good pays the highest dividends in individual pleasure.

Thinkers who followed Locke sought to expand this position so as to include others, and to make morality dependent upon the happiness of others as well as upon the happiness of the individual. RICHARD CUMBERLAND, founder of the Utilitarian school of thought, argued that man is not wholly selfish, but is basically sympathetic. Thus, the welfare of the group, of society, determines the good and the bad. LORD SHAFTESBURY taught that man is interested in the welfare of both himself and society and that good actions result when both of these interests are properly balanced. FRANCIS HUTCHESON, of this same general opinion, coined the phrase "the greatest good for the greatest number," and made it the criterion of a good act.

LEIBNITZ encountered the same difficulty as did many of his predecessors when he came to the problem of good and evil. In a universe of monads, how is evil possible? His answer was similar to that of earlier philosophers. This world, he taught, is "the best possible world," but it is not perfect. God limited himself when he expressed himself in finite beings. These limits result in suffering and sin. Further, evil serves to make good really good. It is like the shadows in a picture, shadows which serve to bring the colors into bolder relief and greater beauty.

Further, in the human soul, he suggested, there are certain innate principles which, if followed logically, lead to criteria of good and bad. One of these principles is that we should seek pleasure and avoid pain. Reasoning from this principle, we can prove that certain acts are good and others are bad.

Often men do not obey these innate principles because of their passions and impulses, but this does not prove that they do not exist, Leibnitz held. All that this proves is that such men are ignorant of the principles.

The Ethical Philosophy of Kant

The basic problem of KANT was to discover the meaning of right and wrong, good and bad. He asked, How is duty to be defined, and what are the implications of the definition? In attacking the problem, Kant accepted as fundamental the principle, laid down by Rousseau, that the only absolutely good thing in the universe is the human will governed by respect for the moral law or the consciousness of duty. A moral act is one which is done out of respect for the moral law rather than for selfish gain or sympathy for others.

Thus, for Kant, consequences are not to be taken as determining the rightness or wrongness of an act. Whether the results of an act are productive of happiness or of pain is not the matter of greatest concern. If the actor performs the act with good intentions, out of respect for the moral law, it is thereby good.

This moral law, in the thinking of Kant, is inherent in reason itself. It is *a priori,* before experience, in the very nature of human thinking. Stated in a sentence, it reads: "Always act in such a way that the maxim determining your conduct might well become a universal law; act so that you can will that everybody shall follow the principle of your action." In every instance, Kant believed, this rule, this "categorical imperative," is a sure criterion of what is right and what is wrong. An act which you would be willing that anyone or everyone should perform would be a good act.

This law, if thoroughly understood, is in everyone. It may not be recognized in the terms stated, but anyone who stops to think will discover that human life is possible only on this moral basis. Should man attempt to act contrary to this principle, human association would be chaotic.

Another law, an implication of the categorical imperative, is stated by Kant: "Act so as to treat humanity, whether in thine own person or in that of another, in every case as an end and never as a means." Here the fundamental worth of every individual is affirmed. Our actions should not be such as to use individuals as means for our ends, but rather to serve others as ends in themselves.

Thus, for Kant, there is imbedded in the human reason itself a law which is so basic and fundamental that it directs all moral activity. It demands that everyone act at all times as though he were the ruling monarch of the universe and the principle of his action would automatically become the principle of the action of everyone. If each individual measures a proposed act by this categorical imperative, he will be able to say without question whether it is right or wrong.

The Views of Fichte and Schopenhauer

FICHTE based his entire philosophic theory upon Kant's idea of a moral nature in man which has the right to make certain definite demands. Starting with the moral nature of man, he built a philosophy which would satisfy the demands of this nature.

This moral law, likewise, implies, Fichte taught, the existence of a moral world order in which man can trust. Having the moral law within himself, man is justified in assuming that the world is such that the demands of this law can be met.

Therefore, man must become intelligent, must know what is right and do it because it is right. The ignorant man cannot be good. Being free, not forced by some outside authority, man must know the moral law and its implications, and must at all times govern himself accordingly. Mere respect for the moral law is not enough. Man must act. Therefore morality, goodness, is not a state to be attained once and for all, a condition of eternal blessedness, but is a continuous struggle of the intelligent individual to act in every situation so as to meet the requirements of the moral law. Knowledge is a necessary part of morality for Fichte.

SCHOPENHAUER begins with an affirmation of the will as fundamental to the universe. Kant's thing-in-itself, the source of all our impressions, is will, Schopenhauer says. This will to be, will to live, is the cause of all the struggle in the world and thus of all evil and suffering. A world where blind wills are struggling with each other to live, where the more powerful kill and devour the less powerful that they may live, is a world of evil. Will to live begets selfishness. Each individual will struggle to preserve himself despite what happens to others.

Thus, for Schopenhauer, sympathy or pity is basic to morality. To the degree that one has sympathy for others, he will act not for himself but for them, and thus be good. The way to this good life is through denial of the individual will; self-sacrifice brings happiness and peace. And this can be attained if we stop to realize that every individual is actually part of the whole, the universal will. The one against whom we struggle is actually part of the whole of which we are also members. When we reach this understanding, we will stop struggling and will develop sympathetic understanding.

According to Mill, Bentham, and Spencer

Recent philosophic thought regarding the problem of good and evil has been concerned with man's social relationships. It has been an ethics of the human group rather than that of divine laws. Consequently, it has taken on the tinge of relativity. Goodness and evil become qualities of acts relative to the situation in which they are performed.

JOHN STUART MILL is a good representative of the Utilitarian school in his contention that the measure of good is in terms of "the greatest good of the greatest number." One must ask of an act, Will it bring much good to a great number of individuals? This eliminates selfishness and makes the criterion of good the social consequences of the proposed act.

Further, Mill holds that "goods" differ in quality and that the goods of the intellect are better than the goods of the senses. Therefore, not only is the social factor emphasized, but also emphasis is placed upon the nature of the act.

JEREMY BENTHAM is very close to Mill in his thinking about good and evil. He too bases good upon the Utilitarian principle of "the greatest good of the greatest number." But he does not admit that goods differ in quality. His only criterion is the number of individuals affected by the act. Bentham justifies this position on the basis of self-interest, holding that to so act will actually bring the greatest good to the one acting.

In this modern treatment of the subject, good and bad are not written in the nature of the universe, but are determined by social factors. The emphasis is placed upon the consequences of one's act in the experiences of others. The idea of a God setting down absolutely defined moral laws is gone. Also the idea that an evil act angers God while a good act makes Him happy is missing. Here is a relative morality, and the determiner of good and bad is the effect of the act upon the lives of other human individuals now living or to live in the future.

HERBERT SPENCER attacks the problem from the point of view of the scientist and seeks to discover a scientific basis for right and wrong in conduct at large. From the point of view of evolution, conduct is a developing, evolving thing, a matter of adjustment of acts to ends. For him, the most highly developed conduct, and therefore the best, is that which makes living richer for the individual and for those among whom he lives and those who will come after him.

The social group, for Spencer, is the ultimate end of morality. Goodness is to be determined in those terms. But he distinguishes between conduct that is absolutely right and that which is relatively right. Absolutely right conduct is that which is immediately pleasurable and at the same time produces future happiness for the individual and the group. Relative right is productive of future happiness, but is not immediately pleasurable. The goal is, of course, absolute right.

The Ethical Views of James and Dewey

The social and individual consequences of activity are emphasized by philosophers of the Pragmatic school as criteria of good and evil. Both WILLIAM JAMES and JOHN DEWEY, especially Dewey, are emphatic at this point. The good is that which serves the ends of the group and the individual in the group. A good act is one which considers the individual as an end in himself and not as a means. But, by so considering each individual, we consider the welfare of the group. The human individual, as a social unit, is the ultimate measure of good and evil. That which enriches his life must necessarily enrich the lives of all. Here the individual and the group are tied together, since, it was argued by Dewey, individuality is a social product and no one has true individuality save as a member of the group.

Thus, a survey of the thinking of men down the ages about good and evil reveals two fundamental positions and many shades of both. On the one hand measures of good and evil are thought to be inherent in the nature of the

universe. Man is to discover them by coming to an understanding of the universe and its nature. Whether the universe speak to man with its own voice, or whether the
voice be that of the Creator of the universe, the position
is fundamentally the same. Good and bad are absolute,
having been established from the beginning of time, and
apply in all situations and at all times. When the criteria
have been discovered, either by rational searching of the
universe or by revelation, they are forever true, never
changing.

The other position is that good and bad are relative
terms, and that the measures, the criteria, are to be discovered by a study of the particular situation involved.
Time and place are determiners of good and evil. For a
sick man, certain foods are evil, but for a well man they
are good. In a modern social group, preservation of the
aged and weak is good, but in a primitive group which is
beset by enemies and must be on the move to escape destruction, to preserve the aged and infirm is bad since it
slows down the group and may result in disaster. This
position looks at the consequences of the particular act in
terms of the life of society and determines the ethical
quality of the act in terms of the good of the whole.

Man's thought on matters of ethics has taken these two
lines throughout history, the absolute and the relative.
And, among present-day thinkers both positions are to be
discovered, although the relative point of view is the most
pronounced. It is difficult for modern man, possessed of
great respect for science and human reason, to find adequate ground for an absolute theory of right and wrong.
All the evidence which commands his respect seems to
point away from this to a relative position.

Chapter IV
THE NATURE OF GOD

HESIOD XENOPHANES PLATO ARISTOTLE
PLOTINUS AUGUSTINE AQUINAS
ECKHART BRUNO BOEHME BACON
SPINOZA LOCKE BERKELEY HUME
KANT SCHELLING SCHLEIERMACHER
SPENCER BRADLEY JAMES DEWEY

*What is the nature of God, and how is he related to
the universe? Is God a person, like man but more
ideal? Or is God a name for the force or forces which
have brought the universe into being and sustain it?
Can the human mind know God, or is God so far
above man that nothing can be known about him?
What is God's relation to us?*

The idea of gods came before the idea of God. The
earliest peoples known did not think of there being only
one god but rather believed in numerous gods: gods of
trees, rivers, winds, the sky, the earth, and hundreds of
others. In some cases one god was more powerful than the
others, but he was one of many.

As mankind developed, belief centered on a few powerful gods who were looked upon as ruling the more important areas of life. The other gods were reduced to the state
of lesser spirits, elves, or beings very much like men but
with more power than men.

The early Hebrews were among the first to conceive of

there being one god and to eliminate all other gods. But this conception was not won easily. We are told in the Bible that Moses introduced the Hebrews to this one god when he delivered the Ten Commandments to his people from Mount Sinai. Gradually the people came to believe in this god, whom they called Jehovah, and to ascribe to him all the power and influence which had belonged to the many gods of their early history.

When we first hear of the Greeks they were believers in many gods. As they became more civilized, some of the gods of their fathers were forgotten and the few who were left were thought of as constituting a community very much like the human community except that it was more ideal.

At the head of this community was Zeus who ruled as a sort of super king. On his throne with him sat his wife, Hera. Zeus was a glorified man with all the weaknesses of men, all human passions and defects, but also with many human virtues. Among the other gods were individuals with specific duties and specific areas of power. There were Apollo, Hermes, Aphrodite, and many others, principally offspring of Zeus. The divine community was full of jealousies, bickerings, intrigue, and other human frailties. But the early Greeks feared and worshiped these divinities.

This is known as the period of mythology in Greek history. Behind it the record is dim and uncertain. No one knows where these ideas about the gods came from. It is believed, however, that they were originally conceived as forces or spirits concerned with various phases of life in the environment of the ancient Greeks and their ancestors.

HESIOD, a Greek writer about whom we know very little, wrote a Theogony or book of the gods in which he attempted to account for things and the coming of the gods. He taught that in the beginning was Chaos who gave birth to Gaea, the earth, and Eros, love. Then Chaos gave birth to Erebos, darkness, and Nyx, night. These two were united and gave birth to Aether, light, and Hemera, day. The earth begot Pontus, the sea, and, in union with the heaven, Uranos, begot Chronos, time.

If we are to believe Hesiod, the early Greek gods were things of the universe conceived of as alive, as beings very much like humans. By the time of the first Greek philosophers these ideas had been organized into the Greek religion in which the vast majority of the people believed completely. Temples were erected to the gods and there had grown up a whole class of people devoted to conducting worship before the altars of these gods. They claimed to understand the gods better than the laymen and gave advice to the people as to how they might keep the gods happy and win their favor and help in various undertakings.

The Views of the Early Greek Philosophers

When the Greek philosophers began to write and teach, they did not attempt to overthrow the gods or to question them directly. Most of the early philosophers believed in the gods as the popular mind and tradition conceived them. However, they did seek to account for the existence of things in ways different from the gods. THALES, for example, sought to explain the coming of the world and all other things in natural ways and without appeal to divine beings. Although ANAXIMANDER taught that the original substance from which everything came was "the infinite," he did not tie this idea up with the popular belief about the gods.

Nevertheless, there was always in the back of the thinking of these early philosophers the hovering belief that the original creation and the ordering of the universe were results of the working of God. We find them often referring to God as the source of the original stuff of the universe and as the power which in some way established the order of the universe. However, these philosophers are never very clear about this point. It is highly possible that most of these men were deeply religious and were attempting to carry their religion in one basket and their philosophy in another and often getting the contents of the two baskets mixed up in their thinking.

HERACLITUS, however, had a deep contempt for the re-

ligion of the masses and did not hesitate to write, "And to
these images they pray, just as if one were to converse
with men's houses, for they know not what gods and heroes
are." No doubt Heraclitus believed that he did know what
gods and heroes were.

XENOPHANES, a rhapsodist and philosophical poet of the
sixth century B.C., attacked the popular religious beliefs
of his day and countered them by proclaiming that God
was one and unchangeable. He was extremely bitter in
condemning the popular idea that the gods were like mor-
tals. "Yes," he wrote, "and if oxen or lions had hands, and
could paint with their hands and produce works of art as
men do, horses would paint the forms of gods like horses
and oxen like oxen. Each would represent them with bodies
according to the form of each." And in another place he
says, "So the Ethiopians make their gods black and snub-
nosed; the Thracians give theirs red hair and blue eyes."

In place of these beliefs about gods, which seemed crude
to him, Xenophanes taught that God is unlike human beings in every way. God is one who governs the universe
without any effort. He lives in one place and never moves.
He is a whole, without beginning or ending, an eternal
unity. As a whole, God does not move; but his parts do
move.

For Xenophanes, God is thought of as the fundamental
principle of the universe. God is the world, the whole of
living nature. Thus Xenophanes holds to a clear pantheism,
a belief that everything in the universe is God, and God is
everything in the universe. God is the "One and All." For
him there is only one God, and this God is the universe. As
the universe, God is a whole, a unity, One. But within the
universe, within God, there are many parts which change
place with each other while the whole changes not. Xenophanes discards the popular polytheism or belief in the
existence of many gods for a more advanced monotheism
or belief in one god.

Thus, it is clear that during the pre-Sophist period of
Greek philosophy the popular religion with its many gods
was being countered with a more philosophic conception

of one god, the source in some way of the entire universe
and the power behind all the phenomena of the universe.
Further, the popular idea of the gods and beings much like
men had been challenged by the idea that the one God
was very different from man in every respect.

This spirit of challenge reached a high point during the
period of the *Sophists*. These practical teachers of young
men made it their business to attack and challenge everything, and belief in the gods did not escape. They appealed
to reason and pointed out constantly that the popular belief in many gods was not reasonable. Although their work
was destructive of the generally accepted beliefs, it was
most valuable, since it made men think seriously about
their beliefs in an effort to meet the objections offered by
the Sophists. It became necessary for thinkers to ask themselves the question, What is the true conception of God?
And out of this questioning there arose a more consistent
and purer conception of the nature of God.

The Concept of God in the Thought of Socrates, Plato, and Aristotle

One of those who sought to develop a more consistent
and purer conception of God was SOCRATES, but he paid
the price of a pioneer in that the masses misunderstood
him, thought he was destroying belief in the gods, and
condemned him to death for his impiety.

His pupil, PLATO, uses the word God, but in a very confused way. Often one feels that he is thinking of the gods
just as the masses think of them, as beings governing
different areas of the universe. Indeed, the popular conceptions of the gods are strewn through his works. At other
times Plato seems to teach the existence of one supreme
God who is master and ruler of the entire universe. In his
book, the *Timaeus*, he accounts for the creation of the universe by using a Demiurge, or sort of architect, who takes
already-created ideas and matter and moulds the universe.
In another place we find him speaking of the Creator as
the source of souls.

This leads us to conclude that Plato believed in the existence of many gods, each of which he thought to be much like a human soul. Among these gods are the idea of the Good, the whole world of ideas, the Demiurge, the world soul, souls of the planets, and all the gods of the popular religion. However, on this matter of gods Plato is never clear. Perhaps Plato was attempting to use the popular beliefs to teach more profound truths. In some passages we are led to believe that he did not attempt to account for the coming into being of either the world of ideas or matter, but takes them as existing from the beginning. Nor does he seek to explain the source of the Demiurge. He also existed from the beginning. Given the Demiurge, ideas, and matter, Plato goes on to teach that the Demiurge, using ideas and matter, created all the gods in whom the masses believed.

In other passages, however, Plato speaks of God as the creator of everything in the universe and the goal of all human life as well as the life of all nature. Holding that the spirit of man is like God and that the body is a prison of the soul, he writes that "we ought to fly away from earth as quickly as we can, and to fly away is to become like God." Here he seems to border on mysticism.

The thinking of ARISTOTLE is much clearer on this point than is that of Plato. You will remember from our previous discussions that Aristotle believed that there were two causes in the universe,—form and matter. For him forms are forces which realize themselves in the world of matter just as the idea of the artist realizes itself in marble. Hence the form is the cause of motion. Matter moves because of form.

Indeed, Aristotle shows traces of the old Greek idea that matter was alive. Not only does form, which is within matter, move matter, but matter seeks to become or realize the form. For example, the oak tree is the form and the acorn is the matter. The acorn grows into the oak tree, it realizes the form "oak tree" which was in it as an acorn but unrealized. As it is growing, according to Aristotle, it is striving to become an oak tree. This is its motion.

But, before the acorn there was matter and an idea or

form "acorn." This form was in matter, and matter was striving to become an acorn because of the presence of the form in it. One might go on tracing this series of events from the crudest matter, each step through the oak tree and beyond, realizing that at each point there is matter and form, and matter striving to become form, being moved by form. Is this series continuous forever?

Aristotle said, "No." At the end there is pure form, form without matter, and he called this an eternal "unmoved mover," the ultimate cause of all motion, of all becoming in the universe. This "God" is the cause of motion, but does not move himself. How is this possible?

We have all had the experience of knowing a person, a hero to us, whom we wanted to be like. We have fashioned our lives after him and have grown into his likeness. Hawthorne's immortal story, *The Great Stone Face*, is illustrative of this experience. The little boy looked at the face so much that he came to be like it. But the face was not moved. It did not change. So with Aristotle's "unmoved mover," it moves men, it draws matter, but does not move itself, is not affected.

All the universe, every object and being in it, desires to realize itself because of God. His existence is the ultimate cause of their striving. Thus, God is the center toward which all things strive, and therefore he is the unifying principle of the universe. Every possibility, form, is realized in him.

Aristotle's God is the ideal of the philosopher, since he is all that the philosopher strives to be, pure intelligence.

The Position of the Later Greek Thinkers

While Aristotle was a monist, a believer in one God, the *Epicureans* were polytheists, believers in many gods. They believed that the gods existed and were shaped like men, but were far more beautiful. Their bodies were believed to be fine bodies of light. The Epicureans also believed that the gods differed in sex, needed food, and spoke the Greek language.

But the gods of the Epicureans were very different from

what the masses thought. The gods did not create the world, were not interested in men, were perfect, did not interfere with the world at all. They lived a peaceful, happy, contented life, free from all the cares and worries which men know.

For the *Stoics* there is one God, related to the world just as the soul is related to the human body. God is corporeal, bodily, but a body of extraordinary fineness. The Stoics believed that all the forces in the universe were united into one force which penetrated everything, the soul of the universe. All life, all movement stems from this soul. This is God. This doctrine, of course, is pantheism, the belief that everything in the universe is God. In God is to be found the whole universe, just as all of the flower is contained in the seed.

This God of the Stoics is very different from the gods of the Epicureans. He is the father of all things, is one, and is not divided; he loves man and knows all that is going to happen, he punishes the evil and rewards the good. The Stoic God is very interested in the world of men. God lives at the farthest circle of the universe, and, from there, pervades the whole universe, the Stoics believed, just as the soul is situated in a particular place in the body but pervades the whole of the body.

CARNEADES, one of the Skeptics, attacked this Stoic idea of God, showing its inconsistencies. He denied that the human reason is able to know God at all, and cannot even know that God exists. We must be skeptical about the matter, he argued.

The Greco-Religious Ideas About God

When PHILO, and his Jewish-Greek contemporaries, appeared on the philosophical scene, the conception of God became paramount in philosophy. Philo, for example, came from the great Hebrew religious tradition, a tradition at the center of which was the idea of one all-good and all-powerful God. He brought this tradition into contact with Greek philosophy, and sought to show that it was consistent with the best in Greek thought.

For Philo, God is so far above man in greatness, goodness, power, and perfection that we cannot know what he is. But we can be certain that he exists. Philo taught that God is the source of everything, is absolutely good, perfect, blessed. Being so exalted, God cannot come in contact with matter. But he gives off, as light from a candle, beings or powers which combine in one power which he called the "Logos" or divine Wisdom. This Logos created the universe, and is the intermediary between God and the world. Here God is separated from the world, a sharp distinction being made between the all-pure God and the impure world of matter, the world in which we live.

For PLOTINUS, who attempted very much the same things as did Philo, God is the source of everything in the universe. But, God is so perfect that we cannot affirm anything about him. We can say what he is not, but can never say what he is. Anything that we think about him is too poor to be true of him. He is far above anything we can think.

Further, as with Philo, God created the world not directly, but by means of emanations, beings coming from him but not him. God, for Plotinus, is like an infinite stream which flows out but is never exhausted. The world depends upon God, but God does not need the world.

Creation, for Plotinus, is a fall from God. At the bottom of creation is pure matter, the farthest thing from God. Here, again, we note the sharp division between God and the world, pure God and impure world.

The Early and Medieval Christian Conception of God

Christianity, as we have already seen, began very early in its history to feel the effects of Greek philosophy. The Gospel of John, written about 100 A.D., shows very definitely this influence. The book begins with a distinctly Greek doctrine, the doctrine of the Logos or world spirit which emanates from God and creates the world.

As Christianity grew and influenced more and more the Greek and Roman world, it became necessary to bring in a great deal of Greek philosophy. Thus, the *Apologists* arose to attempt a joining of Christianity and Greek thought. They taught that the order and reason in the universe point to the existence of a First Cause, a being who is the source of everything, is good, and is eternal. This First Cause, or God, is the eternal principle in all changing things. He emits the Logos as the sun emits light, and through the Logos created the universe.

God, for the Apologists, is pure reason personified, thought of as a person. Thus, for them, Reason is the underlying principle of the universe, its cause and directing and controlling force.

In the teaching of SAINT AUGUSTINE the vast difference between God and the world is emphasized. God is eternal, is transcendent, all good, all wise, absolute in every way. He is the cause of everything, the creator of the universe out of nothing. Further, Augustine taught that God, in the beginning, predetermined everything, so that he knew from the first what would happen to all his creatures throughout eternity.

The God of Augustine is the idealization of everything that man considers good and worthy. He is absolute power, perfect goodness, the source and creator of everything. He knows everything and has so controlled the universe that everything is determined by him forever.

For several centuries the idea of God held by the Christian Church remained very much like that of Saint Augustine. JOHN SCOTUS ERIGENA taught that God was the source of all things, but went somewhat further than Augustine when he took the position that God and his creation are one. For him, God is in the world, the world is God, but God is also more than the world; he is the world plus. The world, Erigena held, is only a slight revelation of God who is far more than all the universe.

By this view, Erigena is able to hold with the Church that God is perfect goodness, power, wisdom, and is never wholly known by men. Man may know something about God from looking at his universe, but this is only a small, insignificant part of God. Indeed, for this early thinker, God is in reality unknowable and undefinable. Man cannot expect, with his little brain, to understand God or to comprehend his ways.

As Christianity developed during the first centuries of the Christian era, a very difficult problem came to the fore. God, as we have seen, was conceived as pure, holy, perfect. Thus it became necessary to introduce an intermediate being, the Logos, to account for the creation of the universe. Many thinkers identified this being with Christ. Further, Christian thinkers held that there was a Spirit or power of divine origin permeating the universe, the Holy Spirit.

As philosophers struggled with the problem of the nature of God, they found it necessary to account for the existence of the Logos, Christ, and the Holy Spirit. Some theory of their relationship with each other and with God had to be developed. Out of the thinking on this problem came the conception of the Trinity. God is thought of as One, a Unity, a Whole. But he is also Three: God, the Logos or Christ, and the Holy Spirit.

The Apologists taught that both the Logos and the Holy Spirit were emanations from God and that Jesus Christ was the Logos in the form of a man. Consequently, they held that although God is One, he is also Three Persons. The Godhead is a Unity, but expresses itself in the world as the creative Logos or Christ and as divine reason which permeates everything.

A little later there came into prominence a group of thinkers, the *Modalists*, who maintained that all three persons or the Trinity are actually God in three forms or modes. The Logos is actually God creating; the Holy Spirit is actually God reasoning; and God is actually God being. This led to a prolonged discussion as to whether the Logos was of like nature with God or was of the same substance as God. Is the Logos an emanation from God or is it God in another form?

Augustine held to the orthodox conception of the Trinity. He believed that God was One, but expressed himself in the universe as three persons, emanations. This was known as the Athanasian position from the fact that ATHANASIUS, the leader of a group of early Christian thinkers, developed the point of view. According to Athanasius, Christ is the principle of salvation and was begotten, not made, by the Father, God. He is eternal with the Father, and is of the same substance as the Father. Further, He shares the full nature of the Father. In Jesus this Logos or Christ was united with a human body. The Holy Ghost, he maintained, was a third being. Thus the one Godhead was conceived to be a Trinity of the same substance, three persons of the same nature: Father, Son, and Holy Ghost.

ROSCELIN, one of the first Nominalists, applied the doctrine of Nominalism to the Trinity. He argued that single things were the only realities and that universals, or general concepts, were mere names or words. Consequently, he held that there could be no reality corresponding to the name God. But there are only three different substances or persons equal in power. Thus, for him, the Trinity is not One in Three, but is three distinct beings.

This was a denial of the orthodox official doctrine and drew great opposition from the Church. It became evident to the Church officials that preservation of the Trinity as a doctrine of the Church rested upon adoption of the Realist position, the position that Universals are the only reals and that individuals are forms of the universal. Thus, this position became the dominant one among the Scholastics, the foundation upon which was built a great deal of the intellectual and ecclesiastical structure of the Middle Ages.

The work of ANSELM hinged largely on the idea that universals exist independently of particular objects. On the basis of this idea he argued for the existence of God. He taught that the idea of God as a being who exists implies that God must exist. If God did not exist, the idea would not be the idea of the greatest thing thinkable. Man could still think of something greater, something that did exist. Thus, the perfection of God, the idea of a perfect being, he held, implies the existence of God, because perfection must include existence.

This argument, of course, could not be made to hold up, as many thinkers have shown. The mere idea of a thing, an idea which includes the concept of existence, does not guarantee that there is an object which exists. GAUNILO, a theologian of the times, showed that one might have an idea of a perfect island without any proof that the island existed.

In his "Theology," ABELARD taught that the Trinity consists of the Father, who is One or Goodness, the Holy Ghost or World Soul, and the Logos or the mind of God. He also taught that the three persons of the Trinity are the power, good will, and wisdom of God.

While these thinkers were attempting to make religion a rational system, and God, at least in part, understandable, there was another movement which despaired of understanding God. This was known as *Mysticism*. For Mysticism, God is not so much to be known as experienced. We do not understand Him with our minds, but we come into direct contact with Him through a mystical experience. God is reached by contemplation. This approach to God gives one an understanding of Him which no amount of reasoning can ever reach, so argued RICHARD OF ST. VICTOR. The goal of the mystic is "the mysterious ascension of the soul to heaven, the sweet home-coming from the land of bodies to the region of spirit, the surrender of the self in and to God." But, this absorption into God is not something which man can attain of his own will. All a man can do is to prepare through certain exercises for this "plunge into the ocean of infinite truth." Then he must wait. If God favors him, He will permit him to make the plunge.

THOMAS AQUINAS was influenced greatly by the thinking of Aristotle, and he sought to adjust Aristotle and Christian theology to each other without destroying the fundamental doctrines of the Church. Indeed, he believed that the teachings of Aristotle could be made to support these doctrines.

God, said Aquinas, is pure form. We infer His existence from the facts of His creation. For example, everything that moves must have a mover. We find movement in the universe. Therefore, the ultimate source of this movement must be an unmoved principle, the Unmoved Mover of

Aristotle, or God. Further, the universe reveals that things are related in a graduated scale of existence from the lowest forms of existence upward toward more or less perfect objects. This leads one to infer that there must be some thing that is perfect at the very summit, God.

God, for Aquinas, is the first and final cause of the universe pure form or energy. He is absolutely perfect. He is the source, the Creator of everything out of nothing. In this creation he has revealed Himself. Further, God rules the universe through his perfect will.

Aquinas, in developing this theory of the nature of God, set the pattern for Catholic belief about God for all times. Even to the present the Catholic Church follows this position practically as outlined by Aquinas.

The teaching of JOHN DUNS SCOTUS is very similar to that of Aquinas. God is pure form or pure energy. He is the cause of the universe, a cause that is conscious and has a purpose in creating and ruling the universe. He is infinite will which is completely free, so free that he can will or not will just as he wants. All this, Scotus argues, is to be proven from the experience which we have of the world about us.

MEISTER ECKHART, a mystic of the thirteenth and fourteenth centuries, taught that God is inconceivable, an indefinable spiritual substance, a something in which all things are united. As such, God cannot reveal himself but becomes known only through the Trinity. Constantly the Three Persons of the Trinity flow out of God and back into him. He is the ground of the universe. All things are in God, and God is in all things. I am God communicating himself. I am immanent in the essence of God. He works through me. As I return to God in the mystic experience, I become one with God again.

Bruno, Boehme, and Other Forerunners of the Renaissance

As the Renaissance began to dawn, and men undertook to think themselves free from the long dominance of the Church and its doctrines, they became aware of the numerous inconsistencies in the doctrines of the Scholastics. They saw that some of the ideas about God held by these philosophers would not stand up under the impact of searching reason. However, although they attacked the reasoning of the Scholastics, they were unwilling to abandon the idea of God.

NICHOLAS OF CUSA, for example, held that man could have an immediate intuition of God, something resembling the mystic's experience. This experience solves the many contradictions and inconsistencies which appear in any attempt to think about God. Through reason we cannot know God, but beyond reason is this "learned ignorance," this supersensible experience of God.

GIORDANO BRUNO, fascinated by the immensity of the universe which the astronomy of his day was revealing, held that God is immanent in this infinite universe, the principle of activity. He taught that he is the unity of all opposites in the universe, a unity without opposites, which the human mind cannot grasp.

In this same tradition was the uneducated German mystic, JACOB BOEHME, who taught that since God is the ground of everything, he is the union of all the opposites in the universe, the original source of all things. Through the objects of the universe God becomes conscious of himself. A divine blind craving gives rise to the universe with all its opposites. But in God all these opposites are united.

The Position of Bacon, Hobbes, Descartes, and Pascal

This despair of reason on the part of many as a means for reaching understanding of God was part of the trend toward freeing mankind from the bonds of the Church so that he could devote himself to the study of the world in a scientific manner. Theology and science were gradually separated, each taking its place in the scheme of things. Nevertheless, the endeavor to understand God continued, though the interpretations of God were in many instances very different from those of the Middle Ages. It became obvious that reason's God was very different from faith's God. Consequently, it happened many times that the philosopher's God was not the theologian's God.

The position of FRANCIS BACON is a clear illustration of

this development. He divided theology into the natural and the revealed. Natural theology, he taught, is that knowledge of God which we can get from the study of nature and the creatures of God. It gives convincing proof of the existence of God, but nothing more. Anything else must come from revealed theology. Here we must "quit the small vessel of human reason and put ourselves on board the ship of the church, which alone possesses the divine needle for justly shaping the course. The stars of philosophy will be of no further service to us. As we are obliged to obey the divine law, though our will murmurs against it, so we are obliged to believe in the word of God, though our reason is shocked at it."

THOMAS HOBBES, interpreting God in terms of his materialistic philosophy, tells us that at the creation God gave motion to all things. Further, he suggests, God is body, a corporeal being, but of this he cannot be certain since he doubts that we can know what God is. We must limit ourselves to the assurance that God exists. However, Hobbes does speak of God as starting the universe in motion and of Him as ruling the world through the human rulers of the world.

DESCARTES, through his method of reasoning, seeks to prove the existence of God and tell us a great deal about Him. He found the idea of God among his ideas, an idea of an absolutely real, perfect, infinite being. The cause of this idea, he argued, must be as real as the idea. Therefore God exists. The idea had to be placed in him by God, he held. This God is self-caused, is eternal, all-knowing, all-powerful, perfect goodness and truth, and the creator of all things. Nor will God deceive man. Whatever he has put into man is real, even the ideas which man finds in his thinking.

Further, for Descartes, God is the basic substance of the universe and the two relative substances, mind and body, depend upon him. God gives motion to body. "God," he wrote, "originally created matter along with motion and rest, and now by his concourse alone preserves in the whole the same amount of motion that he then placed in it." God is the "prime mover" of the universe.

Descartes' conception of God is highly confusing and confused. He made God independent of Nature, thus raising the problem of how God can impress himself upon Nature so that man can know anything about God. Further, how can God, as pure spirit, give motion to matter? This problem, among many others, was left to Descartes' followers. It was the problem of harmonizing the mechanical theory of the new science of the times with the theology of Christianity.

BLAISE PASCAL attacked the problem and suggested that it was impossible for man to demonstrate the existence of God, that philosophic proofs were of no real value as regards God. We know God, he taught, only through religious feeling. God is pure spirit and we can know him only through a spiritual experience.

The Nature of God According to Spinoza

It was SPINOZA who worked out what seemed then a masterful solution of the problem left by Descartes. For him God is the sole independent substance of the universe. Outside of God there can be no substance. Mind and body, thought and extension, are attributes of God and not independent of him. God is the cause of everything in the universe. He is both thinking and extended substance. God is a thought in the human mind and he is a tree in the forest. Thus, God is all, and all is God. There is nothing outside of or independent of God. God is a single, eternal, infinite, self-caused principle of nature and of all things. God and the world are one. Here is clear pantheism.

We can perceive only two attributes of God, thought and extension. We know God, then, through ideas and bodies. But this does not exhaust God. He is far more than this, and we can never know God completely.

God, for Spinoza, is neither personality nor consciousness. He is not characterized by intelligence, feeling, or will. His actions are not directed by purpose; but all things follow from his nature according to strict law. All the ideas in the universe added together constitute the thinking of God. My thoughts and your thoughts, and the thoughts of everyone in the world, make up God's thoughts.

Spinoza had sought to solve Descartes' problem by making God everything and more than everything. Mind and body are not two wholly different things, but are God seen in two different ways. Thus, God can influence both the world of thought and the world of things because actually he is both and is thus being himself.

The Views of Locke, Berkeley, Hume, and Leibnitz

With JOHN LOCKE a new attack was made on the problem of the nature of God. True to his belief that we can have no innate ideas, Locke had to take the position that we cannot have an innate idea of God. However, he held that we may know about God if we use our natural abilities correctly. We can build the idea of God, he taught, out of other ideas which we have. If we take, for example, our ideas of existence, duration, power, pleasure, happiness, and the like, and think of these as extending to infinity and being gathered together, we will have an idea of God. God is, then, certain ideas which we have gathered from experience and extended to infinity.

God, said Locke, most certainly exists. Man studies himself and realizes that he must have been produced by some being who is greater than he. Thus, God is "real being," thinks, is all-knowing, powerful, and just. For Locke, God is spiritual substance, a third substance in addition to mind and body.

As creator of the world and man, God has established certain divine laws which man may discover through studying nature or through revelation. Further, God can enforce these laws either by punishments or rewards in this and in the next world even to eternity. Morality is based upon the will and laws of God, and only by knowing his will and laws can one say whether or not a thing is right or wrong.

GEORGE BERKELEY, Bishop of Cloyne near the middle of the eighteenth century, took the position that God is the Supreme Spirit and the source of everything in the universe. He argued that, on the basis of Locke's theory, one must admit that things exist only when they are perceived. But, to say that a table exists only when he perceived it, did not satisfy him. Consequently, he reasoned that although he might not be at the moment perceiving the table, God is perceiving it. Therefore, the table continues to exist as a thought in God's mind even though he left the room. The natural world is a creation of God's mind, is mental, and impresses our senses so that we have ideas, just as Locke had argued. God, then, is the cause of the natural world; however, this world is not material, it is spiritual, mental.

In this way Berkeley believed he had solved the problem of Descartes and Spinoza. Both of those philosophers had struggled with the two things, mind and matter. Descartes taught that mind and matter were two secondary substances coming in some way from the primary substance, God. Spinoza argued that mind and matter were two aspects, two ways of looking at the same substance, God. Berkeley eliminated matter by holding that God, spiritual substance, is all there is. That which we have thought to be matter is actually an idea in the mind of God.

God, thus, is spiritual, the creator of everything in the universe through his own mind. The dualism of mind and matter which had worried philosophers since the beginning was eliminated. Matter is gone, and only mind remains. And we can operate on the principle that this Author of Nature will always act uniformly, although we cannot prove this since God is free to change his way of acting at any time he chooses.

DAVID HUME was a skeptic. Consequently he sought to show that human reason cannot demonstrate the nature of God. All the arguments which past philosophers had used to prove the existence of God and his attributes were examined by Hume and held to be faulty. Human reason, he held, is far too weak, blind, and limited to construct any adequate conception of God.

However, Hume felt that one must believe in the existence of God since such a belief is the basis of all human hopes, of morality, and of society. Since we find nothing in the universe existing without a cause, Hume argued, we may go on to the position that the cause of the universe must be God, a being of absolute perfection. But this cannot be proven by reason. Nor can we say anything about the nature or characteristics of God.

Nevertheless, Hume suggests a probable way of thinking of God. It is possible, he said, that God is related to the world somewhat as the soul is related to the body, and is the active principle of the universe. But, he hastened to say, this is purely a probability. There is no proof of it which man can substantiate.

Belief in God, Hume taught, does not come from man's reasoning but from human desire for happiness, fear of death and future misery, and the thirst on the part of many for revenge. Because we have these emotional and impulsive characteristics as human beings, we construct a belief in God and then seek to prove that such belief is justified by reason. Hume writes at length in his attempt to show that while, from the point of view of reason, we must be skeptical about God, from the fact of our impulsive and emotional nature we do believe in God and construct a theory about God which is necessary for us. This approach to the problem of the nature of God was, as we shall see later, the part of Hume's philosophy which stimulated Immanuel Kant to make a distinction between pure reason and practical reason.

In developing his theory of monads, LEIBNITZ took the position that these self-contained units of the universe are arranged in a continuous series of increasing clearness. At one extreme is the dullest monad, and at the other extreme is God, the highest and most perfect monad, pure activity, the "monad of monads."

Further, God, for him, is the ultimate cause of everything. Although monads are shut off from everything and can in no way influence each other, God has so constructed the universe that each monad acts as though it were influenced and were influencing.

Man is unable to form a clear idea of God, since God is

the highest, most perfect monad and man is lower and less perfect. Only another perfect monad could know God. However, man can have an idea of God by taking those qualities which he finds in himself,—goodness, power, knowledge,—and raising them to infinity. The result is the idea that God is infinite goodness, power, knowledge, and the like.

Again, since God is perfect and complete, he cannot undergo change or development as do all other monads. He comprehends all things and all time at a glance and completely. He created the world which is "the best of all possible worlds."

The Concept of God in the Thought of Kant

God, for IMMANUEL KANT, is the notion or highest Idea which man can have, the idea of the highest unity, of the one Absolute Whole including and encompassing everything. This idea transcends experience and cannot be obtained from experience. It is one of the results of reason which brings under one head all happenings.

Kant insists that we must never forget that we have formed the idea of the whole of experience. It is nothing that we can know as we do one of our ideas arrived at through experience, for we cannot experience the whole universe. After we have formed this idea, we make an entity of this whole and personify it. Thus, for us it becomes God.

Kant attacks the arguments for the existence of God advanced by philosophers before him, seeking to prove that each one is full of inconsistencies and logical fallacies. But, although it is impossible for one to prove the existence of God by reason, belief in His existence is necessary for the moral life. We need this Idea of the Whole, this transcendent theology, as a foundation for our ethical principles.

Although Kant criticizes the arguments of others for the existence of God, he offers his own argument, or proof, which he believes to be on a truer philosophical foundation than the others. He believed that each individual found inherent in reason itself the categorical imperative: "Always act so that you can will the maxim or determining principle of your action to become universal law; act so that you can will that everybody shall follow the principle of your action." This is a command that one live according to an absolutely good will. Further, to live so is deserving of happiness. Thus, happiness and the good life should go together in the world. But they often do not. We see good people very unhappy and very evil people happy.

Consequently, there must be a God who is perfectly wise, good, and powerful to join happiness and goodness. God, for Kant, is able to know everything, is a Being who possesses our moral ideals, and has absolute power.

Kant's theory, as you will recognize, is a further development of Hume's position. We cannot know by our reason that God exists or what he might be if he did exist. No one can prove anything about God by argument or reasoning. But, we can, on the basis of our meager experiences, form an idea of the Whole of the universe and can personify it. Further, we need the idea of God to serve as a foundation of our moral life. Kant called this idea of God "transcendent" since it transcends, goes beyond, experience. It is also a necessary idea, necessary for the living of the good life, for morality.

This point of view is Kant's answer to skepticism. The philosophers, led by John Locke, had argued earnestly that man can know only that which he experiences. But man cannot experience God. At best, he can blow up or inflate his meager and small ideas to infinity and call that God. Kant agreed with those who held that we cannot know God through reason. But, he added, we need God. Therefore, reason can bring God back as a necessary unknown.

Fichte, Schelling, Schleiermacher, Hegel, and Later German Thinkers

Kant's influence reached deep into the thinking of those who followed. FICHTE came to the conclusion that the source of the universe was universal reason, intelligence alone, pure "ego." This ego is distinct from the self of each individual human being. It is the universal active reason which has created and cannot be kept from creating. This he called God. It is to be thought of as a "universal life-process" dominating the consciousness of every individual.

Further, this universal ego or God is, for Fichte, the universal purpose of the universe and its existence is to be proven, as with Kant, by the moral law. Morality demands such a being, therefore God exists.

The conception of God held by SCHELLING is very similar to that of Fichte. Schelling teaches that God is to be understood as the creative energy which is the absolute ground of everything. This force or principle is the soul of the universe and is realized through the universe. Indeed, the theory held by Schelling is pure pantheism. The world is alive and it is alive because it is God and he is, of course, alive.

FRIEDRICH ERNST DANIEL SCHLEIERMACHER took the position that God, the Absolute, and the world are one. For him God has never in all time or eternity been without the world. Whenever God has been, the world has also been. Further, the world cannot be without God. Nevertheless, there is an important distinction to be made between God and the world.

While God, for Schleiermacher, is to be thought of as a unity, a one, without space and time, the world is, as we conceive it, many things in space and in time. Thus, while this philosopher was in that school of thinking which we have called pantheism, he did make a distinction between God and the world.

Further, he held that it is impossible to ascribe to God the usual attributes of personality, thought, will, and the like. For him, God is to be thought of as the universal creative force in the universe, the source of all life. He is such that man can know him only through religious feeling, a feeling of absolute dependence. Man does, he argued, come to this feeling of dependence and recognizes that the thing upon which he is dependent for all that he is must be a "world ground," God.

The theory of God as held by HEGEL is part of his

whole theory of evolution to which we have referred previously. God, Hegel tells us, is Idea. By this he means that God must be thought of as the entire process of evolution, past, present, and future. The dialectical process which is unfolding in evolution is contained within God. (By "dialectic" or the "dialectical process" we mean the reasoning process.)

Thus, God is the creative reason of the universe and reveals himself in the world and as the world develops through evolution, he becomes self-conscious, comes to know himself more fully. In man he reaches the clearest self-consciousness. It is evident that Hegel's God is not complete, but is developing with the world. His is a developing God.

The world which RUDOLF HERMANN LOTZE believed in, a world of spiritual realities, could not, Lotze held, be thought of unless one admitted the existence of a universal substance of which all the spiritual units are modes or expressions. In this world of many interrelated units he saw the expression of some absolute will which unified these parts, which kept them from being all tangled up in endless confusion. All nature, then, is in some way controlled by the Absolute, a substance of which all the processes of nature are states. This, of course, is pantheism.

We interpret this Absolute in terms of what we conceive as the highest and best possible. Thus, we think of it as a personality that is absolutely good, as a God of love.

GUSTAV THEODOR FECHNER taught that God is to be thought of as the highest soul, a world soul, which is related to the world just as the human soul is related to the human body. For Fechner, nature is the body of God. Fechner began his thinking from the fact of mental processes which he discovered in men. The human individual thinks, he engages in what are called psychic processes. Also, according to Fechner, there are higher forms of psychic processes in the universe. All of these, united, are the world—soul or God.

This group of philosophers thought of God as the underlying source or cause of the universe. He is, in some way, that which is behind the universe. Some have told us that we can know him through our reason while others have held that reason is unable to penetrate behind the universe to its cause. A few have held that we can know God only through feeling.

The Position of Comte, Spencer, and Bradley

The later philosophers have tended to abandon the attempt to know God and turned the matter over to the theologians or religionists. AUGUSTE COMTE, as representative of the Positivists, held that all attempts to get at the essence of things were symptoms of immature development of the human mind. When one reaches the stage of positivism he gives up all attempt to discover God and busies himself with discovering the relations which exist between things, phenomena.

SIR WILLIAM HAMILTON held that one might believe in God if ho wanted to do so, but that it is impossible for one to know anything about God since the ultimate must be unconditioned and the human mind can know only that which is conditioned by something else.

HERBERT SPENCER argued that all we can know is that which is finite and limited. But we can relate things to an Absolute or something unrelated. However, we cannot know this Absolute, the substance which underlies all that we know. Therefore, the Absolute is, according to Spencer, the Unknowable. It exists. This he would not deny. But what it is, he argued that no one can know.

F. H. BRADLEY disagrees with Spencer and maintains that the Absolute is knowable. Further, he holds that this Absolute is a harmonious system, a Whole which is in some way in every part of the universe.

The Views of James and Dewey

WILLIAM JAMES, true to his Pragmatism, holds that a belief in a God is necessary for the satisfaction of man's nature. We cannot prove that God exists, nor can we prove anything about him, but we have a will to believe in God, and we must satisfy this will.

The God in which James holds that man must believe is part of the universe, not divorced from it. He is working with man in the realization of man's ideals. James speaks of him as man's great Companion, his helper. Often he speaks of God as a being very much like man,—conscious, personal, and good,—but somewhat more powerful than man.

JOHN DEWEY would not use the term God without defining it in such a way that it ceases to have any real meaning. He recognizes that the universe exists and that men do have certain experiences which they have interpreted in terms of God. Dewey holds that such an interpretation carries with it too much that cannot be proven and, therefore, should not be made.

Thus, man, in his thinking, has found himself within a universe which he does not understand and which deals out to him much that is evil in his sight. Man has attempted to account for this world and, at the same time, to save himself from the evil of the world. The result is many theories of God, the source of the universe and the salvation of man.

From the earliest of men to the present we discover theories of how the universe came into being and continues to function. Many of these theories are centered about a God or powerful being, very much like man but far greater, who created the universe, usually out of nothing. This God is often thought of as the force, principle, or power, which is working within the universe to keep it going.

In many philosophies, as we have seen, this God is also more or less concerned about man. He offers man salvation from the world and its evils. He cares especially about man.

The religious tradition has, with only a few exceptions, held to a more or less personal God who cares for man and who, at the same time, is the creator of the universe. Another tradition, the scientific, has not been so sure that there is anything in the universe which cares for man or that the creative force of the universe is anything like personality. Science knows forces, drives, energies in the universe, working and creating, and destroying. It sees man, with his values and hopes, coming into being as these forces operate and going to pieces as they continue to operate. Scientists will not dispute if someone wishes to give these forces a name and uses the name "God." But they are quick to state that the word "God" must not be applied here with all its traditional connotations.

Modern philosophy has been moving in the direction of the scientists. Either it denies directly the existence of God and insists that the name be saved for the phenomenon in history to which it has been given originally, or it redefines the term so that it loses all its original meaning and becomes merely a name for the forces of which the scientists speak. Although there is a vast body of people who hold to a belief in the God as developed by Saint Augustine and Thomas Aquinas, and although there are some philosophers who hold to that position, the bulk of modern and present-day philosophy has abandoned the traditional Christian conception of God and put in its place a theory of the Absolute either as the ground of the universe or the unity of the universe, a substance of which all else is created or just the universe taken as a whole and with its consistencies and likenesses emphasized.

You and I are left to make our own choice from among these many theories. We may follow the tradition, or we may accept the scientific approach.

Chapter V
FATE VERSUS FREE WILL

PYTHAGORAS SOCRATES PLATO ARISTOTLE
BACON DESCARTES SPINOZA
LOCKE HUME VOLTAIRE ROUSSEAU
KANT SCHELLING HERBART SCHOPENHAUER
MILL JAMES DEWEY

Is man free to mould his own destiny, or is he a mere straw in the wind of fate? Do our ideals, hopes, acts, and wills mean anything in the universe? Is it true, as some hold, that we come from the unknown, are buffeted around by forces of which we have no control, and at last return to the unknown?

The generally accepted belief that the life of the primitive man was free and happy is not supported by what is known about the ideas and thoughts of the earliest of men. The most general belief found among the most ancient peoples is called "animism." This is the belief that every object in the universe is actually a person very much like man himself but far more powerful. Further, early man was certain that many of these living objects were not friendly to him.

This early man believed that the river, the mountain, each tree, the sun, moon, and each star, in fact everything in the universe was either a living being or else the home of a spirit. Each being or spirit was thought to be very powerful, jealous of this power, easily offended, and mighty in anger. Therefore the primitive man was constantly afraid lest he unwittingly offend and anger one of these beings or spirits and suffer the most fearful punishment.

These beings and spirits ruled him at all times along with numerous other spirits which might be loose in the universe and might enter him at any time. Disease, madness, and all the other disasters which might come to man were the workings of spirits within him. Thus primitive man's world, both inside and outside of himself, was swarming with beings and spirits who determined everything which he did or which happened to him.

In such a world of "powers and principalities" man was never free. That he might have or be a free will acting on his own never entered his mind. The beings and spirits of the universe directed and determined his every act and thought.

Later mankind passed beyond belief in animism, but not to a belief in free will. If the powers which governed all man's actions were not thought of as living objects in nature or spirits occupying natural objects and man himself, they were believed to be the Fates, beings of great power and influence who determined the destinies of every man. In the earliest Greek mythology we find the conception of the Fates, individuals weaving the web of destiny in which all mankind is caught and from which we cannot free ourselves.

Both the idea of spirits and the idea of the Fates are expressions of a basic feeling among early peoples that in some way the destinies of each and every human being are determined by forces beyond the power of his control. It is the idea that all life is a consistent pattern determined by powers outside of man and to which man is completely and absolutely subject. Here no place is left for anything like free will on the part of man. Man is a marionette whose every action is controlled and determined by the pull of strings in the hands of powers far above and beyond him. He must follow their lead and can do nothing else.

The Idea of Fate Among the Early Greek Thinkers

Throughout Greek thought we discover the belief in the absolute power of the forces of the universe. Man's destiny is determined by these powers and, although he may not be happy about it, man is helpless. He must obey.

The *Pythagoreans* were convinced that the universe, including man, was a closed system. This system could be understood if one understood the relations of the parts. Further, these relations could be expressed in terms of numbers. Consequently, if one could penetrate the secrets of numbers one would know the secrets of the universe and the destiny of man. This led to a careful study of numbers in an effort to predict man's future.

In the thinking of PYTHAGORAS and his followers, the nature of the universe is such as to determine man's fate. The secrets of this fate are locked in numbers and can be unlocked if one understands the meaning of numbers. Consequently the way to know what will happen to man, each man, is to comprehend fully the language of numbers. The Pythagoreans devoted a good deal of their energies to this task.

HERACLITUS took the position that the cosmic process is according to law. He writes: "This one order of things neither any one of the gods nor of men has made, but it always was, is, and ever shall be, an ever-living fire, kindling according to fixed measure and extinguished according to fixed measure." All change, he held, is according to a fixed and unalterable law, a law which is the basic principle of the universe. Man is completely subject to this law. At times Heraclitus speaks of this law, or principle, as "Fate" and at other times as "Justice." But, whatever name is used, the meaning is simple. At the base of the universe is inevitable law, to which all things, including man, are subject. Man has no choice but to follow the dictates of this law. "This alone is wise," he says, "to understand the intelligence by which all things are steered through all things." When man understands his fate, he does not rebel, but accepts it as inevitable.

A similar point of view was taken by all the philosophers before Socrates. They all thought of the universe as constructed by some underlying power or force, which, in building the universe, set its pattern so that the parts functioned with a complete inevitableness. Man, as part of this universe, was governed by this inevitableness. Although, in their philosophies, they did not make this inevitableness into a person with the title of Fate, nevertheless they held to the belief that man's destiny was determined not by what he did but by the facts of his creation. Thus, the Fates of popular Greek religion and the belief in the inevitableness of nature were the same in principle.

The first break in this tradition came with the *Sophists*. They centered their attention upon man, and found in him unrealized possibilities. Man, "the measure of all things," could not be wholly bound to an inescapable process or law. Although they were not clear about the matter, it seemed impossible to them that man should not have some effect upon his own destiny. At least, they were certain that man could shape his destiny among his fellows. He could learn how to succeed as a member of society, to defend himself in the courts, and to win a position for himself in the state. Whatever his eternal destiny might be, at least he could shape his worldly existence to fit his desires. Man was not wholly enslaved to the Fates.

According to Socrates, Plato, and Aristotle

This approach forced philosophers to rethink the problem of man's relation to the universe and the forces responsible for its existence and activity. Man would no longer be content to accept the inevitableness of the universe without a challenge, without a fight, without a valiant attempt to defend his own integrity.

SOCRATES added strength to this concern with man. He held that man's crowning achievement is knowledge. Having attained knowledge, man would do the right thing, he would be good. Without knowledge man was in danger of acting wrongly. Further, he believed that man could, through knowledge, have some influence upon his destiny here and hereafter. Man might influence to some degree at least the fate which was his. Here was the beginning of a belief, vague though it was, that man was possessed of some degree of freedom of choice. This freedom was not a mere sham, but upon its proper use might hinge man's future.

In Socrates' thinking, many people made wrong choices and would consequently suffer. They used their freedom to reach evil ends. With Socrates and the Sophists we see the Fates loosing their grip on man. Man was rising up and declaring his belief in his own ability, his strength even against the powers of the universe.

The belief in man's freedom is shown clearly in the writings of PLATO. Man can and does defeat the purposes of the universe. Although he is a creature of the divine Creator, he may so order his life as not to live justly and wisely. The appetites or the passions may gain control of him and refuse to obey the dictates of his highest part, reason or mind. The ideal is a just man with each part of his nature functioning in its proper way. But man can destroy this harmony.

Indeed, in his later writing, the *Laws*, we find Plato insisting upon freedom as a necessary basis for the good life. He would have men free to build a life that is worth while. In this it is evident that Plato believes that a life that is good because it can be nothing else is not in reality good. Goodness comes because one has met evil and overcome it, has made a real choice and has chosen well. This implies that man is not determined by the universe, but is able to choose, is free to determine in the last analysis his own fate.

Central in the thinking of ARISTOTLE is the belief in the freedom of man. Morality, for him, is not a matter of some inevitable law, but is a matter of free choice. He writes that "Virtue, as well as evil, lies in our power." We are free to do that which is good or to do that which is evil. There is no power in the universe forcing us either way.

In another place he says, "Virtue is a disposition, or habit, involving deliberate purpose or choice."

Further, Aristotle held that the supreme end of man was the realization of that which is highest and best in him as a human being, his reason. Man may choose to debase this or to realize it to the fullest. He is free to strive to become all that is in him to become, or to become less. The ultimate choice lies within man.

Thus, both Plato and Aristotle were certain that a world in which fate ruled completely could not be a good world. In such a world man could not be held responsible for his actions. Whether good or bad, he would be determined by a power beyond his control and could not therefore be blamed. Morality, in the thinking of both philosophers, demanded a free will, an opportunity for choice which was real and not a mere sham. The good man, they held, was one who made the right choice and through the force of his will realized the best. The bad man was one who made the wrong choice.

Although both these philosophers recognized the existence in the universe of certain laws and consistencies, they were not willing to close the universe so tightly that man's actions were determined in all things. They had to leave room for free will or freedom, lest they deny the actual existence of the good life.

The Views of the Later Greek Philosophers

The value of freedom was recognized by EPICURUS and the Epicureans. However, following the atomic theory of Democritus, they were in danger of making such freedom impossible. If man, as all nature, is a result of the coming together of atoms and if he disappears when these atoms separate, then man would be subject to the nature of the atoms. To meet this difficulty, Epicurus held that the atoms were endowed with spontaneity. They were not pushed and pulled by forces of nature, but had the power to move as they willed. Thus, if man is a composition of atoms, he too would have the inner power to move and act as he willed.

Believing that the universe of man cannot be explained as the result of blind fate, Epicurus was unwilling to leave man as the pawn of inexorable forces. Free will seemed important to him. As a result, he gave freedom to his atoms so that they might, in turn, give freedom to man.

Thus, man can make choices, determine his fate. He may strive for prudence. He may seek pleasure which comes through the satisfaction of desires and through the elimination of all desire.

ZENO and the Stoics took the other extreme position as regards human freedom. For them the universe is a result of fixed and unchanging law. Everything in it is determined with an absoluteness that permits no break. Even man's will is determined. In the entire universe there is nothing that can happen by chance. From the first beginning to the last end there is an unbroken chain of causes determined by the nature of the universe.

Man can have no freedom of will in any true sense of the term, the Stoics taught. Man is part of this causal chain and all his actions are the result of factors over which he can have no control.

It is possible, Zeno asserted, for man to obey graciously or to obey ungraciously, but in either case he must obey. His only freedom, then, is to accept his fate, to assent to what fate has decreed for him.

According to the Stoics, everything in the universe has its beginning and source in the will of God. God is the ruler and the determiner. Everything which has evolved has been the result of God's purpose. Thus fate and God's will are the same.

However, when the Stoics come to the problem of ethics or the good life, they abandon the complete determinism of their metaphysics. (By "metaphysics" we mean the philosopher's conception of the universe and of reality.) In their ethics the Stoics teach that man may determine for himself whether or not he will obey the moral law, whether or not he will follow reason and seek to realize the supreme good. Man may give himself to his passions and become their slave, or he may escape from his passions and rise to a moral life above them. As he conquers his passions he becomes free. This, for the Stoic, is true freedom.

Thus, while the Stoic, in attempting to hold to a universe in which cause and effect are determined, must deny freedom in his metaphysics, he is unable to carry this theory to its logical conclusion. When he approaches the ethical problem he realizes that man must be free if good and bad are to mean anything in reality. Here the Stoic is in the tradition of Socrates, Plato, and Aristotle.

The Position of the Greco-Religious Thinkers

PHILO, in his attempt to reconcile Jewish religion and Greek philosophy, conceived of the body as the source of evil. When the soul comes into the body it partakes of the evil of the body, an evil that has been of the body from the beginning. Thus, the incarnation of the soul in the body is, for Philo, a fall.

But the soul possesses what Philo thought of as pure intelligence, an addition which the soul receives from the divine, from God. This makes man akin to God, to the divine. However, even though the human soul is connected with the divine and is, in a sense, part of the divine, it has the power to freely accept or reject the rule of God.

The divine does not exercise complete control over man, but makes it so that he can give himself over to sense and the bodily passions or conquer these and rise to the divine. Thus, man has a real freedom, and can exercise it to determine his own destiny in a real sense.

Likewise, PLOTINUS conceived of the soul of man as part of the world soul and as thus partaking of the freedom of the world soul. But man's soul had the desire to shape and mould matter, and thus became enmeshed in matter and fell. In this fall each soul loses its original freedom. As the real soul turns away from the life of sense in the body, it regains its freedom. The nearer it returns to God the more freedom it has.

The soul, for Plotinus, has an original freedom just as one outside a prison has freedom. As it becomes entangled in matter it enters the prison house of matter and loses its freedom. But, it can turn away from the body and regain its freedom. It can escape from the prison house of the body, of the sensual, and return to God who is perfect freedom.

Whether or not each soul does this, Plotinus believed, rests with the soul itself. There is no compulsion on the part of a fate or an inescapable law. Man is free to sell his soul to the sensual or to free it from the body and strive upward to union with God.

These early religious philosophers never doubted but that God was perfect freedom and, in so far as man or the human soul is godlike, it partakes of this freedom. Thus, for them, man is fundamentally free. But, because of their almost universal contempt for the world as the seat of evil, they believed that the incarnation of this free soul in a body or in matter was a fall and a loss of freedom. However, in this incarnation the soul did not lose its ability to rescue itself. It was still free to become free from the body if it so willed. All of these thinkers were unwilling to give matter absolute power over the soul.

Early and Medieval Christian Thinkers

This conception was carried over into early Christianity. The *Apologists* without exception taught that man is basically free and that he has fallen through his contact with body. At the creation, they believed, the soul was endowed with the ability to choose between the good and the evil. As a result, some souls chose to turn from God and give themselves over to the sins of matter. But man is able, through the aid of the divine and the living of a Christian life, to return to God. Man can make a choice which will determine forever his destiny. This choice is real and eternal. Thus, the freedom of man is real in that it enables him to determine his estate forever.

The early Christian doctrine of the work of Jesus is in line with this theory. Jesus, the Apologists believed, came to save man from sin. But sin implies guilt on the part of man and guilt is meaningless unless man is in some way responsible for his sin. You cannot hold a man as guilty of an act unless he is able to act differently. Thus, only if man is free to choose can he be condemned for his sin. If man has sinned, he must be free.

Further, the early Christians argued that God, who is all good and perfect, cannot be responsible for evil and sin in the world. Thus, man must shoulder this responsibility, and must be free. The early Christian monk PELAGIUS taught that God had given freedom to man so that he may make a choice between good and evil. Each man makes his own choice, but he retains his freedom of choice. Thus. he may turn away from sin by an act of his free will, repudiate evil, and receive divine forgiveness.

It is obvious, then, that freedom was believed by these early Christians to be necessary to account for the work of Jesus and the whole scheme of salvation.

The conception of individual freedom was denied by SAINT AUGUSTINE. According to him, mankind was free in Adam, but since Adam chose to sin, he lost freedom not only for himself but for all men and for all time. Now no one is free, but all are bound to sin, are slaves of evil.

But God makes a choice among men of those whom he will save and those whom he will permit to be destroyed because of sin. This choice is not influenced by any act of an individual man, but is determined only by what God wants.

In Augustine we find both fatalism and predestination as far as the individual man is concerned. With Adam there was no fatalism. He was free. But God knew even then how Adam would act, knew that he would sin. Thus, from the beginning God made up his mind whom he would save. These were predestined from the first to salvation, and all the rest were predestined to eternal punishment. Adam's sin, for Augustine, became hereditary, with the result that the future of every man is completely determined and has been so from the beginning of time.

The doctrine of original sin, so prevalent in the early Christian church, led in Augustine to a belief in fatalism as far as the individual man is concerned. His future is sealed not by any act of his, but by the act of the first man and the free will of God himself.

ABELARD was not in complete agreement with Saint Augustine, but held that man is actually free to choose between good and evil. Sin, for him, consisted in the consenting to do an evil act which is recognized by the individual as evil. If one does wrong, but intends to do right, he is not a sinner. But, if he knows that an act is wrong and persists in doing it, he is sinning. This choice of act is a matter of the free will of man. He can actually decide on the basis of his knowledge and can act in terms of his decision.

While Augustine took from man all choice, Abelard gave choice back to man in order to preserve the fact of guilt and sin. Without choice sin could not exist, he held.

With THOMAS AQUINAS we find a clear belief in the freedom of the human will. Man, he taught, is a being with a will and with intelligence. He is not pushed from without like the animals, but can determine his actions. His will may follow his intellect, doing what the intellect says is right. But the will can choose to act or not to act. When his reason tells him that a certain course of action is good, man can decide which particular acts are best suited to the realization of the end proposed.

However, when Thomas Aquinas turns to a consideration of specific religious doctrines, he modifies his doctrine of free will somewhat. He believed, as did Augustine, in the doctrine of original sin. Adam's sin, for him, was transmitted to all men, and carried with it the natural consequences of sin. Only divine grace can bring salvation. But, even where God wishes to bestow this salvation, the human will must co-operate. God foresees that some will not accept the offer of grace, and predestines them to eternal punishment.

JOHN DUNS SCOTUS taught that if the human will were inferior to the human intellect, as Aquinas had believed, it could not be free. If the will had to look to the intellect for direction, it would be subject to the intellect. Therefore, to make the will wholly free, he taught that it was superior to the intellect.

The will, then, for Scotus is completely free and can make decisions between sense and the moral law. The will is the highest faculty of the soul, higher than intellect. This leads, of course, to the position that the will is the final determiner of right and wrong. What the will determines as good is good simply because the will has said that it is good.

Carried over to the idea of God, this doctrine leads one to the position that God's will is superior to his intellect, and that right is right simply because God wills it to be right and not because it is right in terms of reason. God has made certain things right. He could just as well have made the opposite things right since it is his arbitrary will which determines the right. The will of God is arbitrary.

This is the extreme of the position that the will is free. As long as will is influenced in its action by the intellect or reason, it cannot be wholly free. But, if it is free also of reason, it has reached the peak of freedom. This is the direction of Scotus' thinking, although he tends to draw back from the final logical results of his position, complete chaos since every human will would become a law unto itself. That which I will is right, and that which you will is right. There can be no measure above the human will. Scotus drew back when he found himself approaching this conclusion. But he held tenaciously to the idea that the human will is free and is not subject to the intellect. Indeed, he took the position that if it was necessary for him to have either intellect without will or will without intellect, he would choose the latter. He was, in this, one of the great champions of the freedom of the will.

With the Renaissance, man undertook to free himself from the dominance of the Church and its doctrines and to study the world freely. This was an assertion in fact of man's freedom. The human mind refused longer to be tied to the doctrines and beliefs of the past, but aspired to search the universe with unblinded eyes and tell what it found there.

It is a curious fact, however, that as man undertook this search he began to discover inexorable laws and mathematical consistencies by which everything in the universe seemed to be controlled. The early scientists turned from the Church and from Aristotle to the world round about. There they found things happening in what appeared to them mechanical ways. Galileo, Kepler, Sir Isaac Newton, each found the events of the universe following what appeared to be definite laws.

And into this system of laws man seemed to fit of necessity. His being, his actions, even his thoughts were conceived to be subject to the laws of the universe, laws which brooked no interference or change. Thus, man was freed from the authority of the past and of the Church to find himself again in bondage to a master more powerful and unyielding than any he had known before. He became, in the philosophies of many of the Renaissance scientists, merely a part of a mechanical universe controlled by forces in the universe and of no meaning save as a unit in the inexorable whole.

The Views of Bacon, Hobbes, Descartes, and Spinoza

FRANCIS BACON is typical of man's earnest desire to be free from the traditions of the past and to approach the universe without religious or intellectual bias. Fundamental to his thinking was the belief that man must free himself from the forms and prejudices of the past and follow a new method in studying the universe. His aim was to free the mind from the "idols" which the past has foisted upon it so that it might consider its universe clearly.

Then, having been freed, the human mind will, he was certain, be able to discover the laws which govern the universe and determine its every action.

Nevertheless, Bacon was not wholly able to escape the notions of the past. Although he relegated religion to a realm of its own outside of and different from philosophy, he held that there were religious laws which man must obey whether they appeared to be reasonable or not. By separating theology and philosophy, Bacon was able to free philosophy so that it might undertake an unbiased study of the universe. But he left man subject to the will of God and thereby shorn of his freedom. It is obvious that this condition could not long satisfy the thinking mind. It was far too contradictory.

THOMAS HOBBES saw the unsatisfactory results of the position suggested by Bacon, and went a step further by holding that all in the universe was subject to a purely mechanical series of cause and effect. Everything, even the actions and destiny of man, he argued, can be explained mechanically. All the universe is motion. All thoughts or ideas are simply motions in the brain.

Thus, for Hobbes, to hold that man is a free will is absurd. An individual finds himself the scene of alternating desires and aversions. He wants to do some things and does not want to do others. As these opposites play across his mind, he is deliberating, thinking. The last desire or aversion is called will. He completes his deliberation and decides to act or not to act.

Each desire or aversion is caused. Consequently the last desire or aversion, the point at which one stops, is also caused. Thus, the will is caused and cannot be free. A man is, Hobbes held, free to act after he has willed, but is not free to will or not to will. The very nature of his being makes him a willing being. He must will. But he can choose to act or not to act on the willing which he does.

The problem of DESCARTES was, as we have seen, to reconcile the mechanical theories of his time with the ideas of God, soul, and freedom. He was not contented to accept the mechanistic view of the universe, including man, which the science of his day seemed to demand. At the same time, he was unwilling to discredit science altogether and return to the older spiritualistic tradition.

His solution lay in making a sharp distinction between mind and body. The body, for him, was part of the organic universe and was governed by purely mechanical processes. He believed that here cause and effect was supreme, that there were no breaks in the chain of causes, and that everything was determined by what went before. All the universe, including man, could therefore be explained mechanically.

The mind, or soul, however, is free. It wills an active principle. It is free, for example, to will to love God or not. It is free to think pure thoughts or not. It is free to create imaginary pictures and to move the body in any way it cares. The volitional part of man's nature, then, is in the soul, and can be influenced by the body only indirectly.

The will, according to Descartes, is independent of the body, and can, if it so desires, produce states of the body. The will is free. Further, the ideal for which man should strive is to keep the will free from influences of the body and any other outside influences.

While Descartes had separated mind and body in an effort to reconcile the mechanistic science of his day and the religion of the times, he left unanswered the question of the relationship between mind and body. How can the free will of the individual influence the body? This was the problem which his immediate successors attacked.

The *Occasionalists,* of whom GUELINCX is a representative, held that God is aware at all times of what an individual is going to will, and he arranges the universe so that the thing which I will happens. The human will is free, but God has foreknowledge and thus can act so that it looks as though the will was influencing the body or other bodies.

Other successors of Descartes, BLAISE PASCAL and PIERRE BAYLE for example, placed freedom in the realm of religion and held that though we cannot prove man's freedom by reasoning, we can know that man is free through a direct religious experience.

In SPINOZA we find a complete abandoning of the idea of freedom. His philosophic system is absolutely deterministic. Everything in the universe follows from something else in a definite causal chain each link of which is necessarily connected with the one preceding and the one following.

God, or Substance, for Spinoza, is absolutely independent, self-caused and self-determined. God is wholly and completely free. However, all finite objects and all thoughts form two lines each interconnected in strict causal sequence. Thus, while the underlying substance of all things and all thoughts is free, the individual thing or thought cannot be free but is determined by its history, its past.

Thus, there cannot be any such thing as a free will. The will, for Spinoza, is simply the soul affirming or denying what is true and false. The intellect and the will are essentially the same. The will is nothing more than an idea which one might have affirming or denying itself. And the affirmation is determined by the idea. Consequently the will is under the dominance of the intellect and cannot in any sense be free.

Further, the will can have no effect on the body. Both body and mind are attributes of God or Substance, and each is independent of the other.

Man, Spinoza holds, is fooled into thinking he is free because he does not see the chain of causes which determine his action. Indeed, any object equally ignorant might think that it was free. But when man comes to understand the causal chain, he realizes that he is in no way free.

Spinoza also teaches that we have different stages of the will. At one level are the passions. These are confused and inadequate ideas. Here we will before the idea is complete and definite. Adequate ideas result in will proper, the adequate action upon ideas. As man attains to these adequate ideas he is freed from his passions and acts in the light of clear understanding. When a man knows, he is free from hate, fear, anger and the like. But his will is always determined by his understanding and therefore cannot be thought of as free.

The Position of Locke, of Hume, and of Leibnitz

To ask whether a man's will is free or not is, according to JOHN LOCKE, a foolish question. "It is as insignificant," he writes, "to ask whether a man's will be free as to ask whether his sleep be swift or his virtue square." This is true, he argues, because the will is the power of an individual to think his own actions and to prefer their doing or not doing. If one is able to think about his actions and is able to prefer one action over and above another, he has will. On the other hand, freedom is also a power, the power to do or not to do any particular thing in terms of what he wills.

Man may have both powers. He may be able to think clearly about his actions and reach a preference among possible actions. Further, he may be able to do that which he prefers or he may find himself unable to act in accord with his preference. But these are two powers and must be recognized as such, Locke urges.

God, Locke holds, has endowed man with certain desires or uneasinesses of the mind for want of some absent good. These desires determine the will. The individual determines to do that which is most pressing. He sets about to realize the desire which is paramount. This he wills to do.

DAVID HUME held that the idea of necessity and the idea of cause which men have are the result of observation of the uniformity in nature. As men see the world about them, they recognize that certain things always follow other things. This leads them to reason that there is a necessary causal connection between the two things.

Likewise, as men watch themselves they discover that when they desire something, actions follow which are directed toward securing that something.

Thus, because of these experiences, men move to the conclusion that the universe is characterized by causal necessity and that there is a relation of cause and effect between a man's desires and the actions in which he engages. However, men find a necessity in the causal relationships of nature but do not find a similar necessity when they study their own actions. While they believe that nature is characterized by a rigid cause and effect relationship, their own actions are not so rigidly determined by their motives.

But, wherever there is uniformity of action, Hume holds, there is necessity. There is uniformity in nature and there is a like uniformity in man's actions. Consequently, we can infer from one act to its cause just as we can infer from one thing in nature to its cause. Man's actions result from his character and are necessary results of that character. Give him another character, and his actions will be different.

Freedom, for Hume, is merely this necessary connection. So long as man's actions arise from his own character, nature, or desires, they are free. If, however, he acts because of some external compulsion contrary to his character or desires, he is not free.

For example, a man strikes another. If this action is a result of his inner nature, his character or desire, it is brought about necessarily from the nature which is his, but he is free in so acting. However, if someone else forces him to strike the individual against his own desire and character, he is not free. In both instances there is necessity. But, in the first case the necessity is that of the very nature of the man acting, while, in the second case, the necessity comes from without him and is not in accord with his nature.

GOTTFRIED WILHELM LEIBNITZ tackled the same problem as did Descartes. He realized that, in some way, philosophy must reconcile the achievements of science and the elements of Christianity which were considered valuable. But, while Descartes conceived of one universal substance and two attributes, Leibnitz believed in the existence of an infinite number of minute units or substances, the monads.

Each monad, he held, is completely insulated from any influences outside of itself. It cannot be determined by anything other than that which it is. It "has no windows." Therefore, whatever it does is a result of its own nature and not because of forces outside it.

Man, like all objects in nature, is composed of a number of monads intricately organized. Since each monad is insulated from without and is thereby free from outside influences, so man must be free from such influences. However, just as the monad is determined from within by the law of its own inner nature, so man is determined from within, by his own nature, his own impulses and desires.

Will, for Leibnitz, is simply the conscious striving of an

individual, striving that is guided by a clear idea. Man knows what he wants, and strives to attain it. This striving is his will. Thus, will is always determined by the idea which the individual has of what he wants. Choice is simply the selecting of the desire that is strongest. Man is never free, in any absolute sense of the term, to decide for one action or for another regardless of his desires. He must decide for the desire which is strongest, and must strive to realize it through his actions. We will what our nature tells us is best.

Leibnitz believed that in this theory he had saved man from the mechanism of science and made possible the realization of the values of Christian thought. The monad was not open to influence from the outside and therefore not mechanically determined. Its actions were determined by its own inner nature, and thus were free.

Fate and Free Will According to Voltaire and to Rousseau

In his earlier writings the great French propagandist of the movement in philosophy known as the Enlightenment, VOLTAIRE, taught a doctrine of the freedom of the will that bordered on complete irresponsibility, but in his later works we find him abandoning this for an almost equally complete determinism. He wrote, "When I can do what I will, I am free; but I will necessarily what I will."

There followed a long list of brilliant thinkers who, influenced more by the scientific side of the philosophies of their predecessors, sought to prove that man was wholly and completely a machine devoid of anything which might in any sense be called freedom of the will. They saw man in all his parts a being similar to the intricate machines which inventors were constructing. JOHN TOLAND, DAVID HARTLEY, JOSEPH PRIESTLEY, LA METTRIE, BARON D'HOLBACH, and many others taught that thought is merely a function of the brain and that the human individual is wholly and completely determined by the play of forces in the universe so that he is tossed here and there as these forces meet and separate. He has nothing that could be called a will which might have power to shape these forces to ends which might be his.

The general position of all the Enlightenment philosophers was that man in all aspects is governed by the same laws which govern the natural world. For them man was just another, but more intricate and amusing, machine.

A bomb was dropped into the midst of this brilliant group of thinkers by JEAN JACQUES ROUSSEAU. He took issue with the basic positions of all these men when he affirmed that the truest characteristic of man was not the scientific mind but the feeling heart. Man, for him, is not a toy in the hands of natural laws, but is a free soul striving to live according to the dictates of this freedom. Rousseau saw in this trend toward the sciences the inevitable destruction of all that man had come to believe was of most value. Thus, he threw himself against this flood and sought to stem the tide which threatened to engulf mankind.

Kant, Fichte, Schelling, Schopenhauer, and Other German Thinkers

It is said that when KANT received his copy of Rousseau's *Emile* he was so fascinated by the arguments there developed and the point of view taken that he neglected to take his afternoon walk. To so neglect was almost a major tragedy in the community since the old philosopher was so prompt each day that villagers could set their watches by his appearance at his door. It was Rousseau who stimulated Kant to his great attempt to save man's freedom in a world of science.

Kant took the position that, so long as one sticks to experience, there is no proof of freedom. In experience we find necessary connections, cause and effect. Thus, we are not able to prove theoretically the existence of free will. So far Kant was in agreement with the mechanists, those who saw the world as an interlocking series of mechanical laws and their operations. From the point of view of pure reason there is no evidence to support a belief in free will.

But, Kant believed that the mind had the faculty of Reason, a faculty engaged in bringing together the various processes, events, or occurrences into wholes or Ideas. These Ideas, though not matters of experience, are legitimate bases for man's reasoning. And, the results of such reasoning are to be accepted as legitimate bases for beliefs and actions.

The Idea of freedom is not to be found in experience. Here we find only cause and effect *ad infinitum*, on and on as far as we can go. But, Kant argues, it is legitimate for us to go beyond experience to "transcendental ideas," ideas created by Reason independently of experience.

Further, to preserve the moral life, it is necessary for man to believe in freedom. This is a practical idea, a necessary belief. Freedom of the will, then, is an idea which man erects because of the demands of his moral nature. It is necessary, and thus legitimate, even though it cannot be proved by experience.

Man, then, for Kant, is a free agent. He is capable of acting voluntarily so that his acts are not links in a chain of natural causes. Man, a free agent, originates the act which, when seen by the mind, is part of an intricate web of cause and effect.

It is impossible, Kant held, ever to prove that the will is free. Nevertheless, because such a belief is necessary, we can act and live as if the will was free. When we so act and live, we discover that certain moral insights are possible. For example, we are then able to hold each individual responsible for his actions, and we are in a position to strive for a better life. We are not drowned in complete moral despair, not caught in the inevitable tangle of cause and effect which characterizes the world of nature. Life becomes meaningful for us as human beings when we can believe that what we do is the result of free choice, and has, thereby, a moral meaning. The moral consciousness of man implies that the will is free.

Kant, in this position, makes a place for the values which the science of his day was fast pushing out of the picture. He agreed with the scientists that experience left no room for these values. But, they were so necessary that we are justified in acting as though they were real.

Basic to this position was the thesis that there is a higher truth than that of the sciences, the truth of the moral nature of man. The moral law within man is a guarantee of the world beyond the senses, a world in which freedom applies. Faith in this world was Kant's way of escape from the deadening world of experience.

FICHTE began his thinking at this point. Fundamental to Fichte's point of view was the belief in freedom, the idea that the will, or as he called it "the ego" (meaning the "I"), is not a link in the scientific chain of cause and effect, but is free, self-determining activity. This will is, for him, the only real thing in the universe.

The ego, being pure activity, creates the world which it knows. My world is not something given to me from the outside, but is a creation of the pure, active, free ego, of which I am a part. The Absolute ego, or God, is free and self-determined. Each individual ego, or will, is a part of this Absolute ego and is likewise free and creative. What I do, as an individual, is simply the Absolute ego acting, and, as it is free, so am I free.

If, some will ask, what I do is merely the realization of the purposes of the Absolute ego, am I not a slave of this ego? Fichte's answer was to the effect that we can decide whether we will be blind tools of this Absolute ego or will be conscious, willing instruments of its purpose. In making this choice we, as individuals, are free. But, having made the choice, we are no longer free. My freedom lies, then, in my choice as to whether I will willingly or unwillingly serve the Absolute ego. It is freedom of choice.

SCHELLING took very much the same view as Fichte. For him, likewise, the ground of the universe was a creative, free, living ego or principle of which everything is an expression. As man sets up his idea freedom, he reads freedom into the universe and comes to know the Absolute ego as a principle of freedom. As we live a life of creative freedom, he held, we realize that the universe is at heart free. "Freedom," he writes, "can be comprehended only by freedom."

In the philosophy of SCHLEIERMACHER an attempt is

made to salvage human freedom from the doctrine of the Absolute. Here the individual egos are thought of as in the Absolute. They are parts of the universe, and, thus, are controlled by the universe as a whole. They must fit into the universe, conform to its laws and requirements. However, each individual is endowed with its own special and particular abilities or talents. If these are not allowed to develop and reach full bloom, the universe will not develop to its fullest. Therefore, the individual is free to develop itself, to grow in terms of its inner nature or talents.

Schleiermacher, because of his basic theory of the dependence of the individual upon the "world-ground" or Absolute, was in grave danger of so merging the individual with this Absolute as to leave him wholly determined by the laws of the Absolute. He saved himself from this complete determinism by putting emphasis upon the specific contribution which each ego must make to the development of the whole if the Absolute is to realize itself fully.

HEGEL held that the universe is a process of evolution in which that which was inherent at the beginning is finally realized. In this realization the whole becomes itself to the fullest. The rose, for example, is inherent in the seed, and is the result of the process of evolution from seed to rose. However, the seed is not fully itself until the rose has bloomed. This is true of the universe, Hegel believed.

Since God is, for Hegel, the living, moving reason of the world, he becomes fully conscious and the universe becomes fully realized only in the minds of human beings. The self-conscious individual is the fullest realization of the universe.

But this individual must be free. Freedom is inherent in the universe from the beginning and is realized fully in a human being in a society which makes for freedom. Progress, for Hegel, is the development of the consciousness of freedom.

Hegel saw freedom as the end and goal of his dialectical process, a process of development from the simplest and most primitive to the Absolute Mind. Man is free, but he is free to realize the nature of the universe. In realizing this nature, he is realizing himself. Therefore, man is free to realize himself to the fullest.

HERBART refused to follow the lead of Fichte, Schelling, and Hegel in defending the doctrine of freedom. He could see no freedom for man. His ambition was to build a science of the human mind which would be parallel to the physical sciences. In endeavoring to do this, he believed that he had found certain definite laws of human behavior which were so absolute as to allow no freedom on the part of the individual. Everything, he argued, follows fixed laws, the laws of a definite science.

On the other hand SCHOPENHAUER taught that the heart of the universe is will. Striving or will is to be found in everything, the principle of its existence. As we move from the rock, for example, to man, we see will becoming conscious of itself. Will is constant, persistent, eternal in everything.

This will to live, will to be, is the cause of all struggle, suffering, and evil in the world. In such a world, to be moral is to have pity for others. Sympathy prompts good acts. But, if man can evidence sympathy and remorse, his will must be free. Indeed, he is free to negate his will.

Schopenhauer sees man's will as the basis of all evil, in that it makes man selfish. He wills what he wills and thus is self-centered. But he is also able to show sympathy, to suffer remorse for his deeds and those of others. In this he denies his will. Man is happy and at peace when, and only when, he has suppressed his selfish desires, when he has denied, negated his will, when he wills not to will.

The Position of Mill and of Green

JOHN STUART MILL agrees with the views of Hume when he asserts that all the confusion in modern thought as regards the problem of free will is due to a misunderstanding of terms. It is true, he points out, that human actions are the result of many factors. There is a sequence of events which, if wholly known, will enable one to predict the future acts of an individual.

One of these causes or factors is the desire of the individual. It is possible for me to resist other factors, to desire something to be different and to work toward that end. This fact makes possible a sense of moral freedom. Without this ability to desire, and the power of desire in shaping results, it would not be possible for us to hold our fellows guilty of their sins. A fully deterministic universe has no place for praise or blame. But, Mill sees the basis for praise and blame in the fact that one of the causes of an act is the desire of the individual.

Freedom, then, is a fact of human existence, according to Mill.

THOMAS HILL GREEN saw that past experiences determined the factors which an individual accepted as good and those he accepted as evil. But, even in these past experiences, man has been a factor, and has, thus, had a part in determining his experiences. Therefore, he is responsible for the kind of good which appeals to him now.

Further, Green finds man able to think of a better kind of world. He is able to build ideals of and for himself, visions of what he may strive to become. Indeed, having constructed these ideals, man is able to strive to realize them, strive to be better in the future. Therefore, Green argued, man is free, free to will a better existence.

This ability to will, to strive, and in some degree to accomplish, makes man a moral agent and responsible for his acts. Man is free, therefore he must accept responsibility for his deeds.

The Views of James and Dewey

WILLIAM JAMES found in man a will to believe, and this he put at the base of his thinking. Every system of philosophy, he argued, depends in the last analysis upon the will to believe. Man wants to believe in a certain way, because the belief seems to satisfy him most completely. This is the pragmatic test. It fits and works.

Now, if the will to believe is so fundamental, man cannot be bound down by immutable laws and conditions. He must be a part of the picture in a real sense. Thus, he must be free. Man, in this world, is free to build his ideals and to risk all on their realization.

JOHN DEWEY goes even further. He conceives of a world

which is in the making, and man as doing some of the creating. Unless this is all a sham, a play before an audience, man must be free to make decisions and to have his decisions count in the ultimate nature of things. Human wants, desires, willings are determiners of the universe.

Though subject to the factors of the universe in which man lives, he is able to inquire, think, plan, reach decisions and act upon them with the result that the universe is changed by his action. For Dewey, the pivot of progress is the intelligent human being freely foreseeing the possible consequences of events and throwing himself into the stream in order to, in a degree at least, change the course of the stream so that it conforms more fully to his ideals.

Thus, throughout the history of human thought man has struggled with the question: Am I a mere pawn on the chessboard of universal forces over which I can have no control, or am I able to determine my fate, my destiny, to some degree at least? Philosophers have taken both sides of this issue, and many have ranged themselves between the two extremes. By far the great majority of philosophers have endeavored to find some freedom for man. Nevertheless, there have been many who have more or less willingly turned man over to some inscrutable fate. But, the human mind cannot long be content to place itself wholly in the hands of fate. It inevitably rises up to proclaim its freedom and challenge whatever forces there be to beat it down.

Inevitably death must overtake man. The pessimists stand up to assert that death has proven their point, and that man, no matter how he may protest, is at last forced to bow to a fate which he can no longer challenge. But the optimists will answer back that death is no defeat, but is actually a victory for the will of man.

Though beaten down time and again by forces in the universe, man rises up again and again to proclaim

> *I am the master of my fate,*
> *I am the captain of my soul.*

Chapter VI

THE SOUL AND IMMORTALITY

EMPEDOCLES PLATO ARISTOTLE PLOTINUS
AUGUSTINE AQUINAS BRUNO
DESCARTES SPINOZA LOCKE LEIBNITZ
KANT SCHLEIERMACHER SCHOPENHAUER
LOTZE COMTE JAMES DEWEY

*Is death the end of human existence? Or is there more
for man in a land beyond the grave? Can we find in
man a soul, something distinct from his body, which
can survive the event of death and live eternally?
What can we believe about heaven and hell?*

Death is a universal experience. All men, whether great
or small, wealthy or poor, high or low, must inevitably
move toward that hour when life will cease and the body
return to the dust from which it came. To the eye, this is
the end, the finale, the conclusion. The body, if left to itself, will disintegrate and disappear, so that, in time, every
trace of its existence will be gone.

And so it has been since life first appeared on this earth.
Living is but a short span and is soon done with. Death
writes "Finis" to life, and the living of yesterday is soon forgotten. Man is born, grows, struggles, dreams, plans, and
builds, only to surrender at last to death.

But the human mind has never been content to let the
matter rest here. Throughout the history of mankind there
has persisted a conviction, sometimes dim and at other

times very vivid, that death cannot be the end, that the grave is not a victory of man's foes, that death does not inflict a cosmic sting. In every age there have been millions firm in the belief that what is truest in humanity persists in some form or state after death.

Early man had his dreams. In these he roamed far and wide, hunted and fished, and had many adventures and endured many perils. But, when he awoke his friends assured him that he had not moved from his cave or tent. Since this happened so often, he came to believe that there was something about him which could free itself from the body and live its own life. This was probably the beginning of a belief in the human soul.

But, if man had this soul, other things must also have souls. The early men believed, as we have pointed out, that all nature was alive. The tree had a soul or spirit; the river had a soul; and everything else in primitive man's universe had a soul, a spirit which could leave the body and return to it after going where it would and doing what it cared.

It was a very early belief that what affected the body had little or no effect upon the soul. The freedom which the soul enjoyed to come and go and the special nature of the soul made it immune, more or less, to the happenings of the body. Thus, it was but natural that man should believe that the soul survived the body and continued to be active long after the body had been lost.

In this way mankind gradually built up the belief in the human soul as something distinct from the body, and in the immortality of this soul, the existence of the soul after death had destroyed the body.

But, for many early peoples this immortality of the soul was not necessarily eternal. Having left the body, the soul, some believed, remained near by for some time, returning to the place of the body at intervals. Therefore, food, drink, and other necessities were placed with the body so that the soul might be cared for.

Other peoples believed that the soul left one body only to take up its abode in another body. Here we find the idea that the former life of the soul determined what kind of a body it entered. A good soul entered a better body or one higher in the scale, while a bad soul had to enter a body farther down the scale.

Still others believed that the soul went to a place of shades and ghostly forms, there to pine for the world of men. The early Greeks and the ancient Hebrews, among others, held to such a belief. Their dead spent eternity in a dark, uninviting, and cheerless region in misery and remorse.

The Soul as Viewed by the Early Greek Philosophers

Most of the early Greek thinkers built their theories of the soul and of immortality upon the popular beliefs which were native to the culture in which they lived. That all nature was alive, few questioned. Nor did they question the belief that man had a soul which was, in some way, the real part of him. The earliest Greek philosophers thought of this soul as the least material form of the particular substance out of which everything in the universe was made.

For example, ANAXIMENES, who taught that the underlying substance of the universe was air, likewise held that the soul was very thin or rarefied air and that this substance was the thing which held the individual together. When it left the body disintegration set in and the body was destroyed.

PYTHAGORAS, and his followers, the Pythagoreans, held that the destiny of the soul after leaving the body was determined by the life in the body. Consequently, they prepared long and involved rules which each man should know and follow with the utmost severity in order to insure a desirable existence after death.

In the teachings of HERACLITUS we find the belief that the vital principle of the universe is the ever-living fire. This is, also, the principle of life or soul of the individual human being. The soul is the finest (most rarefied) form of fire, ever-changing, but never being destroyed. To this basic belief, Heraclitus added the idea that souls varied in quality. Some souls are very dry and warm. These are the best souls since they are most like the great cosmic soul, the soul of the universe, the purest fire. Other souls are not so dry and not so warm. They are less like the cosmic fire and, thus, are less good.

Souls, according to EMPEDOCLES, leave one body at its death only to enter another body and continue to live. This is known as the doctrine of the transmigration of souls. Instead of leaving the body and going to some place reserved for souls, or instead of being destroyed with the body, this doctrine holds that the soul migrates, moves on, from one body to another when its present abode is no longer habitable. This belief was general among members of a famous early religious group, the Orphics, who influenced many of the early thinkers and had a wide following during the pre-Christian and early Christian eras.

LEUCIPPUS, DEMOCRITUS, and the other Atomists, taught that, just as the entire world is composed of atoms, or very tiny bits of matter, so the soul is composed of the finest, purest, most perfect fire atoms. These atoms are, they held, scattered throughout the body, a soul atom placed between two other atoms. While man lives, he breathes soul atoms in and out. When he dies, the soul atoms are scattered throughout the universe. The body is likened to a jar in which are many soul atoms. When the jar is broken at death, the soul atoms are spilled out.

But these atoms are not lost or destroyed. Indeed, for these philosophers, the destruction of atoms is impossible. Soul atoms may be scattered, but they enter into other bodies, rearranging themselves and thus creating another being. Change, these men believed, is not absolute. We cannot create or destroy in any real sense of the term. Actually the only change possible is that of reassembling of atoms into new patterns or beings. Soul atoms live forever, but are constantly being rearranged in the universe just as are all other atoms.

Democritus taught, as did some of the early Atomists, that the soul is to be identified with reason, the thinking and judging part of man.

The Soul and Immortality According to Plato and Aristotle

PLATO distinguishes between the soul of the world and individual souls of human beings. In his book, the *Timaeus*, he describes, in somewhat mythological terms, how the Demiurge, or world architect, endowed the world with a soul, the cause of motion, beauty, order and harmony. This world soul is between the world of ideas and the world of things which we see and experience. It acts according to definite laws, the laws of its own nature, and is the cause of all law, harmony, order, of life, mind, and knowledge.

This Demiurge also created, according to Plato, souls of all the planets and all individual souls. These individual souls, he taught, are eternal, having existed before they came into bodies. In this pre-existence each soul saw all pure ideas in a realm of perfect ideas. But, coming into the body is like entering a prison. The body clouds the soul and it forgets all that it has seen. It is pulled down and debased by the body.

Thus, the goal of the soul, Plato held, is to free itself from the body in order that it may see truth clearly. Further, by certain experiences, the soul recalls the pure ideas which it saw in its pre-existent state. Knowledge, then, is not a new thing for the soul, but is simply a recall of what has been forgotten because of the body.

The human soul, then, is a part of pure reason. But it is debased by the body. However, since it existed before it came into the body, it may free itself from the body and continue to exist after the body has been destroyed. The soul, for Plato, is immortal.

Plato offers several proofs of the immortality of the human soul. In the first place, he holds, the soul is in absolutely simplest form and thus cannot be divided or destroyed. Further, the soul is life and it is not possible that life can become not-life. Life must always remain life, and not-life must always remain not-life. Neither can become the other.

Having a desire to possess a body, the soul, which had

occupied a star, leaves its heavenly abode and enters into matter, or body. From then it has to struggle to free itself from the body. If it succeeds, it will return to its star and dwell there forever. But, if it fails, it will sink lower and lower, moving from one body to another. Here again is the familiar early idea of the transmigration of the soul.

The ultimate goal of life, according to Plato, is release of the soul from the body so that it may return to its star and there spend eternity contemplating the beautiful and pure world of ideas. But, whether or not the soul succeeds in becoming free from matter and its evils, it cannot be destroyed. The eternal pre-existence and immortality of the soul is a fundamental doctrine of Plato.

ARISTOTLE taught that soul is to be found wherever there is life and, since everywhere in nature are to be found signs of life, soul must be throughout nature. If we examine nature we will find, so said Aristotle, a series of souls beginning with the lowest or plant souls and moving upward to the highest or human souls. Plant souls are concerned with eating and digesting food, or nutrition, and with the growth of the body as well as with reproduction. The soul of man has additional and higher powers.

As we study man, Aristotle held, we discover that his soul is very much like that of a plant in that it governs the life functions of the individual. But it also resembles the animal soul in that by means of it man is able to receive sense impressions and deal with them. It is by means of this function of the soul that man comes into contact with and knows the world outside of his body.

However, the human soul is higher, in that it has the power of thinking in terms of concepts, is able to think about the inner nature of things. Thus, the soul of man has the power of reason. This reason perceives concepts just as the lower part of the soul perceives objects in the world.

Here Aristotle divides reason into that which he calls passive reason and that which he calls creative reason. The former is possibility which is turned into actuality by the latter. Just as throughout the universe Aristotle believed that matter and form were together so that form was constantly realizing itself in matter, a doctrine which we have discussed previously, so in the soul. Here he taught that creative reason was the form and passive reason the matter. Creative reason, the form, existed, he held, before either body or soul were created. While passive reason, or the matter part of the soul, is connected with the body and will perish when the body is destroyed, creative reason is not influenced by the body, is immaterial, and will continue to live after the death of the body. This creative reason is a spark of the divinity, a part of God, which comes into the soul from without and is not influenced by the baser side of the soul.

Since all but the creative reason perishes with the body, personal immortality is impossible in Aristotle's system. The only part of the soul which survives death is actually part of God and simply returns to God. All else perishes.

The Position of the Later Greek Thinkers

Since the *Epicureans* based their metaphysics on the work of Democritus, they were logically bound to hold that the soul is composed of atoms just like all other things in the universe. But, the atoms of the soul are extremely fine (thin) and are of various kinds. There are atoms of fire, air, breath, and very fine matter. These atoms are scattered throughout the body and are controlled by a rational part which, according to the Epicureans, is located in the breast. Further, all sensations of the body are a result of the soul.

Since the soul is, for these philosophers, material, it cannot be immortal. When the body dies and disintegrates, the soul atoms are scattered throughout the universe. Death, then, is the end for both body and soul. As Lucretius, one of the later Epicureans, wrote, "A fool will not make more out of the hereafter than he has made of this life."

The *Stoics* held that man is both soul and body, and that the soul is a spark from the divine fire controlled by a ruling part situated in the heart. It is a sort of blank tablet upon which things write by means of impressions just as one might write on a wax slab. This is the source of our knowledge.

The soul of man, the Stoics taught, is the source of what we know as perception, judgment, feeling, and willing. At its best, it becomes rational, able to think in terms of concepts or ideas. Thus, the soul makes it possible for man to deliberate and make choices before he acts.

Various Stoics held different ideas of immortality. Some taught that only the good and wise souls continued to exist after death of the body. All others perished with the body. Other Stoics held that all souls, regardless of their goodness or badness, lived until the end of the world.

The Views of Plotinus

In PLOTINUS we have an attempt to interpret the teaching of Plato in terms of the later religious interests. In doing this, Plotinus becomes one of the school known as Neoplatonism or the new Platonism. For Plotinus the human soul is part of a world soul. At first this human soul was in a realm where it saw the pure world soul and knew all that was good. But it turned toward matter and fell because of its desire to mould matter.

From this state of degradation, the soul must struggle to free itself from matter. If it fails, it must, at the time of the death of the body, enter another body of a man, a plant, or an animal. However, to the extent it succeeds in freeing itself from matter, it returns to God and thereby realizes itself.

Being part of the world soul, which is itself an emanation from God, the human soul is immortal, and will continue to live after death. If it has not purified itself, it will continue to live in another body. If, however, it has been purified, it returns to the God of which it is a part and lives as does God.

The Early and Medieval Christian Conception of the Soul

Christianity, as interpreted by the *Apologists*, taught that the soul and body were separate things, and that the soul was that part of the individual which most nearly represented the good in the universe. Thus, for them, the soul was immortal but continued to live in a resurrected body. Death, for these thinkers, was not a separation of body and soul, but rather a purification of the body so that it might be a fit place for the soul to dwell in throughout eternity.

This point of view was developed further by AUGUSTINE who taught that man is a union of soul and body. But, for him, the body is a prison house of the soul, the source of all evil. The soul, on the other hand, is immaterial (not made of matter) and is wholly different and distinct from the body. Although he taught that the soul directs and forms the body, he was unable to tell how this happens.

Further, Augustine taught that each individual has his own soul, and that it is not an emanation from God. A soul does not exist before the body in which it dwells. How the soul was created was a mystery. However, after the soul came into being, it continued to live forever. The human soul is, for Augustine, immortal. Nevertheless, the life of the soul after the death of the body may be either happy or miserable, depending upon how the individual lived during his earthly existence. If during this earthly existence he has won the favor of God, he is given blessedness. If not, he is eternally condemned to misery.

Throughout the so-called Dark Ages, in the teachings of the Schoolmen and their followers, the belief was held generally that man possesses a soul which is distinct from the body but which may be, in some way or other, influenced by the body. Indeed, the eternal destiny of the soul was thought to depend to a degree at least upon its experiences while in the body. That the soul was immortal was not questioned. Whether it had an existence before it entered the body, as those influenced by Plato had held, or whether it came into being at the time the body was created, there was no doubt that it lived eternally after the body perished.

If good, the soul was rewarded by being permitted to continue its existence in a realm of complete blessedness. But, if the individual possessing the soul had lived an evil life, the soul was condemned to eternal suffering and torment. Immortality was certain in either case. Since the body was thought of as a source of evil and a danger to the soul, most thinkers held that the soul should, in so far as possible, free itself from the body and its temptations. In many instances, men sought ways to torture and deny the body so that the soul could live its own good life and thus prepare itself for an eternity of happiness.

THOMAS AQUINAS was the philosopher who brought this general point of view into a complete and thorough statement. He taught that the human soul was created by God. This soul was, for him, immaterial, the intellectual and vital principle of the body. This intellectual soul was added to the body at birth. While there are other souls, the human soul is different from all these in that it is intelligent and can will.

This intelligent soul is not dependent upon the body for its existence or functioning, but can continue to act after the body has perished. Further, the soul continues to exist just as it did while the body was alive. Thus, it forms for itself a new body, a spiritual body through which it functions throughout eternity.

This point of view was the pattern which orthodox Catholic Christianity accepted and made fundamental to its belief. Later Christian thinkers did not alter it in any significant detail. Heresies came forward from time to time, but were beaten back by the strength of the orthodox position.

The Soul According to the Forerunners of the Renaissance

LUDOVICO VIVES, forerunner of the interest in science which marked the Renaissance, urged that doctrines should be abandoned and man should make a careful scientific study of the soul to discover, not its essence, but the manner in which it acts. BERNARDINO TELESIO attempted to explain the soul mechanically and materially in a way resembling the early Greeks. He held that the soul was a very fine substance, resembling heat, centered in the brain but diffused throughout the body through the nerves. As such, he believed the soul caused the parts of the body to remain together and to move as an individual. Besides this material soul, he held that an immortal soul existed, a soul added to the material soul by God.

GIORDANO BRUNO taught that the soul was an immortal monad or uncaused element similar to the monads or elements composing everything in the universe.

These men, standing at the opening of the new age of mankind, the Modern Period, were not contented to accept the theories of the soul developed by either the ancients or the medieval Churchmen. They felt that these earlier theories and ideas did not stand the tests of science. Consequently, these men sought a theory of the soul and of immortality which would square with the new learning that was flooding in upon the age.

The Views of Bacon and Hobbes

The attempt to break with the past is clearly seen in the writings of FRANCIS BACON. He taught that the human soul was actually two souls, one divine or rational and the other irrational. The divine soul was, he held, a matter for religion to handle. The irrational soul, however, was open to study and understanding by man using the methods of science. By these methods Bacon believed that we would find this soul to be material but invisible, residing in the head and running along the nerves to all parts of the body. This soul was the seat of reason, imagination, understanding, memory, appetite, and will.

HOBBES broke completely with the past. He held that the entire universe was material and that in such a universe there could be nothing corresponding to the human soul as described by earlier philosophers. His materialistic position left no room for an immaterial soul that could survive the disintegration of the body.

The Views of Descartes and Spinoza

DESCARTES felt that the logical result of science was a mechanical and materialistic universe, but he was equally certain that this was not the complete explanation of the universe. Consequently, he was anxious to discover a way

by which he could take account of all that science seemed
to demand and at the same time hold to the existence of
the human soul. The result of this desire was his theory of
one absolute substance, God, and two relative substances,
mind and body. Having made this distinction, it was easy
for him to maintain that the soul was distinct from the
body and therefore not subject to the same laws as the
body.

The soul, he taught, is a unit or single principle which
expresses itself in numerous ways. Among these are willing,
feeling, and reasoning. Thus, the soul is seen as acting
and also as having passions.

Since this soul is part of the Whole, part of God or
Absolute Substance, it cannot be thought of as disappear-
ing, but continues as long as God continues. Death of the
body is but a change, and the soul, being free of the body
and never actually influenced by it, is not affected by its
disintegration.

Although Descartes held that God is the only substance,
he felt it necessary to make a clear separation between
soul and body and thus he left an ultimate dualism. This
did not satisfy his followers. Two ways of solving the problem were easily evident. On the one hand, a philosopher
might turn away from the body and concentrate upon the
soul. MALEBRANCHE did just this. The soul was, for him,
the only reality, and what we think of the body is merely
an idea of the body in the soul. This is pure idealism.
Hobbes had taken the other position: to deny the existence of the soul and concentrate upon a materialistic view
of the universe.

It remained for SPINOZA to offer a solution of the problem without sacrificing either the results of natural science
or the soul. Since, for him, God was the only substance,
the soul could be nothing else than a mode of God. As
such, it was identified with the spiritual side of the universe. Soul was perceived when one looked at Substance
from the side of mind rather than from the side of body.
Thus, it was subject only to spiritual laws and not to the
laws of science or of the material world.

Further, as a mode of the absolute substance, the soul could not be immortal in an individual sense, but it did have immortality as a mode of God which could not be destroyed any more than God could be destroyed. If it be a mode of God, it would of necessity continue even though the visible form of the body, also a mode of God, changed.

Locke, Berkeley, Hume, and Leibnitz

The position of JOHN LOCKE resembles very much that of Descartes. He thought of the universe as being composed of two substances, bodies and souls. The souls, for him, are spiritual substances with the power of perceiving, thinking, and willing. Man arrives at the idea of soul by combining the various operations of the human mind, such as willing, knowing, and the like, and supposing a support for them. This support or ground is soul substance. His argument for this is: "Having as clear and distinct ideas in us of thinking as of solidity, I know not why we may not as well allow a thinking thing without solidity, i.e., immaterial, to exist, as a solid thing without thinking, i.e., matter, to exist, especially since it is no harder to conceive how thinking should exist without matter than how matter should think." The soul is this immaterial thing which thinks.

This soul of man is both active and passive for Locke. It is able to influence and move bodies and, at the same time, it is influenced by bodies so that it has ideas. Thus, the soul interacts with bodies.

That the soul is immortal, lives after death of the body, is, for Locke, a matter of faith, and not anything of which we can have a clear and distinct idea. It is above reason, but can be believed on faith.

Mind and soul are terms used interchangeably by BERKELEY. The universe, as we have seen, is, for him, all mind or spirit. Following Locke's position that all we can know are our ideas, Berkeley takes the thesis that mind, the creator and source of ideas, is all that exists. Ideas which are not the creation of the individual mind are the creation of God who is also mind. Thus, man's soul is the

beginning and end of the universe. And, of course, it cannot die but will live on as part of the spiritual essence of
the universe.

HUME, carrying the Lockian position to its logical conclusion, as he saw it, held that we can have no certain
knowledge either of material or spiritual substance. We
cannot know that either the outer world or the soul exists.
All we know is that there is a succession of ideas, one following another. That there is a ground or support of these
ideas, a soul which has them, cannot be known. We must
therefore be agnostic (that is, without definite conviction)
as regards the soul.

No investigation, Hume held, will reveal an immaterial,
indivisible, imperishable soul-substance. He writes, "When
I enter intimately upon what I call myself, I always stum-
ble on some particular perception or other, of heat or cold,
light or shade, love or hatred, pain or pleasure. I never
catch myself, at any time, without a perception, and never
can observe anything but the perception." Mind, then, is
nothing more than a succession or jumble of perceptions.
Thus, any idea of the immortality of the soul is wholly
without foundation and cannot be accepted.

This line of reasoning was pure skepticism. As such it
could not satisfy thinking men. Rather than accept it at its
face value, philosophers were certain that somewhere
along the line reaching from Locke to Hume there was
something wrong, something important omitted. Thus,
they set about searching for the mistake, the missing part
which would make an entirely different picture.

The position of LEIBNITZ seemed to many to offer more
promise than the skepticism of Hume. The universe, for
Leibnitz, is composed of an infinite number of monads or
units of force. Even the soul is such a substance, a unit of
spiritual force. Indeed, the soul atom is the model of all
monads in the universe.

The human organism differs from all other beings in
that it contains in addition to other monads a "queen
monad" or soul, which is the guide or controlling monad
of all the other monads which make up the organism. This

soul monad organizes the monads of the organism into a unity, a whole. But, this control which the soul monad has over all other monads of the body is not a matter of direct influence. No monad can influence another. Rather, God has so created all monads that in man there is a pre-established harmony between soul monad and other monads. As we see it, the soul monad seems to control other monads just as one man might control another. But this is an illusion. Actually the two act together because of this pre-existent harmony.

The soul monad, just as all other monads, develops and moves toward self-realization because of its own nature, because of what it is internally.

Further, all knowledge comes to the soul monad not from without, but from within itself. It is implicit within the soul and is a matter of the development of what is latent in the very nature of the soul itself. Experience simply stirs the soul to realization of what is within it.

No monad can be destroyed, and this is therefore true of the soul monad. It is eternal, and therefore lives on even though the monads which make up a particular body separate at death. The soul, then, is immortal.

During the 18th century the influence of Leibnitz was strong in Germany, where philosophers were striving to prove the existence of the soul and its immortality. However, in England, where the influence of Locke, Berkeley, and Hume was dominant, there was a trend toward a mechanistic theory of man and his universe. Here the idea that man was nothing more than a machine was prominent. Of course, such an idea left no room for the conception of a soul. Men like Toland and Hartley strove to show that any idea of the soul was out of the question.

The Soul and Immortality According to Kant

It was KANT who drew the many strands of thought together into a system which has proved to be one of the most important accomplishments in the history of human thought. Kant held that the understanding cannot know anything but that which is experienced. However, reason

can go beyond this and conceive of a world of which we
can have no actual experience. Thus it transcends, rises
above experience, and gives us transcendent principles.

Reason gives man an idea of soul as the summation of
all mental processes. Although we can never experience
the soul, the idea of soul has value and therefore it is
legitimate for us to think of it.

Since there can be no knowledge without a knower, it is
legitimate for us to conclude that there is such a thing as
a soul, and act as if it existed. Although we cannot prove
the existence of an immortal soul, we may act as though
one existed since there is real value in so doing. Kant held
that this idea has regulative use in that it unifies many of
our concepts, it systematizes many of our concepts or ideas.
The Idea of a soul serves as a focal point to which we
may refer our conscious experiences.

Further, the idea of the soul has ethical value. It is a
result of the moral law and serves as a basis for moral life.
The moral law, which we have discussed previously, demands the good will, one so regulated that it acts always
in such a way that its action might well become universal
in principle at least. This good will must be realizable. But,
man cannot become absolutely good at any moment during his mortal existence. Consequently, this principle makes
the immortality of the soul necessary so that the demands
of the moral law may be met. During this endless time
made necessary and possible, the human soul goes on and
on to perfection, to a complete realization of the demands
of the moral law.

Fichte, Schleiermacher, Herbart, and Schopenhauer

Kant's contention that the moral law is the basis for acting as though there is a supersensible world, a world beyond that of science, of experience, was the starting point
of the philosophy of FICHTE. On this principle, Fichte and
those who followed him built what has become known as
post-Kantian idealism. The ego, or will, for Fichte, is the
source, the creator of the world that we know. Man can
understand only that which he has created.

But, the ego is pure activity, universal reason, an absolute principle different from the ego of each individual. It is the basis for the individual ego, the ego of each person who lives. It is a universal life process dominating every individual consciousness. This ego is broken up into bits which are the egos of individual persons just as light might be broken up into bits but is not broken off from the source. Thus, that which is the individual self is but a manifestation of the universal ego or creative principle.

This individual ego, because of the moral law which it finds within itself, as Kant had held, must go on struggling and therefore must be immortal. It is the part of the individual which others had called the soul and it cannot be thought of as dying with the body.

Though unwilling to accept the doctrines of idealism to the same extent as Fichte, SCHLEIERMACHER did, however, believe that the individual ego has an independence which makes it self-determining. It is able to develop its own particular talent and thus contribute to the development of the Whole or the Absolute of which it is a part. But, even this freedom is not enough to admit of immortality of the ego or soul. The only immortality which Schleiermacher is willing to admit is that of union with the infinite. The soul, for him, is immortal when it becomes "eternal in every moment of time."

HERBART opposed the entire idealistic point of view. For him, there are many simple, unchangeable "reals" or substances which combine to form objects. The soul, he taught, is a real which may be characterized as simple, absolute, timeless, and spaceless. The body of a man is a mass of reals with the soul established in the brain. Although all souls are essentially alike, they do differ in development due to the nature of the body in which each soul resides.

As a soul bumps up against another soul sensations arise which are organized in the soul and form its content. Originally the soul is empty, and its furnishings are sensations which result as the soul seeks to preserve itself in contact with other souls.

Since the world of reals is unchanging and the only change is a mixing and remixing of reals, the soul does not disappear when the body goes to pieces, but continues to exist.

The "will" of SCHOPENHAUER corresponds to the soul of other philosophers. It is the "thing-in-itself" of Kant, the foundation beneath all experience, all things. And the individual will is immortal in that it is part of the universal will. At death the individual will ceases to be individual as a particular expression of the universal will. But will does not die. It is basic to all the universe, and will continue to be forever.

The external world, according to RUDOLF HERMANN LOTZE, is a creation of the soul in the soul. This soul is situated in the brain and can contact the body only in the brain. While the body is alive, the soul is the ruling and controlling principle. After death of the body it is not clear, Lotze argues, what happens to the soul. However, he believes, as an act of faith, that each individual must sometime and somewhere receive his just reward or punishment. Therefore, although he is not able to prove it, he does believe in some kind of an immortality of the soul.

Recent and Present-Day Conceptions of the Soul and Immortality

More recent philosophy has abandoned the conception of soul and that of individual immortality. As one reads the pages of modern philosophers, one is struck with the fact that soul is seldom mentioned and the word "immortality" is almost never admitted. In a recent anthology of modern philosophy, a book of some 650 pages selected from the writings of the present-day philosophers, there is no mention of the soul and only a very few mentions of immortality.

The position of most modern philosophers is that the body is able to act in certain ways which show a high degree of intelligence. This is called "minded action." Some few writers will use the general term "soul" to describe this action, but if they are pressed for a more accurate explanation, will admit that they know nothing of a soul which is distinct from the body and which can claim anything like immortality.

The basis for this general position is to be found in the present-day interest in science and the general conviction that it is dangerous to go beyond observable action. Interest and respect characterize modern man's attitude toward the scientific method. This method, if applied carefully, does not lead to the soul nor does it lead to a belief in immortality.

The Behavioristic psychology as championed by John B. Watson and others centered modern attention upon behavior as the thing to watch. Although many thinkers were not willing to go the whole limit of Behaviorism and admit with its most enthusiastic advocates that behavior as seen by an observer is the beginning and end of a scientific study of man, nevertheless the influence of this position has been great.

Further, the older attempt to account for man's ability to think and to reason on the basis of his possessing of a mind or soul has been largely abandoned. It is felt that such an explanation is no real explanation, but rather a dodging of the issue. Thought, it is held, is an activity with a certain quality, the quality of mindedness. Man who thinks does not have a mind distinct from the body with which he thinks. But, because of his finer organization and construction, he is able to perform acts which are characterized as thinking.

We find this general position taken by representatives of both the *Positivistic* and the *Pragmatic* schools of thought. Among the Positivists is AUGUSTE COMTE who believed that the search for a soul and a belief in immortality were characteristics of an earlier and more childish stage of human development. As man becomes more mature in his racial development, he recognizes that such beliefs are not exact, that they are mere wishes which cannot be proven or founded upon fact. Consequently, he argues, they must be abandoned.

Pragmatism follows in this same tradition. WILLIAM

JAMES recognized that many men believe in the existence of a soul which has immortality and that such a belief has a certain usefulness in man's moral life. But he was not able to make a place for this belief within the structure of careful thought. JOHN DEWEY is more certain than was James that there is no basis for such beliefs. Indeed, he is convinced that the doctrine of the soul may be definitely harmful since it carries a load of tradition which weights man down or causes him to give up altogether the attempt to understand experience which has the quality of the religious.

While there still remain many philosophers, influenced almost to a man by the religious tradition, who attempt to interpret the term "soul" and the accompanying term "immortality" in such a way that both can be fitted into the scheme of modern science without too much twisting and turning, the modern trend is toward abandoning the ideas altogether as far as philosophy is concerned.

Soul is held to be nothing more than a name for a kind of activity, an activity which is spiritual. It does not mean an entity or thing which one may possess as he possesses hands, eyes, and the like. Further, immortality does not mean for most modern philosophers the eternal continuing of a thing or the eternal living of the individual entity which we know as ourselves. Biological immortality or the continued existence of the germ structure of man, the immortality of influence or the continued effect of one's influence after his body has died, and the immortality of the group or the continuation of the whole of which each individual is for a time a part, are positions taken by modern thinkers.

But the older traditional idea that there is a dualism of body and mind or soul, both entities with more or less separate lives, has been almost wholly abandoned. Thus, the conception that one member of such a dualism, the mind or soul, can continue to live and function after the other member has ceased to function has been abandoned also.

In the place of these traditional ideas, conceptions which

have a long and honored tradition, we find today the more scientific conception that man is a being who, because of his long and highly specialized evolutionary development, is able to do certain things wholly impossible at any other level of the evolutionary process. He is able to reason, think, plan and carry out the results of his planning, is able to conceive spiritual values and strive for their realization. He is able to make fine adjustments to his environment. Indeed, he is able to conceive the universe in the compass of his thought and make far-flung plans to master it and turn it to his desires. These abilities are far above anything which we know in the universe. Thus, they have a quality different from that of any other activities which man knows. However, modern thought is not willing to go from these facts to the theory that such acts are not the result of body but are rather the result of another thing which man has and which can be called mind or soul. Modern thought holds that these activities are minded or spiritual activities, and part of the complete activity of the individual.

An illustration will help to make this position clearer. One man will be called ugly while another will be called handsome. What, modern philosophers ask, produces the difference? Does the second of the two men possess a thing which we may term "beauty," and because of which he is beautiful? No. Beauty is not a thing, but a quality. Because the features of one individual are so constructed and organized, we say he is beautiful. There is no thing, no entity, such as "beauty" which makes one individual beautiful.

Likewise, man does not have a soul or a mind. Rather, his acts are of such a nature that we characterize them as minded or spiritual.

This position makes it necessary for modern philosophy to abandon the idea of immortality as it has been held in the past. If there is no thing, no entity, which corresponds to the soul, then there can be no immortality of the soul. This necessitates the abandonment of the conception of a place where souls go after death. This conception extends all the way from the old Hebrew idea of Sheol, and the Greek idea of Hades, the land of the shades across the river Styx, to the highly imaginative idea of Heaven held by the Christian tradition. Indeed, almost every religion has held to the belief in a land beyond the grave where good souls go to receive and to enjoy their reward. Many religions have also conceived of another land to which the evil souls go to receive their punishment. But, if there is no soul, there can be no lands of reward and punishment.

Modern thought, therefore, turns to man and to his life between birth and the grave, for a locus (that is, locality or realm) of its values. Within this span the modern philosopher finds all that he needs in order to understand man. Many individual thinkers will allow for beliefs or hypotheses regarding after-grave experiences, but they do not include them in their philosophic schemes, nor can they find sufficient evidence to make such beliefs other than hang-overs from an older and less scientific tradition or the wishes of those who are not satisfied with the scientific interpretation of life.

Chapter VII
MAN AND THE STATE

PYTHAGORAS DEMOCRITUS THE SOPHISTS
SOCRATES PLATO ARISTOTLE
THE EPICUREANS THE STOICS AUGUSTINE
MACHIAVELLI GROTIUS HOBBES
LOCKE ADAM SMITH ROUSSEAU HEGEL
MARX MILL NIETZSCHE DEWEY

*Is society made for man or is man made for society?
Is the state a divine creation which man must not
question, or is it a result of a "social contract" among
men and subject to change when it no longer serves
men? How do the rulers get their authority? Is revolution justifiable? Is totalitarianism or democracy correct?*

Man is a gregarious being. By nature he lives with his
fellows and likes it. Indeed, no more cruel punishment can
be inflicted upon an individual than to isolate him from
other men for a long period of time.

Whether this love of being with other men is due to
man's basic and original nature, no one can say. However,
it is clear that the earliest men of whom we know anything
lived together. It may have been in a cave, or it may have
been in rude shelters constructed of branches and leaves,
or it may have been squatting beneath a tree or in the
protection of some overhanging cliff; but wherever it was,
the most primitive of men wanted to be near those of their

kind. The reason may have been the inherent desire for security and the realization that one man alone is dangerously exposed to his enemies, while two or more men together are better able to protect themselves.

But, whatever the reason and whatever the location, wherever we find evidence of man we find evidence of a number of men and women all living in a group. And, since all living together, whether it be of man or of beast, brings conflicts of purpose and desire, it is almost certain that the earliest of men organized some form of society, established some rules which were accepted by each one. Probably the first rules were not consciously determined or set down so that all might learn. They were possibly accepted as right and necessary without much if any thought on the matter.

It was out of these simple provisions for living together that the first social requirements grew. Gradually an accepted body of customs and procedures evolved. These became tribal laws or rules of the social group. Those procedures which were found to preserve the group and protect it against enemies without and within were held to tenaciously, while those which did not serve this purpose were abandoned.

By this process tribal or group organizations developed with their ways of living which were handed on from the older generation to the younger. Some of these rules were learned by the young as they lived day by day among their fellows. They saw others act in certain ways and accepted these ways as right. Other rules were transmitted to the young in solemn ceremonies conducted by the members of the group on special occasions, the chief of which was that conducted when the young man was admitted into full membership in the tribe at puberty.

These unwritten customs and laws held the group together solidly, and anyone who dared to disobey even in the least was severely punished. Often death was the penalty for failure to follow the tradition. Here was a closely knit society, with laws, customs, and penalties, a society which passed on its traditions to each generation by example, word of mouth, and ceremonial rites.

Then came the time when these laws and customs were written down and a code of laws resulted, laws which were binding because they had proved themselves to be necessary for the preservation of the life of the social group. These were the beginnings of society and the state.

It was many centuries later that the philosophers turned their attention to this social organization and asked how it came into being and what was its nature and meaning. "Is it," they asked, "a natural result of man's living together, or does it have divine origin? Is it a mere convenience which is to be changed and revised as times change, or does it have a permanent status such that man changes it at his peril? Where is the power of the state, in the people or in the rulers who receive it from God? What is the best form of the state, and how shall man attain this?"

These questions and many others have occupied the attention of many of the great philosophers. Not only have they been the cause of much philosophic speculation, but they have served to stir men to wars and threats of war. Revolutions have arisen because men have differed in their answers to these questions and have been willing to die to prove that they were right. In our own time men have fought world-engulfing wars because they were unable to agree as regards the answers to some of these questions.

The ancients believed that their gods were the ultimate rulers of the state, and that those of their fellows who held power over them had received their authority directly from the gods. Further, they accepted without question the belief that all the laws by which they lived were given to their ancestors by the gods and therefore could not be changed even in the least.

Illustrative of this position is the belief of the early Hebrews that Moses, their great lawgiver, received the laws written on tablets of stone from their god, Yahweh (Jehovah). The Ten Commandments, the basis of their law, was believed to have divine origin, and Yahweh was their only ruler. Moses and the others who ruled over them did not hold this position by their own power but as representatives of Yahweh. Punishment for breaking the laws was not man-given, but was inflicted by Yahweh.

All early peoples held these same beliefs, substituting the name of their god for the Yahweh of the Hebrews. They saw the state as a divine creation and the laws as divine commands which man broke at his peril since divine punishment was sure and just. The god was made angry and wreaked vengeance upon those who dared disregard his will.

The early Greeks did not have their laws written on tablets of stone but rather in the minds of their leaders. The customs of their forefathers, customs developed through generations of tribal and group experience, were passed on to the group and interpreted and enforced by the old men. In time these customs were brought together and written down by Lycurgus. Here the rules for living together in a group or state were presented clearly so that everyone would know what they were and could obey them.

Among all these early peoples the group or the state was more important than any member or citizen. These ancient people recognized that the individual man could not live long and could not enjoy many advantages unless he lived in a group. Further, they realized that the greatest good for the greatest number depended upon the preservation of the group as a unit. Consequently, anyone who by his acts threatened the safety of the group committed a crime deserving of the most severe punishment. It was necessary, they saw, to preserve the group even at the expense of the individual. When the individual and the group came into conflict, it was the individual who had to yield or be destroyed. It would be fatal to all if the group was destroyed.

The State as Viewed by the Early Greek Philosophers

The *Pythagoreans*, representative of this early point of view among the Greeks, taught that the individual should subordinate himself to the whole and should act at all times for the good of the state. Thus they taught their members respect for authority, the laws and civic virtues of the times, and the ideal of sacrifice for the good of the whole.

This same general position was taken by DEMOCRITUS. He held that each one should devote himself wholly to the good of the state because "a well-administered state is our greatest safeguard." In another place he wrote, "When the state is in a healthy condition, all things prosper; when it is corrupt, all things go to ruin." Since, he argued, the ultimate welfare of everyone depended upon the state, it was but reasonable to hold that the welfare of the state was man's first concern.

After the Persian Wars (500 to 449 B.C.) Athens became the center of ancient Greek culture. The events leading up to these wars and the developments during the wars developed in the Athenians, among other peoples of the times, an interest in the problems of government and an interest in the democratic form of human living. This led naturally to a growth of independent thinking which eventually resulted in a growing concern for theories of government. Men began to question the older blind loyalty to the powers of the state, and many began to assert their own independence and their right to a life more or less free from the dominance of the established government. Individualism was in the air. Some suggested that man should divorce himself from the authority of the group and hold himself free to challenge the group and criticize freely the older traditions.

The *Sophists,* as we have pointed out before, led this advance into individualism. They centered attention not on the group, but upon the individual member of the group. They asserted his ultimate worth and independence. They proposed to teach the individual how to succeed, how to gain his own ends, under the law, and even to dodge the law by skillful argument.

Indeed, there were Sophists who argued that the laws were mere inventions of the weaker members of the group, of society, to enslave and hold down the stronger. In Plato's dialogue entitled *Gorgias,* a well-known Sophist argues that "The makers of the laws are the majority who are weak; and they make laws and distribute praises and censures with a view to themselves and their own interests; and they terrify the stronger sort of men, and those who are able to get the better of them, in order that they may not get the better of them." He goes on to assert that the great men of history have been those who refused to obey the laws of the weak majority who have organized to hold them down. The bait which they held before the people of Athens was stated by Callicles in this way: "If there were a man who had sufficient force, he would shake off and break through, and escape from all this; he would trample underfoot all our formulas and spells and charms and all our laws which are against nature." This was a challenge to the spirit of independence which was abroad in the land to assert itself and refuse longer to be repressed by the weak, the ignorant, and the fools.

It is obvious that this position might easily be interpreted as a call to anarchy, an incentive to rebellion against all authority. And many individuals took it for just that. Thus, much of the Sophist influence led to unreasoned refusal to be subject to the dictates of the group and thus threatened the solidarity of the Athenian state. But, there were many Sophists who did not intend that this should happen. They were not satisfied with the older traditional idea that man should be subject to the state wholly and unconditionally, and against this they rebelled. But they did not want to go to the other extreme of complete anarchy (that is, lack of any form of government). The tragedy of their thinking was that although they saw the problem and the danger in the traditional philosophy of the state, they were unable to counter this tradition with something better. They were not able to offer a solution to the problem of society which would make for social unity and at the same time avoid blind subservience to the state.

However, in their efforts to solve this problem they etched clearly on the minds of their age the issues involved, and challenged better minds than theirs to attempt a solution. They made it impossible for those philosophers who followed them to dodge the problem of developing an adequate philosophy of the state. And the great minds who worked during the next two hundred years made many significant contributions to a solution of the problem.

The State According to Socrates, Plato, and Aristotle

SOCRATES first asked the important questions involved in the problem. Xenophon, in his *Memorabilia*, recounts that Socrates never tired of asking of everyone he met, "What is a state? What is a statesman? What is a ruler over men? What is a ruling character?" Although he did not answer these questions, he laid the basis for answering them in his major position that the greatest concern of any citizen should be knowledge. The good citizen was one who constantly searched for true knowledge, who was forever questioning. When, Socrates argued, a man discovers true knowledge, he will act on it and will conduct himself rightly in all his relations with his fellows.

Although Socrates saw defects in the Athenian state and spent a good deal of his time pointing to them and criticizing the rulers for their mistaken ideas about government, he was intensely loyal to Athens. When he had been condemned to death by the Athenian courts, a condemnation which he with many others believed to be wholly unjust, he refused the offer of his friends to bribe the guards and escape. His argument was that should he do that he would be breaking the laws of the state and thus making it that much weaker. The state, despite its mistakes, was to him a mother who had given him life and had made him what he was. He could no more betray the state than he could betray his mother. His method was not that of rebellion. Nor would he accept exile and turn away from the state. Rather, he counseled his followers to remain loyal to the state, and through this loyalty to help the state correct its faults and mistakes.

The illustrious pupil of Socrates, PLATO, took up the problem where Socrates had left it and endeavored to find a solution. He held that the state was necessary for the highest development of the individual. Goodness, for him, was not goodness in isolation, but was goodness in the group. The good man was the good citizen. Thus, the state should be so constructed that it would make possible the good life for all.

He argued that the individual should subordinate himself to the state, but that this was simply a means by which the individual could reach his most perfect development. The good of each man, he believed, was tied up with the good of the group. Laws were necessary only because some people refused to co-operate with the good state. They served to bring these people in line and thus make the whole good.

In the state, he argued, the best minds and the finest souls should rule. They formed a class of philosopher-rulers whose authority should not be questioned by the rest of the group. He believed that since they were philosopher-rulers their rule would be good and just. They could understand the right, and would do it without question. The rest of the members of the state he would place in classes suited to their talents. Those who had a talent for war should be placed in the warrior class. Those who had a talent for mercantile pursuits would be in the trade and merchant class. The slaves should be placed in the slave class. Plato believed that such an organization would give the best possible state and that in it each individual, doing his assigned job to the best of his ability, would be happy and would develop to his fullest.

This ideal state is developed in Plato's famous book, the *Republic*. In a book written somewhat later, the *Laws*, he argues that all citizens should have a voice in the government and that all work should be turned over to the slaves.

This theory of the state is fundamentally aristocratic. Plato was wealthy, a son of the most favored class in Athens. Being such, he never was able to be wholly democratic, but aligned himself with the more aristocratic thought of his day. Further, his theory was socialistic in that it provided for complete control by the state of the lives of its members. The wealth of all was to be devoted to the use of all as they needed and deserved it, and the rulers could say in what class each individual should work and live. The state was supreme, but this doctrine was robbed of its sting by his added argument that in such a state each person would be happy and develop to his fullest.

ARISTOTLE, the pupil of Plato, developed a philosophy of the state which resembled that of his teacher very much. He held that man is by nature a social animal and, as such, can realize his truest self only in society and among his kind. Although the earliest forms of social living were the family and later the community, the goal of social evolution was, for Aristotle, the city state such as was known in Greece during his lifetime.

Since Aristotle believed, as we have pointed out before, that the whole is prior to its parts, he held that the state was prior to the individual member of the state. The individual is born into the state which has existed long before he became a member. But, the goal of the state, he maintained, is to produce good citizens. Therefore, it should be organized and conducted so that it enables each member to become wholly good. To the extent that the state does not enable the individual to live a virtuous and happy life, it is evil.

Any constitution, he argued, should be adjusted to the nature and the needs of the members of the particular group. But, in any group there are individuals who are unequal in many ways. Therefore, a good constitution must recognize these natural unequalities and confer rights accordingly. In so far as all men are equal, the constitution must confer equal rights, but in so far as they are unequal, it must confer unequal rights. Among the unequalities which he would recognize are those of personal abilities, property, birth, and freedom. You treat slaves differently from free men and those born of slaves differently from those born of free men.

Aristotle held that a monarchy, an aristocracy, and a "polity" in which the members are nearly equal, are the best forms of the state. On the other hand he condemned as bad a tyranny, an oligarchy, and a democracy.

Aristotle believed that slavery was a just practice in a good state since it was, for him, a natural institution. However, he would admit only foreigners to the slave class. He took this position because he held foreigners of all nations to be inferior to the Greeks and thus not fit to enjoy the same rights as Greeks.

Socrates, Plato, and Aristotle were all unable to solve the problem of the state and the individual. Their theories were interesting on paper, and many thoughtful men of that time studied them and were interested. But the spirit of individualism as championed by the Sophists was sweeping Greece, and each man was concerned primarily with himself and his own success. Slowly but surely the unity of the state was destroyed. Individualism was no pathway to unity against the enemies of Athens and other Greek city states. As a result, these enemies were successful and the Greek city states fell under their yoke one after another. Athens, Corinth, and Sparta, the three great Greek city states, fell, and eventually all Greece came under the domination of Philip of Macedon at the battle of Chaeronea in 338 B.C. Individualism had proved an internal poison which eventually so weakened the Greek city states that they could offer no effective resistance to their enemies and their fall was inevitable.

The Positions of the Later Greek Thinkers

Amid the gradual crumbling of the city states of Greece the *Epicureans* sought to develop a theory of the state which would fit the situation. They taught that all social life is based on the self-interest of the individual. We become members of a social group simply because we find that in such a group we can get more for ourselves, because the group will give us better protection from our enemies. Therefore, there can be no absolute justice or natural rights and laws. That is good which men agree to call good. The laws are simply rules which the group accepts and by which the members are willing to live. If the members of the group decide that a certain law is no longer of value in getting what they want, it can be changed or thrown out altogether.

Injustice is not an evil in itself, they held. We are just, only because it helps us to be so. When obedience to laws does not help us longer, we may break the laws, if we can escape punishment.

The Epicureans did not believe that participation in public life would contribute to the happiness of the individual; therefore, they held that the wise man would shun public office and public responsibility as much as possible. This position, as is evident, is one of pure individualism and selfishness. The individual associates himself with others only because it is to his advantage to do so, and he breaks away from the group and its requirements as soon as it is to his advantage to do so. Further, the individual helps the group and participates in group responsibility only to the degree that it is to his advantage to do so. This point of view certainly does not build strong group loyalty or solidarity. It is the complete opposite of the earlier Greek position of loyalty to the state. Indeed, it is a clear expression of the doctrine of "enlightened self-interest." Each person is told that he is to make his own happiness, and that alone, the goal of all that he does.

The *Stoics* took a position wholly opposite to that of the Epicureans as regards man's relationship to the group. They held that man is more than merely an individual interested in his own welfare. He is also an individual with an inborn social impulse which makes necessary group life. Indeed, all men are members of a great cosmic society, the universal state. We all have duties and obligations in this state, and its laws are the natural laws which we must all obey whether we like it or not.

The Stoic state is universal and thus dominates every individual completely. Indeed, each member must be willing at all times to sacrifice himself for the good of the state. Individual interests are always subordinate to the interest of the whole, and the state must be preserved at all cost.

Thus, the Stoics taught that everyone should participate in public affairs and contribute as much as possible to the welfare of the group. However, and this is most important, the Stoics never taught a narrow nationalism in which a small state could be superior to the general-welfare of humanity. The good state was, for them, one whose laws and practices were in harmony with the good of all mankind and with the natural laws of the universe.

The Stoic, then, was to be a universal citizen, a member of the Great Society which includes all men and the laws of which are the universal laws of nature itself. Each man must subordinate himself to the universal ideal and live in such a way as to serve the good of all men wherever they might be. A world society rooted in nature was their ideal. This was, obviously, wholly different from the position of the Epicureans and the other individualists of the day, and was equally opposed to the position of those who would have man subordinated to a particular state or social group. The Stoic ideal of universal brotherhood was the highest point to which the thought of the Greek period arose, and to which other thinkers in days to come were to strive.

Indeed the Stoics taught much which has become central in modern thought. With the loss of Greek independence they began to look at all men as brothers and to teach universal brotherhood and equal rights for all men. They sensed the doctrine of the solidarity of the human race and the dignity of man regardless of his position in society, his wealth, his birth, or his education. Their position may be summed up in the words, "Virtue despises no one, neither Greek nor barbarian, man nor woman, rich nor poor, freeman nor slave, wise nor ignorant, whole nor sick." This was certainly close to our modern view.

The Views of the Early Christian Thinkers

This point of view was also central in the thinking of most of the Christian thinkers and philosophers. For them God was the Father of all mankind, thus making all men brothers. The Christian community was a social group in which the customary distinctions of race and social status were eliminated. Further, the Christians thought of the temporal state as an institution subject to God and deriving its power from God. Man, therefore, was loyal to the state only in so far as it obeyed the laws of God. His first loyalty was to God.

However, in the thinking of many, the temporal state had so far failed to square itself with the will of God that man was more or less free from any obligation to it. The "contempt of the world," which characterized the metaphysics of many of the *Apologists*, likewise characterized their attitude toward the state. The corruption of the age drove many to seek a life of seclusion from the state in the monastic life. They turned from social obligations to a personal striving to save their souls through a life of isolation and contemplation.

Throughout most of the early Christian period loyalty to God and His laws was first in the thinking of the Christians. In so far as the state was obedient to God, they could be loyal to it also.

But, with the development of the Church as an institution and with the spread of Christianity throughout the Roman Empire, it became necessary for Christian thinkers to revise their notions regarding government and human associations. For a while we find Christian writers hesitating between the older contempt for the world and the things of the world and the opposite attitude of interest in the world and all that it contained. In SAINT AUGUSTINE, for example, this inability to make a choice between world denial and world affirmation is remarkably evident.

While AMBROSE, an earlier church thinker, had held the possession of property and wealth to be "damnable," Augustine admitted that one had a right to gain wealth. But, he did feel that such wealth might be a hindrance to the Christian life.

In Augustine's theory of the State we find the same inability to decide between the world and contempt for the world. For him the state is based on self-love and often leads to a contempt for God and all his laws. But the "City of God" is based upon contempt for the self and complete

love for God. Thus, his ideal is this City of God. Nevertheless, he writes that the state is an ethical community and
that its chief end is the happiness of mankind. In it justice
may rule.

Despite this hanging, as it were, between two states,
Augustine holds firmly to the position that the Church, as
a worldly incarnation of the City of God, is to be supreme
over the state, and the head of the Church is to rule over
the rulers of the states. Further, while the ruler of the state
may make mistakes, the ruler of the Church can never
make a mistake. His word and his rule are infallible since
he is the representative of God on earth.

Thus, while Augustine feared the state and saw in
it dangers to the soul of man, he was never able to turn
his back on it completely and condemn it as wholly sinful.
The older Christian contempt for the world haunted him,
but was never able to master him completely. Although
the monastic life was for him the ideal, he was practical
enough to realize that most men could not attain the ideal
and thus had to do the best they could as members of a
temporal state.

The Views of the Medieval Christian Thinkers

During the so-called Dark Ages, after the northern tribes
had overrun the Roman Empire and destroyed a great deal
of the culture and social organization of the first four centuries of the Christian era, the principle of authority was
supreme. During the entire Middle Ages man was subject
to some authority. The state and its rulers assumed control over the people, so man found himself everywhere
under the command of some authority. Thus obedience to
the law, whatever its source, became a settled practice.

Gradually there grew up the idea that the king received
his authority from God and thus could not be questioned.
Any disobedience to him was actually disobedience to the
supreme authority of the universe, God. Indeed, authority
was superior to public opinion and the state superior to
the individual. Here the individualism of the later Greeks

was conquered completely, and in its place stood almost complete domination of the individual by the state.

The thinking of the *Schoolmen*, as was pointed out earlier, was confined to interpreting the dogmas of the Church. Although they were at times keen of mind, these philosophers were confined within the walls of Church doctrine and tradition and had to spend their talents in careful analysis of the meanings of these. Thus, their thinking about the state and the place of man in the social structure was limited by what the Church was willing to accept as authentic.

But, as in all ages, while the great majority of thinkers followed the standard pattern, there were those who, often without understanding the entire import of their thought, planted the seeds of a later breakdown of tradition.

Among the Scholastics were two groups known as the Realists and the Nominalists. The Realists held that the whole was the only real thing, and that the parts, the units, were not truly real. The Nominalists held that the parts, the units, were the real things, and the whole merely a name. Applied to our immediate problem, the State, this would mean that the Realists held the State to be the only reality, and its members, men and women, to be mere units with no true reality. The Nominalists, on the other hand, held man to be the true reality, and the State a mere aggregation of men which had no existence or reality of its own apart from its members.

The logical result of these two strains of thought was that some would hold that the real authority rested in the State as the only reality while others would hold that the real authority rested in the individual man and not in the State. Realism and Nominalism were doctrines applicable to the problem of the State and its members.

JOHN SCOTUS ERIGENA was a realist. Although he did not work out his doctrine in its application to the state, he conceived of the universal, the whole, existing prior to the particular individual. Thus he was in the tradition of Plato and Aristotle and those others who saw the state as eventually supreme and prior to any individual member.

Likewise ANSELM was in this realistic tradition. He devoted much time and thought to proving that universals were prior to individuals.

ROSCELIN represents the other point of view. He taught that the individual is the only reality and that any universal is nothing more than a mere name for a group of individuals. Take away the individuals and you have nothing but a name left. No reality remains.

As with any two extreme positions, and Realism and Nominalism were extreme positions, there arises sooner or later someone who seeks to effect a compromise. ABELARD was that man at this time. His theory has been called "conceptualism." He taught that universals cannot be realities apart from things, but that they are concepts in the mind of man. He was interested particularly in things and wanted to point with emphasis to them, but recognized that ideas of groups had a certain reality in the mind of man.

Thus, for him, the individual was extremely important, but the group had its importance also and could not be ruled out altogether. Both were significant factors in any understanding of man and his relations with his fellows.

Thus, the thinkers of the Middle Ages planted the seeds which were to destroy the supreme authority of the social group. After this doctrine had won out over that of individualism and had dominated man's thinking for several centuries, the spirit of individualism again asserted itself and began to demand recognition. Gradually it gained the ascendency and man began once more to question the authority that ruled him.

THOMAS AQUINAS, the last of the great Church thinkers of the Middle Ages, sought to fuse the thinking of Aristotle with that of Augustine. He taught that man is naturally a political being and seeks to be in society. Further, the supreme purpose of the state was, for him, the good of the group. This can be attained only if the society is strongly united and is able to present a solid front against its enemies. Thus a monarchy in which the rule is strongly centralized is, for him, the best form of government. But this

government must not be oppressive of the members. There
must be no tyranny.

Rebellion against the government can never be justified.
St. Thomas Aquinas taught that any change in government
should come through legal means, since government is of
divine origin. If it is not possible for the member to obtain
redress of his grievances through legal means, he must
leave the matter to God who will work out good in the end.

But Aquinas held that the church was superior to the
state and the ruler of the state was to be always obedient
to the ruler of the church. The state, then, was thought of
as an institution divinely established and drawing its power
over men from God through His church. Man's ultimate
loyalty was to the church and God, but he had to obey
the state since the state in turn received its power from the
church.

The position of JOHN DUNS SCOTUS is interesting in that
it is developed upon the premise that God is absolutely
free and supreme. Society is a creation of God and is what
it is because God has made it so. God could have made
another type of society just as well and could have made
different laws. Then this type would have been right and
its laws just. This is a far cry from the Sophistic conception
of the state as a result of an agreement among men and its
laws as established because men wanted them so. The
state, for Scotus, is a creation of God, not of necessity but
of his own free will. It is as it is because God wills it so.
Thus, man must obey the laws of the state or suffer divine
punishment.

Although Scotus did not foresee the result, this theory
gave great power to existing states and rulers. They could
claim direct authority from God and could use the fear of
eternal punishment to enforce their authority.

But man was not contented to accept this domination of
the state even though it was based upon the theories of
great churchmen. The nominalistic position persisted and
there were those who arose constantly to assert the freedom
of the individual over the authority of the state. WILLIAM
OF OCCAM was one of this group. He stressed the reality of

the individual and thereby gave man a strong argument for asserting his dignity and for questioning the power of the state when it seemed to violate the will of its members.

This, along with other things, led to a growing battle between the state and the church. Men arose to hold that the state was a temporal institution receiving its power and authority from the governed and thus free from any domination by the church. At times the church was in the saddle and ruled the states then existing. At other times the states overcame the church and asserted their freedom.

The State as Viewed by the Forerunners of the Renaissance

It was at this time that man began to assert his own freedom and to challenge the power of rulers who held key positions in the state. The democratic spirit was afoot in the land, and absolute rule was being effectively beaten in many places. Indeed, everywhere the spirit of freedom was breaking through the heavy crust of the Middle Ages, and man was struggling to become a true individual and obtain some power to rule himself.

Added to this was the growing feeling of nationalism evident on all sides. Groups of individuals with common language, customs, and traditions began to appear and to assert themselves over against other such groups. But there was opposition to all such nations on the part of the Church, which saw its world domination threatened. Thus, a struggle ensued out of which gradually developed the nations of the modern world, large groups of individuals with a common concern and a growing desire to establish themselves as units.

In addition, the individual began to assert his own independence of thought, and to believe that human reason was superior to authority. Slowly the idea took form that truth was a thing to be reached by the operation of human reason and not something handed down by an authoritative Church.

All these movements tended to weaken the power of the Church and place the individual man, both as an individual and as a member of a political group, in the center of the stage. In this setting philosophers began to dream of a perfect social group in which ideal conditions would exist. An example of this trend is the *City of the Sun*, a utopian treatise by TOMMASO CAMPANELLA. In this volume Campanella sketches the outline of a socialistic state similar to that found in Plato's *Republic*, a state in which knowledge is the governing force and power. Everyone in this state is equal since there is only one class. However, Campanella does make distinctions between men on the basis of their knowledge. The philosophers, who are also priests, are the rulers. In making this assertion, he shows his desire to effect a compromise between the Church and the growing national feeling of the times. In his state there was to be a sort of papal monarchy, a religious unity as the basis for political unity.

Campanella's work is typical of the preliminary work toward thinking through a new theory of the state and its relations with its citizens. However, the general trend of the times was away from the authority and dominance of the Church, a trend in the direction of political independence.

Machiavelli's Conception of the State

The most violent attack upon the Church and its hitherto generally accepted dominance over the state was made by NICCOLÒ MACHIAVELLI. His ambition was to establish a united Italian nation wholly independent of the Church. He took as a model for this state the old political forms established by Sparta, Rome, and Venice.

Since the general situation of his day was one of corruption, Machiavelli argued that such a state could be established only by a strong and absolute despot. Although such a political structure would destroy civic freedom, Machiavelli thought of this as a necessary intermediate stage out of which man could eventually work as he became less corrupt. His ideal was a free, independent nation in which civic rights would be cherished and the independence of each individual guaranteed.

To accomplish his ends, the prince or ruler had the right

to use any means necessary, even force, deceit, or breach of the moral law. He had to fight trickery with trickery, deceit with deceit.

Grotius, Hobbes, and Other Thinkers of the Renaissance

Another thinker of the period, JEAN BODIN, taught that the state is founded upon a contract which the people make with their ruler. The fundamental article of this contract is one which gives over to the ruler all authority and which permits the people under no circumstances to take it back.

JOHANNES ALTHUSIUS attacked this position, holding that the people could never give away their authority. Rather, he argued, the contract which the people make with their ruler lasts only so long as the ruler fulfills his part of the bargain. When he violates the contract he may be dethroned and executed and another ruler set up in his place by the people.

HUGO GROTIUS, a leader of the aristocratic party in Holland, developed the theory of absolutism in great detail and with many cogent arguments. He taught that man has certain natural rights which are rooted in his very nature and which even God cannot change or destroy. But these natural rights may be limited, and indeed are limited by the positive law which results from man's voluntary agreement to live in groups. We give up the privilege to exercise certain natural rights in order that we may live together as members of a state. Thus, the state is a result of the free agreement among its members. Consequently, at no time can man give up his natural rights unconditionally. But, he may delegate these rights to a ruler forever.

Therefore, during this early modern period the tendency was toward absolutism. The ruler had power which, though originally given him by the people, was more or less absolute from then on. Of course, there was opposition to this point of view. When the practice of more or less absolute sovereignty reached its climax in the reign of Louis XIV in France, a climax expressed in his famous saying, "I am the state," there was sufficient opposition to effect an overthrow of the whole position and to begin building the more modern idea of democracy. But that is getting ahead of our story.

The materialist, THOMAS HOBBES, based his theory of the state upon the fundamental principle that man has the natural right to do anything which he pleases. The most primitive urge of all men is that of self-preservation. To accomplish this end, man may use any means he deems necessary. In this state of nature man may invade the rights of others with the result that chaos reigns.

Man is, then, fundamentally a ferocious animal, one who engages in war and pillage, seeking always his own gain. But, in such a state no man can be strong enough to preserve himself for long. Each man will destroy the others and he in turn will be destroyed by others. Thus, to escape from this inevitable end, man creates a society in which he voluntarily gives up his rights in many matters. This is a contract which men make with each other by which they give up certain rights in order to obtain others which they desire. To insure this mutual contract, men transfer power to one ruler or an assembly. After the ruler has been set up and given power, men must obey.

It is true, Hobbes recognizes, that at times the ruler will be unjust and will wreak hardships upon men. But they have no right to rebel. Hobbes justifies this position by holding that even at their worst, the injustices of a ruler are never so bad as the original state of man before power was given to the ruler.

Hobbes believes that the absolute monarchy is the best form of government. But, there are certain things that even the king cannot force men to do. Among these are suicide, murder, or the confession of crime. These the king has no right to impose upon any man.

Hobbes argued further that the king was God's representative on earth and that God spoke through him. Thus, freedom of religion cannot be tolerated. The religion of the king must be the religion of all the people.

This theory of Hobbes is actually an attempt to defend

philosophically the power of the English king and the general structure of the English monarchy. The defense led to the theory of the "divine right of kings" and to the position that the king can do no wrong. So long as the king can protect the people he is absolute and no one has the right to challenge his authority.

The Views of Spinoza, Locke, and Adam Smith

The belief that the state is in some way a result of a social contract among men is also seen in the teachings of SPINOZA. In the natural state, he held, might makes right, and man has the right to do anything which he is able to do. He may destroy others to gain his ends, cheat, lie, or engage in any activity which will help him. But, in such a state, conflict will inevitably arise and many will be destroyed.

Consequently, men give up many natural rights so that there may be a degree of peace in which they can realize other desires. The state is the result. By general agreement, men in a state agree to limit their natural rights for the good of all. Therefore, only in a state can justice and injustice have a meaning. According to natural rights anything may be just. However, in a state, disobedience to the laws set up by virtue of the social contract is unjust. The just is that which makes social life possible.

JOHN LOCKE was in complete disagreement with Hobbes and others who believed that the natural state of man was one of war and self-seeking. Further, he was opposed to the doctrine that the king rules by divine right and that he has absolute power to govern men as he wills. Locke held that the original and natural state of all men is one of perfect freedom and equality. Since all men are free and equal, no one has the right to take away another's life, liberty, or possessions.

Further, the original nature of man is that of peace, good will, and mutual assistance. Thus, men naturally move toward social living. In a society, men set up law, an impartial judge, and one with executive power in order to attend to matters of common interest. This structure is established by a social contract agreed upon by the members of the group.

After the society has been established, each member is under obligation to submit to the authority of the majority. This is necessary for efficient living together, since unanimous consent is next to impossible in a large group.

The main purpose of law, Locke taught, is to preserve the social group and thus it must be limited to the public good of society. Beyond this, men are to be left free. Locke said that there are certain areas into which law cannot come. He specifically excluded the right to enslave, to destroy, or to impoverish men.

Locke did not think it good that those who made the laws should also have the right to execute them. Consequently, he would divide the powers of government into the legislative and the executive and would keep these two branches separate for the public good. The people have the power to remove the legislators whenever they wish since power rests ultimately in the people. They also have the right to punish their legislators or their executive whenever they are convinced that either is acting in opposition to the public good.

It is obvious that Hobbes and Locke were exponents of two very different doctrines. While Hobbes was interested in presenting a philosophical justification for absolute monarchy and the divine right of the ruler to rule without being accountable to the people, Locke was interested in justifying the doctrine of political freedom. Locke sought to prove that the power of the state always rests in the people and that their rulers are merely their servants subject to their will. This power can never be taken from the people nor can they give it up. Hobbes held that once the people gave power to the ruler, they were unable to get it back regardless of what the ruler did.

These were two points of view which appeared often in the political writings of the eighteenth century and the early part of the nineteenth century. They were in constant conflict, and the conflict has not died down even today.

This theory as developed by Locke, a theory of man's

freedom and of the state as an institution charged with keeping order among men, but one very limited, led to the famous doctrine of *laissez faire*. This is the doctrine that the state should not interfere any more than is absolutely necessary with the affairs of its members, that the individual has a natural right to exercise his activity in the economic sphere with the least possible interference from society.

ADAM SMITH wrote his famous *Wealth of Nations* to show that the best state exists only when men are permitted to engage in unrestricted competition, freedom of exchange, and enlightened self-interest. In this work the pendulum of philosophic thought was swinging away from the theory that the state should regulate every activity of men, a theory held by Plato and many other thinkers, to the opposite extreme that the state should observe a strict policy of hands off and permit men to exercise their natural rights in all directions save in those where the safety of the group is threatened.

In Adam Smith, and other philosophical writers who followed Locke, we see the attempt to carry Locke's theory of freedom and natural rights into various fields of human activity and to free men in each of these fields from the restraints of government which had become so common since the beginning of written history at least. In most instances it was felt that the best results would be obtained if each individual was left as free as possible in all his activities. Government was to keep hands off except in those necessary affairs where the safety of the state was in danger.

The Position of Voltaire and of Rousseau

The brilliant VOLTAIRE never tired of condemning the traditional authorities and championing human freedom. Yet, he did not believe that the lower classes had the capacity for self-government. He believed that the "ignorant rabble" was a danger whenever restraint was removed. Thus, freedom was to be the privilege only of the enlightened, the intelligent.

A powerful opponent of this position was JEAN JACQUES ROUSSEAU. He believed in all men and fought for their freedom. Indeed, he would rule out representative government and place in its stead direct government by all the people. The Swiss republic was his model, a small, closely-knit group of people considering every issue as a group and determining their destiny by popular vote. Indeed, "Rousseau took the Lockian idea of democracy seriously" and argued that since all men were created free and equal they should not be robbed or ruled by a privileged class.

To attain this freedom, Rousseau would cast away all the trappings of modern society and return to nature. Natural society, he believed, is based on a "social contract" by which the freedom of the individual is surrendered to self-imposed laws which are the result of the general will. Sovereignty lies, he argued, with the people at all times and cannot be taken from them. Government merely carries out the will of the people, and the people have the right at any time to recall their government and establish another.

Locke, Rousseau, Fichte, Schelling, and many other thinkers, although differing in some details, held the general position that man's true self could be realized only in the right kind of a social group. They saw that human association is not a detriment but is rather a means to the best kind of life. When a man lives among his fellows he develops characteristics which are most worth while. Therefore, they sought the right kind of social group, and reached the conclusion that a group in which the greatest amount of freedom was possible would meet the requirements of this society. Schelling argued that an isolated ego could have no consciousness of freedom. We only know freedom when we live with others and see it in relation to possible restraint.

The State According to Hegel, Marx, and Lassalle

HEGEL taught that universal reason reaches its height in a society of free individuals, each subordinating its individual reason to the universal reason. The individual, if living by himself and exercising his own caprice, is not free. Only as he blends himself with the group does he attain to true freedom. History, he held, has been striving throughout time toward the realization of a perfect state, a state in which each member so blends himself with the whole that the will of the whole is his will.

For Hegel, there is a universal reason to be discovered throughout history. It is seen working itself out in one society and then shifting to another. Thus, when one society destroys or conquers another, the universal reason shifts to another group and continues to work itself out. The conqueror becomes the agent of this universal reason. War, then, is justified in Hegel's mind because it is the means by which progress is made.

The Hegelian system was adopted by the Prussian state and many Prussian thinkers held that the Prussian state was destined to carry forward the realization of universal reason through its eventual conquest of the world.

KARL MARX and FERDINAND LASSALLE, along with other early socialists (founders of modern socialism), derived certain of their views from Hegel, especially his idea that change is but the road to better things. They held that one type of society, which appeared good at one time, would inevitably give way to another which would be seen to be better, a synthesis of opposites. Thus, for example, a society based on private property would give way to one in which socialism was supreme. They saw in Hegel a philosophical justification for the new society which they desired.

De Maistre, Saint-Simon, and Comte

The result of the Lockian tradition of freedom and popular sovereignty in France was the revolution and the accompanying social and political upheaval. This inevitably gave impetus to a great deal of conservative reaction with its emphasis upon the need of authority. JOSEPH DE MAISTRE, for example, held that man had shown his inability to govern himself and argued that a stable society was possible only on the basis of tradition and strong authority.

However, the desire for "liberty, equality, and fraternity" continued to burn brightly and the dream of reforming society haunted thinkers. They recognized that merely to proclaim freedom and equality was not enough, but that actual reforms of society were necessary. CLAUDE HENRI DE ROUVROY, COMTE DE SAINT-SIMON believed that the goal of freedom and equality could be reached if men could build a science of society based upon the laws of group living. Such a scientific society would elevate the poor and the lowly and would bring to the world true Christianity with its doctrine of love for the oppressed. In such a society there would be equal distribution of property, power, culture, and happiness.

But Saint-Simon was not the thinker to develop this science of society. He could see the need for it and could preach this need, but it was left for a man of the intellectual strength of AUGUSTE COMTE to actually attempt the logical construction of such a positive philosophy. He saw that social reform was impossible without a knowledge of the laws of society, the development of a social science equal in logical accuracy to the other sciences of his time.

Sociology, the science of society, Comte held to be the most complex of the sciences, including both an understanding of society as it now is and also a study and understanding of the progress of society.

Comte held that society begins as a way to satisfy man's social impulse which is fundamental to him. As man progresses, his social life passes through the three stages: militarism, in which discipline and force are supreme; revolution; and the positive stage, in which the emphasis is upon social rather than political problems. It is this positive stage in which the expert guides scientific research and controls all phases of living. This expert is not to be dependent upon the ignorant; therefore popular government is not desirable.

The ideal of social living, the positive state, is for Comte one which has passed beyond the stage of chaos represented by the revolutions which followed the Lockian influence. Here the expert has emerged and is able through the strength of his ability to direct society toward more and more perfect living. He sees the needed reforms of society and is able to effect them. The masses of men accept his guidance because he is an expert.

The Views of Mill and Spencer

This dream of social reform and the building of a more ideal society was basic to the thinking of JOHN STUART MILL also. He believed that the phenomena of social living conformed to fixed laws just as other phenomena do. However, he recognized that the factors involved in society are so numerous and are changing so constantly that prediction is impossible. Thus, the methods of study used in other sciences, those of the laboratory, are not applicable to a study of society. By the method of deduction from many instances we can see tendencies in human social development and can point to them as guides to activity, he taught.

Believing this to be true, Mill held that the task of the social scientists was to investigate social groups to discover how the different forms of society develop and follow each other. Thus, by a study of history we can discover the laws of social progress and development. Then we can point to tendencies in the present social structure and predict that there is a high degree of probability that certain social results can be expected.

For example, a study of ancient civilizations will show the reasons for their fall. The historian can point to factors in the social structure which contributed to the downfall of the civilization. Then, if an examination of a present society reveals the same factors as present and operating, it can be predicted with a degree of probability that that society will also fall.

Mill, as many of his predecessors, recognized that social well-being was necessary for individual well-being, that the individual was tied up with the group and that his happiness was dependent upon the status of the group. Thus, he dreamed of a society in which the happiness and prosperity of all was certain, and in which all would share the wealth of the group. In his *Autobiography* he wrote,

"While we repudiated with the greatest energy that tyranny of society over the individual which most Socialistic systems are supposed to involve, we yet looked forward to a time when society will no longer be divided into the idle and the industrious; when the rule that they who do not work shall not eat will be applied not to paupers only, but impartially to all; when the division of the produce of labor, instead of depending, as in so great a degree it now does, on the accident of birth, will be made by concert on an acknowledged principle of justice; and when it will no longer either be, or be thought to be, impossible for human beings to exert themselves strenuously in procuring benefits which are not to be exclusively their own, but to be shared with the society they belong to. The social problem of the future, we considered to be: how to unite the greatest individual liberty of action, with a common ownership in the raw material of the globe, and an equal participation of all in the benefits of combined labor."

Mill was struggling here with a problem that seems to have become more and more clear since his day: the problem of undeserved poverty and equally undeserved wealth. Society, as he understood it, exists for the good of all individual members. Therefore, each must have freedom to work and be rewarded for his effort. But, the raw materials of the world cannot be the exclusive possession of a few. These belong to all, and must be held by society as the representative of all. Mill believed that a time would come when such would be the case and when society could guarantee economic freedom to all.

HERBERT SPENCER accepted the doctrine that each individual had the right to preserve himself. Indeed, he saw in nature a struggle in which the fittest survived and the less fit perished. Thus, men must be free to struggle and prove their fitness to survive.

But, the survival of the fittest among human individuals depends, he argued, upon group life. Isolated from his fellows, even the fittest of men would perish. Therefore society is essential. This necessitates a course of activity in which each individual is restricted by the rights of others.

One may do what he wills in this struggle, but he must not violate the freedom of others. Everyone has the right to act to a certain limit, but no further.

However, Spencer would not accept the socialistic thesis of Mill. For him, the state is greatly restricted. Its chief functions are to prevent internal aggression and to protect its members from foreign invasion. Beyond this it cannot go. To own the raw materials of the world and distribute them for the good of all was not a function of the state, to his thinking. In this direction he saw only danger, the danger of complete state control and the inevitable suppression of the individual.

Competition among the members of society was to be permitted and encouraged. He believed that society, and the welfare of each individual, was better served by the establishment of as few restrictions upon competition as possible. In this, Spencer was an advocate of the *laissez-faire* theory. The best life, he taught, was one lived with only a minimum of regulation by the state.

Nietzsche's Conception of the State

FRIEDRICH NIETZSCHE had no use for equality or anything that suggested democracy. The will to power is his dominant idea. In the struggle of the universe, this will to power is expressed; and the most powerful wins and has the right to win. If others are weaker and are unable to survive, that is good. The weak should be destroyed anyhow to make room for the strong.

He recognizes differences among men and believes that these differences should be magnified. The more powerful should rule, and the weaker should be ruled. Slavery seems perfectly natural to him; and he feels that women, being weaker than men, cannot be expected to have the same rights as men. Thus, he repudiates all that has been held by that long line of philosophers whose constant theme has been the equality of all men and the right of all to share equally in the goods of society. For Nietzsche, society is merely a field in which the strong have a chance to demonstrate their strength and win their rewards, while the weak are defeated and dragged from the arena to be disposed of completely. Since inequality is characteristic of nature and the natural state of man, it is unnatural to replace it with a forced equality.

The Views of Dewey and Recent Thinkers

JOHN DEWEY has shown at all times a strong interest in society and its problems. He constantly attempts to interpret the modern democratic point of view, to reveal its implications, and to forecast its future. He thinks of society, at its best, as a group of individuals sharing their experiences and growing through this sharing. The individual is to be free, but this freedom is not to be that of the older tradition. As the individual becomes a true member of society he is incorporated into the group in such a way that he can contribute to the welfare of the whole and receive from the whole that which makes him truly human.

At all times Dewey recognizes the importance of the individual. He holds that no one should ever be treated as an instrument, as a means to some goal that is not his. Rather, each one should be treated as an end in himself. "Respect for human personality" is the chief doctrine of his philosophy. This is, perhaps, the only absolute known to Dewey and his school of thought.

Man, Dewey holds, is man because he lives in society. To the extent that his activities in the group lead on to richer and more rewarding activities for him and for all members of the group, he is acting wisely and truly. Society, group life, is the way to this complete and full life since here mutual sharing is possible.

Thus, we may say that two points of view are basic to the great mass of recent writing which deals with matters of the state. On the one hand are those who follow more or less completely the lead of men from Plato to Nietzsche and hold that inequality is the natural state of man. This being the case, each member of the state must take his proper place in the social structure. It is perfectly right and natural, these men argue, that some should be rulers and others should be ruled, and the ruled should not question the acts of the rulers. Such writers spurn democracy, socialism, and all other systems of human equality and freedom. Plato saw democracy as the open door to anarchy. He would have the philosopher-king rule, and all others take their places in a tightly organized system.

Hegel carried this idea one step further when he held that certain states or groups of individuals were by nature superior to others and therefore should rule them. This, of course, is the basic point of view of all totalitarian systems of government.

Opposed to this entire trend is the democratic tradition which grew out of the Renaissance and came to fruition in the work of men like Locke, Rousseau, and their followers. It holds that all men are by nature free and equal. This position is basic to the French Revolution and the American Declaration of Independence and Constitution. It affirms that there are certain rights with which all men are endowed by their Creator, and which cannot be taken away from them under any conditions. These rights have been listed in many ways, chief of which is "life, liberty, and the pursuit of happiness."

This position led to the influential doctrine of *laissez faire*, a doctrine which characterized the early years of development in the United States. It limited the authority of the state and magnified the freedom of the individual to work and hold the rewards of his work.

Today philosophers are seeking to discover a balance between these two positions. Complete freedom leads to a crass individualism in which the powerful oppress the weak. Complete regulation leads to the same end, but the oppressors are those who happen to gain control of the government. Dewey—and many modern thinkers agree in this— seeks a freedom within the social group by which both the individual and the group will prosper. A great many of the social experiments of the present are in this direction, seeking to balance individual interests and group interests in such a way that both will be served and neither sacrificed to the other.

Chapter VIII
MAN AND EDUCATION

THE SOPHISTS   PLATO   ARISTOTLE   QUINTILIAN
ABELARD   LUTHER   BACON   HOBBES
COMENIUS   LOCKE   ROUSSEAU
PESTALOZZI   HERBART   FROEBEL   DEWEY

Why do we establish schools and pay for them? Is the fundamental purpose of education the training of obedient citizens of a totalitarian state, or is it the development of free men in a democracy? Shall the church or the state dominate the schools? What shall we teach in our schools?

As we survey the whole course of man's development from the earliest times to the present and from the most primitive and simple to the most complex ways of living, we are strongly impressed by the fact that wherever men have lived together there has been some group interest in education. As the group becomes more complex this interest grows, and institutions definitely charged with the task of teaching are created. Thus the school comes into existence and an educational system evolves.

But, so far as we know from the meager records which have been left, early man had only a very simple educational system. Most of the child's learning was picked up as he associated with his parents and other members of the family, tribe, clan, or larger group. He learned to fish and hunt, to prepare his food, to fight his enemies, and to take care of his simple and elementary needs. In short, he learned to survive in the world in which he found himself.

In time, however, as traditions and customs grew, this simple association together was not enough. The child could not learn all that was necessary by this method. As a result the older men of the group took it upon themselves to instruct the young at certain times in traditions, customs, and group lore. One of the most important of these times was the age of puberty, when the child was initiated into the group as an adult. Special initiation rites were held, and if the young man stood the tests imposed upon him he was told the most cherished secrets of the group and then accepted by the group as a full member. Thus education became a definite concern of the group.

As the life of the group became more complex, certain members of the group took it upon themselves to become thoroughly familiar with the traditions and the customs and devoted most of their time to the teaching of the young. At first, this teaching was done wherever the teacher and a group of learners cared to gather. But later specified places for teaching and learning were set up. These were the first schools.

Often these places of teaching and learning were also the places where members of the group gathered for religious purposes. This was due to the fact that among early people the traditions, customs, lore, and ways of living were tied up closely with their religion. Their gods were believed to be the powers who established customs and traditions. Thus, worship of the gods and compliance with customs and traditions were so closely united that education was largely religious education, and everything that was learned had a religious sanction. Consequently, it was natural that the teachers should be men of religious power and that the places of learning should be also the places of worship.

The ancient Hebrews reveal this fact clearly. Their schools were held in the synagogue or place of religious worship and their teachers were the rabbis. Even though education later became concerned with a great deal more than mere religious matters, the leaders of the religious life of the poeple continued to hold a dominant position in the education of the young, and a large part of the material taught was directly or indirectly of a religious nature.

In time the thinkers or philosophers began to devote considerable attention to the matter of education. They wanted to know what should be taught the young and how it should be taught. They gave thought to the relationship of education to the rest of group life, its importance and necessity. They took up questions of the aims or purposes of education, of the methods of teaching, of what should be taught. In this way education became a major concern of the philosophers.

This development was logical and necessary. If a philosopher believed that a certain thing was true, his next question was: How can others be instructed so as to believe it to be true? Every philosopher, as soon as he developed his philosophy, was confronted with the problem of how to get others to accept his philosophy as true. And the answer was always "through education."

Education as Viewed by the Early Greek Philosophers

Among the Greeks, the *Sophists,* as we have seen, were individualists. They believed that man should be trained to take care of himself at all times and advance himself in his community at all cost. Thus, they advocated a system of education which would promote the happiness and insure the success of the individual. Since a great deal of man's activity at that time hinged upon public discussion and the workings of public opinion, the Sophists based their education upon training in debate and oratory. They wanted the young men trained to argue well and convincingly before their fellows so that they might win their cases.

This training was careful and thorough. The young men learned to build logical arguments which could not be broken down, and to deliver these arguments with a persuasiveness of voice and personality such as to win their hearers. This included training in logic, mastery of the laws and customs of the Athenians, a familiarity with the literature of the past so as to be able to use illustrations from it, great practice in speaking and careful training of the voice, and a thorough mastery of the language of the people so that it could be used with ease and brilliance.

The Sophists, strolling teachers who taught for a fee, held that an individual so trained could rise to high places in the life of Athens and could lead the people. But, there was tied up with this a belief on the part of many Sophists that the best speaker should also be the best man. ProTAGORAS is believed to have said, "If you associate with me, on that very day you will return a better man than you came." Part of the work of fitting a young man for a successful career, as many Sophists saw, consisted in making him a better man in every way.

According to Socrates, Plato, and Aristotle

SOCRATES, although disagreeing with the Sophists in many respects, held this same general belief. He stated that education should make a man a better citizen and thereby a happier individual. However, while the Sophists placed emphasis upon the individual man, Socrates emphasized man as a member of the group. He taught that the most valuable thing a man could have was knowledge, and that such knowledge was to be obtained by removing individual differences and discovering the essentials upon which all men would agree.

This belief lead Socrates to go about Athens challenging the statements and beliefs of those with whom he spoke. He would show that many beliefs were false because they were superficial. Then he would continue the discussion by probing the topic deeply until he discovered the essential truth about it. His method has become known as the "dialectic" or "Socratic" method. It consists of taking a statement made by another and so analyzing it as to reveal its inconsistencies. Then, after the other person recognizes the fallacies in his view, the questioner asks him a series of questions in which he brings out what he believes to be the truth.

Socrates was a great teacher, who devoted himself to the practice of education. His pupil, PLATO, developed one of the first theories of education. In the *Republic*, one of Plato's great works, we find a system of education which, Plato believed, would insure a happy and just state.

Since Plato believed that men were by nature different and should be put into classes corresponding with their basic differences, he developed a plan of education which would meet this need. It was a plan by which men would be selected and trained for work in one of three classes. During the first eighteen years of a boy's life he was to be trained in gymnastics, music, and literature, learning to read and write, to play and sing, and to take part in many sports. At eighteen those boys who showed ability were given further training, while the rest stopped and became tradesmen, merchants, and the like.

Those boys who were retained in the educational system were given two years of cadet training. At twenty, those who were found to be incapable of going on were put into the military class and charged with defending the country. The remainder were given more extensive training in philosophy, mathematics, music, science, and other cultural subjects, and would eventually become the leaders of society.

In this system Plato was endeavoring to use education to pick men for the various duties of a social group. In each case, however, he sought to pick men in terms of their abilities as discovered by a system of education. It is evident that Plato held education to be a matter of state concern. It was supported and controlled by the state and its function was to select and train men for service in the state. Plato believed that if the state would adopt this system of education, it would produce an ideal society in which everyone would be doing the work for which he was suited and trained and thus would be happy.

ARISTOTLE held that the aim of education should be to make people virtuous. Thus, there should be three periods of training fitted to the three periods in the development of an individual. The first period, from birth to seven years of age, should be concerned wholly with the training of the body in preparation for formal schooling. The second period would be that of formal schooling, from seven to twenty-one years of age. This would consist of training in literature, music, gymnastics, and the like.

For Aristotle, as for Plato, education was a state matter and should be controlled by the state. Aristotle would have the state determine what children should live and what ones should be destroyed soon after birth because of physical deformities. Further, he would have the state determine whom a man should marry, so that desirable offspring would be assured. The state, he held, should use education in order to develop citizens who could defend the state and make it better.

The positions taken by Plato and Aristotle, positions emphasizing the use of education by the state as a means for training good citizens, did not have wide influence in the life of Athens in their day. Rather, the Sophist position that education was for individual interests dominated. The individualism of the times was not to be suppressed by a few philosophers. The people listened to the philosophers, but they followed their own interests and demanded a type of education which would make them most successful and happy. They were carried away with visions of personal success and individual happiness and were in no mood to listen to philosophers who suggested that both success and happiness in the long run depended upon the welfare of the group.

The Roman Conception of Education

In Rome, education followed the pattern which had been developed by the Sophists. The ideal of the Roman was the orator who could sway the multitudes with his eloquence. Success in public life was largely determined by the power which one possessed to speak in public and to influence mass opinion. QUINTILIAN, the Roman authority on education, pointed out that the orator had to be more than an eloquent speaker. He must also be "a good man," one of "excellent mind." He believed that "the man who

can duly sustain his character as a citizen, who is qualified
for the management of public and private affairs, and who
can govern communities by his counsels, settle them by
means of laws, and improve them by means of judicial en-
actments, can certainly be nothing else but an orator."

Thus, the heart of Roman education was the training of
the orator. This included knowledge of logic, good morals,
a careful schooling in the laws of the nation, and a character that was above suspicion. CICERO developed this
scheme thoroughly and became himself the model of the
Roman orator.

Early Christian Conception of Education

With the development of Christianity education was
once more concerned with religious questions. Those individuals who wished to become members of the Christian
community needed instruction in the beliefs and rites of
the Christian faith. Thus "catechumenal" schools were established to give such instruction to the "catechumens" or
candidates for admission to the group. Further, as Christianity came into contact with other religions and the philosophies of the world it became necessary to train leaders
who could explain Christian beliefs to the leaders and the
people of the times. This led to the setting up of "catechetical" schools in which instruction was carried on by the
question and answer method, the method of the catechism.
Out of these schools came the *Apologists,* men able to meet
the questionings of those interested in Christianity and to
answer the many critics of the movement. Many of these
Apologists, after receiving training in the catechetical
schools, became teachers in them and instructed a great
number of individuals who spread throughout the then-
known world preaching and teaching the Christian beliefs
and doctrines. Among the most important of these were
CLEMENT OF ALEXANDRIA and the great theologian
ORIGEN.

These men, along with many others, believed in education as the only sure means of protecting the Christian
movement and spreading it throughout the world. For

them education was not an instrument for the state, as Plato and Aristotle had held, but an instrument for the church, to be used in the service of God. The influence of these early Christian thinkers was wide, and schools under the control and direction of the church began to spring up everywhere. By 529 this movement had become so powerful that the Emperor Justinian ordered all pagan schools closed and permitted only Christian schools to operate. Thereby Christian education, a system under the control of the church, was left without a rival in the vast Roman Empire.

St. Benedict and the Monastic Way of Life

As life in the Roman Empire became more and more corrupt, many devout people fled from society and established themselves in secluded groups, living in monasteries. We speak of this way of life as "monasticism." Although the chief purpose of the various monasteries was religious living, education was not neglected. SAINT BENEDICT, head of the famous monastery at Monte Cassino in southern Italy, established a "rule" for the government of the members of his monastery. This included work and study, and emphasized the belief that education was necessary for the continuance of Christianity. As the influence of Saint Benedict spread and his "rule" was adopted in principle by other monasteries, schools became a part of monastic life. At first these schools were devoted to the education of young men who planned to enter the monastery. Later others who wished some education but did not intend to devote themselves to the religious life came to the monasteries for training. Thus, two types of schools developed in connection with the monasteries, one for the "interni" or those who were dedicated to religion and the other for the "externi" or those who came only for education.

At first this education consisted merely of reading in order to study the Bible, writing to copy the sacred books, and some calculation for the figuring of holy days and other church festivals. By the end of the sixth century it had grown until it covered the "seven liberal arts" of grammar, rhetoric, dialectic, arithmetic, geometry, music, and astronomy. These subjects were taught almost wholly by the question-and-answer method.

Thus, throughout the so-called Dark Ages of European history, those centuries when the lamp of civilization burned low in Europe, some learning was preserved in the monasteries, a learning which was wholly under the control of and for the service of the church. Its aim was fundamentally the salvation of the human soul in a world of temptation and sin. This became the general aim of all education during these dark days.

Education in the Middle Ages and Early Renaissance

A light in these centuries of darkness was the work of Charlemagne, Emperor of the Holy Roman Empire during the early part of the ninth century. He called the Anglo-Saxon ALCUIN from the monastic school at York, England, to help him establish a palace school and to reform education in his empire. Alcuin established a monastic school at Tours, and wrote many textbooks on grammar, rhetoric, and dialectic as well as a work on psychology.

Alcuin had great influence in the empire and left his imprint upon many scholars, among them JOHN SCOTUS ERIGENA. Erigena and the others of this group followed the general position of the times in holding that education was fundamentally a matter of religion and the salvation of the human soul. Its purpose was vocational only in so far as it might serve to train young men for the church. Popular education was to be based wholly on religious matters and everything taught pointed to religion in some way or other. This position, of course, helped the church to maintain itself as the dominant institution of these ages.

The education of *Scholasticism* did not depart from this general point of view. Although the Schoolmen studied widely, their aim was to prove the reasonableness of the doctrines of the church. PETER ABELARD, one of the greatest of the Schoolmen, devoted much of his time to teaching and was influential in the founding of the University of Paris. Here theology was the dominant interest, and the core of teaching was the presentation of the doctrines of the church. Abelard never lost the conviction that all the doctrines of the church could be proved to be logical and scientific.

After several centuries, as we have seen, thinkers began to question this complete dominance of the church. It was inevitable, when men began to attempt to prove the doctrines of the church by reasonable means, that some would question the proofs offered.

Further, there began to arise classes of merchants and skilled tradesmen whose interests were largely outside of the church. They desired an education which would fit their children to follow them in their trades or to succeed in commercial pursuits. As these skilled workmen began to unite into "guilds" or early trade unions, they established schools to train young men for service in the particular trades. In this way, guild schools and later burgher or town schools sprang up. Although religious questions were considered in these schools, the main purpose for them was vocational rather than religious.

Thus, as the Middle Ages faded so faded the complete dominance of the church in matters of education. Along with the guild and burgher schools there arose court schools founded and supported by wealthy rulers of the Italian cities. One of the most famous and influential of these was presided over by the noted scholar VITTORINO DA FELTRE at Mantua. He sought a harmonious development of mind, body, and morals, following the teachings of the ancient Greeks. He wished to prepare boys for a practical life in the world of the age. He gave time to Latin, mathematics, fencing, wrestling, dancing, ball-playing and other physical exercise, and also to the Latin and Greek classics which had been rediscovered by such men as Petrarch and his contemporaries.

Schools similar to that of Vittorino were founded at Florence, Padua, Pavia, Milan, Ferrara, and other Italian cities. They all represented a move away from the church and a definite challenge to the religious dominance of education.

Martin Luther and the Protestant Reformation

While the leaders of the Italian Renaissance were challenging the church's control of education, the leaders of the Northern or German Renaissance were substituting the control of the people's church, the Lutheran church, for that of the Roman Catholic church. MARTIN LUTHER, spearhead of the Protestant Reformation, the northern counterpart of the Italian Renaissance, held that everyone should know how to read his Bible and interpret it according to his understanding.

Thus, Luther and his followers were driven by a necessary logic to support education for all people. They advocated training in the elements of reading, writing, and figuring, and held that, though fundamentally this knowledge was to make possible their understanding of the Bible and religion, it was also necessary for good citizenship. Luther wrote that even though there were no heaven nor hell, education would be necessary for the citizen.

This swing away from the dominance of education by the church, and its control more and more by secular forces, led to the establishment of schools and school systems by cities and by interested private groups. An example was the school of JOHANN STURM at Strassburg, which was then in Germany. This institution aimed at "piety, knowledge, and eloquence." Although religion was a prominent factor in the teaching of the school, other matters were also considered, and the control of the school was not in the hands of the church.

As this trend toward secular education grew in strength there began to appear men who attempted to put it into philosophic form, to draw up a philosophy of education to fit the new age and new demands. JOHN MILTON, the great English poet, who was also a schoolmaster, urged students to turn to the ancient writings of Greece and Rome and study them, not for their form, but because they contained all that man needed for a happy life. He believed that the best possible education was to be obtained from the study of these classical writings.

The Views of Bacon and Hobbes

But this devotion to the past did not hold its own in the face of the growing interest in the world in which men were then living. Science was making itself known and respected. Men everywhere saw the value of scientific understanding and began to emphasize the need for scientific knowledge. Thus any philosophy of education which would prove acceptable to the age had to be based on the scientific knowledge then available.

FRANCIS BACON pointed out the need for clear and accurate thinking, showing that any mastery of the world in which man lived was dependent upon careful understanding of the facts of this world. Bacon would first rid the mind of all prejudices. Then he would have one observe carefully and collect all possible data from which to draw conclusions or hypotheses to be tested by other data which could be collected later. As society accumulated more knowledge it should pass this on to the young through schools so that they would start in their thinking where their parents and the older members of society left off. Thus, education was, for him, a passing on of the knowledge of the past, the accumulated knowledge of society, to the young.

The interest of THOMAS HOBBES in government led him to argue that the ruler should have the right to determine the kind of education fit for his subjects; and that the subjects must accept the educational system set up by the ruler. Education, according to Hobbes, is one of the absolute rights of the sovereign power. It serves to strengthen the state, and therefore should be watched carefully and controlled at all times. Here we have education as an instrument of the state, set up and controlled to serve the ruler and his system. Each child should be trained in order to serve the state better.

Comenius' Philosophy of Education

Among the great educators of this period was JOHN AMOS COMENIUS, a Moravian bishop and teacher. He believed that it was possible for everyone to learn everything. Thus he visioned a long period of encyclopedic training during which the student would be introduced to all scientific knowledge. At first everything was to be taught in "a general and undefined manner," while, as the child grew, teaching was to become more exact and specific.

This training, Comenius argued, should follow the "method of nature." His plan was to expose the pupil to the world in which he lived, let him observe, and thereby lead him to an understanding of things about him. As the child grew older his observations would become more detailed and cover a wider and wider area.

Locke and Rousseau

Although the scientific trend in education, as developed by Bacon, Hobbes, and Comenius, interested him, JOHN LOCKE was more interested in the training of the English gentleman, a youth of breeding and wisdom. He condemned the education of his day as being little more than a reproduction of the old interest in the classics and religion. He did not believe that such would fit a man for the manifold duties of the world in which he lived. Consequently, Locke sought a more practical and efficient type of education.

Locke held that the human soul at birth was a blank tablet but possessed of the power to receive impressions from the outside world and endowed with a desire for pleasure. Consequently, he saw education as the process of learning through experience with this outside world and working toward the realization of happiness. His ideal was a sound mind in a sound body.

To realize this ideal, Locke advocated much physical exercise and a hardening process by which the body would become strong and able to endure hardships and long physical strain without breaking. Further, the child should be exposed to as much of the world about him as possible, so that he could receive impressions in great numbers. Travel, teaching by private tutors, and wide experience in the social world were advocated by Locke as methods for training.

The aim of education, Locke argued, should be an individual who knew all the proper methods of association with his fellows, who was wise in the ways of the world so that he could take care of himself at all times, who was pious, and who had enough knowledge to meet the demands of his environment. This, of course, was a practical education which would fit the young man for complete living in the world of Locke's day.

In contrast to this social emphasis in education, JEAN JACQUES ROUSSEAU held that society warps the child and that its influence is wholly evil. Consequently, he would protect the child from society at all times until he is so completely developed that society cannot destroy his inner nature.

In his famous book, *Emile*, Rousseau outlines the education of a boy in a manner which is natural and spontaneous. Emile, the hero of the story, is to be permitted to develop in accord with his own nature, without interference. Education is protective, a means of shielding the child from the influence of society which will warp the natural growth of his real self.

For the first four years of the child's life, Rousseau would emphasize physical training, the development of the body. Then, from five to twelve years, the child would develop his senses. He would live in the world of nature, and observe many things. Intellectual training, through books and the like, would begin when the child is thirteen years old. Even here Rousseau would follow the natural curiosity of the child, and give instruction only as the child naturally came to demand it. During this period the child would learn a trade in order to be economically independent. Between fifteen and twenty the child would be given moral training. Here he would come into contact with his fellows and learn the basic principles of sympathy, goodness, and service to mankind. Here religion would come into the picture.

Although Rousseau emphasized the natural training of

boys, he did not believe that the same training should be given to girls. They should be educated to serve men and make them happy. Girls were to be fitted into a pattern demanded of men, one of restraint. While the boy should be free to develop according to his own inner nature, the girl should be moulded to fit the pattern demanded by the man.

Rousseau voiced the growing belief of his day that life should be freed from the many restraints which had been put about it. Men were breaking away from the past with all its hindrances. They had escaped from the dominance of the church, but found themselves dominated by the restraints of society. Hobbes' point of view, that the ruler as representative of society should set up an educational system which would make the young worthy citizens, was not acceptable to many. They felt that this system warped the original nature of man. Thus Rousseau said and wrote what was in the minds of many of his fellows. They wanted to free themselves not only from the church, but from the many requirements of society. Freedom was their watchword.

JOHANN BERNHARD BASEDOW came under the influence of Rousseau and established an educational institution in which he sought to put Rousseau's ideas into actual teaching. His school emphasized conversation and play. The interests of the child were considered so that this school became in a large measure a "child centered" school. All instruction began with those things in which the child was interested, and moved along as interests grew. The idea spread, and many other educators sought to incorporate Rousseau's ideas into their teaching.

Pestalozzi's Conception of Education

One of the most influential educators to be influenced by Rousseau was JOHANN HEINRICH PESTALOZZI. He sought to understand the nature of children and to build his teaching on the "natural, progressive, and harmonious development of all the powers and capacities of the human being."

As he understood the natural laws, he sought to develop children in accord with them.

Thus some educators supported one and others supported the other of two fundamental principles—the principles of social control and of nature. Which should be dominant? Should education be a matter of building citizens according to a socially accepted and determined pattern, or should it be a following of the inner nature of the child? Here, from another angle of course, is the old problem of the individual and the group. Which should dominate? This was the problem of the eighteenth century, a century in which more and more emphasis was being placed upon the individual and his freedom, in which the ideas of freedom were being realized in the French and the American revolutions.

JOHANN GOTTLIEB FICHTE approached education from the point of view of the state. In one of the darkest moments in the life of the Prussian state he arose to deliver his famous *Addresses to the German Nation*. In these he argued for group unity and social solidarity such as to create a new and strong nation. And, as a basis for this unity he advocated a strong system of education which would mould the people into a whole. Education, for him, was to be a means for building a nation.

Thus, education should concern itself with the greatness of the nation. In a sense, it should be a program by which the people of the nation should come to know and love those factors of national life which were significant. Education, Fichte believed, was necessary to national unity and national progress.

Herbart's View of Education

Another great educational mind of this period was JOHANN FRIEDRICH HERBART. His interest was fundamentally psychological, and this interest colored his thinking on educational matters. Experience, for him, is the sole source of knowledge. The mind receives impressions and organizes them. Then its further reception and use of impressions are determined by the impressions already received and organized.

Thus, the environment in which the child is placed is of greatest importance. From this he receives his impressions. If it is good, his impressions will be good and he will be morally sound. Consequently, Herbart emphasized the place of the teacher in the educational system. It is the teacher who, to a great extent, determines what impressions the child receives. If the teacher is wise and clever, he will so set the scene that the child receives right impressions and will thereby develop a character which is good.

Froebel's Conception of Education

Without doubt, one of the most consistent followers of Rousseau's ideas of naturalism in education was FRIEDRICH WILHELM AUGUST FROEBEL. He believed firmly that the nature of the child was good and that it should be allowed to grow naturally. Education for him was a process of permitting and making possible this natural growth of the child. He called his school the Kindergarten, the garden of children. For him the school was to be operated as one might operate a garden. The teacher should permit and help the children to grow, just as the gardener helps the flowers to grow.

However, Froebel went further than Rousseau did, in that he attempted to take into account the fact that the child is not merely an individual, but is also a member of a group. He would not shield the child from society, but would help him to adjust himself to society in such a way that his social and individual experiences would both be helpful in the development of the complete personality.

Thus, in Froebel we see an attempt to reconcile the two divergent doctrines of education which thinkers before him had held. He realized the value of natural growth and development, and did not want this warped or interfered with. But, he also realized that society plays a great part in making the person a civilized being. Thus, society should not be ignored, nor should the child be educated in complete disregard of the values of society.

Consequently, social participation, work in groups, was a definite part of the kindergarten as conceived and founded by Froebel. At the beginning of the kindergarten day the children gathered in a circle, each child holding the hands of those on either side of him. This circle was supposed to symbolize the unity of the group. Then the circle was broken up, and children played or worked either alone or in small groups. At the close of the day the circle was again formed to emphasize that even though the child was an individual and should develop as such, he was also a member of the whole group.

This problem of the individual and the group is still the major problem of present-day educational thinking. Public schools have been set up by society and are supported by means of taxes. Thus, society has said, in effect, that it recognizes the necessity of education for its preservation. Further, society has designated what shall be taught in these schools. Teachers are certified by society, and must meet certain standards set by society.

All of these factors indicate that society has a major interest in education. Therefore, there are many who argue today that the fundamental purpose of education is to train and mould individuals into service to the state. The whole totalitarian educational system in the twentieth-century dictatorships is of this nature. Education is controlled completely by the state and no one is permitted to do or teach anything except that which will contribute to the building of citizens who will devotedly serve the state and be obedient to the will of the ruler.

But educators in the democratic countries see the danger of destroying the individuality of children. They feel that in so far as the individual is permitted to grow according to his nature and to deviate from the group, he is able to make a contribution to the groups such as will further group progress.

One of the leaders in the field of education in our democracy is JOHN DEWEY. His theories are in agreement with those of men who believe that the center of education should be the individual child. Dewey recognizes, however, that neither the individual nor the group should be given exclusive emphasis. The individual becomes truly developed as a member of society. Further, society has the right to demand of the individual that he prepare himself to serve the best interests of the group. But, Dewey holds that the best interests of the group will be served as the individual develops his own particular talents, as he develops his individual nature. Education is concerned with the individual in society and not with the individual isolated from society.

This point of view has led to the development of what is generally known today as the "child centered" school. In some instances this school has gone to the extreme of the philosophy upon which it is founded and has emphasized the child's interests to the exclusion of all others. Many so-called "progressive" schools are of this type. But, the saner representatives of this movement, under the leadership of Dewey, have attempted to find an adequate adjustment and reconciliation between the two extremes of emphasis—on the individual and on society. The result is a school in which individual interests, talents, and purposes are considered as means for contributing to the good of the whole.

Chapter IX
MIND AND MATTER

ANAXAGORAS PLATO ARISTOTLE PHILO
ANSELM ROGER BACON PARACELSUS
FRANCIS BACON HOBBES DESCARTES SPINOZA
LOCKE BERKELEY KANT
BRADLEY ROYCE JAMES DEWEY

Is the universe actually just a great mind, or is it really matter throughout? Is matter mind or is mind matter? If it is mind and matter, what is the relation between the two? How can mind influence matter or matter influence mind? Have philosophers found a solution to the problem of the relationship between mind and matter?

Anyone who opens his eyes to observe will discover a world of objects which can be kicked about, moved from place to place, broken into bits, shaped and moulded in many ways, but which do not "seem to care." A piece of clay can be shaped into a thousand and one forms. A rock can be rolled about, broken into pieces, or ground into the finest powder.

This individual who has noted these facts knows also that certain other objects seem "to care" what happens to them. Indeed he finds evidence that they make plans for their future and endeavor to carry them out. A man, for example, seems to plan his actions, to resist forces which would turn him from his plan, and is able to shape his

environment to fit his plan. He moves into a barren land,
draws plans for a giant irrigation system, builds the system, and eventually has changed an arid region to a modern Eden of flowers, trees, and green grass.

The difference between the rock and man is, according
to many philosophers, to be found in the fact that in man
there is a mind which is absent in the rock. This mind,
they argue, controls that part of the individual which is
not mind. The not-mind is called matter.

The earliest people of whom we know anything recognized this difference among objects in the environment.
Indeed, they recognized the difference within themselves.
They experienced their bodies as composed of matter, but
they were vaguely conscious that this mass of matter was
animated by something which was distinct from matter,
and different. As far back as we can penetrate into the beginnings of man's thinking, we find that he recognized a
difference between mind and matter and that he placed
mind in a more exalted realm than matter.

The earliest beliefs regarding mind and matter were
tied up with beliefs about the soul and the body. In the
days of the childhood of humanity this thing which made
man different from other things, this soul, was not clearly
defined or understood. Indeed in many quarters early man
believed that all the universe had a soul. The rock, the tree,
the river, all had souls as well as bodies. Later, as man
developed, the idea of mind as a peculiar human possession and distinct from matter became clearer.

The Greeks exhibit all stages of this development, from
the most primitive to a clear distinction between mind
and matter. The first records which we have of the Greeks
reveal them as nature-worshipers believing that everything
in nature was possessed of a soul. Gradually they developed a mythology or group of stories about the activities
of nature which they looked upon as alive. Then, as the
Greeks came to distinguish between the animate and the
inanimate, they no longer looked upon the rocks and trees
as having souls, but they felt that gods presided over them.
This was the period of the great theogonies or genealogies

of the gods who ruled over the various things in nature.

Then, as the Greek mind matured, these inventions of fancy and of the childhood of the race gave place to more careful studies of nature and of man. The gods were put in a realm of celestial glory and more or less peace; nature was held to be alive but not possessed of a soul; man was believed to be a unique combination of soul and body. The Greek was studying his world and himself and was coming nearer and nearer to the belief that there must be a clear distinction between two phases of the universe, between matter on the one hand and mind on the other. But, the final realization of this distinction was a long and difficult process.

Mind and Matter as Contrasted by the Early Greek Thinkers

The first Greek philosophers were interested, as we have already seen, in the problem of the nature of the universe. They saw this universe as composed of one or more original and simple substances. But, to account for the fact that the basic substances became a universe, they introduced a force which in some way or other moved substance. ANAX-IMANDER, for example, held that the basic substance of the universe was "the infinite," an eternal and imperishable substance. But he endowed this substance with eternal motion in order to explain how the universe as he saw it and as his fellows saw it came into being. Here is an early distinction between mass or substance and a force which moves it and shapes it into objects and things.

This distinction runs through early Greek philosophy. Each thinker suggests some basic principle or substance of which the universe is composed, and accounts for its coming into being by adding another factor which is distinct from the basic substance and which makes it take the many forms which we see about us in the world.

HERACLITUS attempted to make the original substance and the cause of the forms which it takes one and the same, when he held that the first principle of the universe was fire as a symbol of change. He saw ceaseless activity everywhere and reasoned that change or activity was all that there was in the universe. Nevertheless, he felt that in addition to the fact of change there was some entity which changed, something different from the principle of change.

When Heraclitus came to speak of man, he revealed this fact clearly. Here he made a distinction between man's body and his soul. The body was material and the soul was akin to divine reason. Thus, even in Heraclitus we find a distinction between that which moves and that which is moved.

In PARMENIDES we find a suggestion that thought or mind is in some way the creator or cause of that which is not mind. This is the principle which much later developed into the great idealistic movement. Parmenides argued that being and thought are one and the same, for what cannot be thought cannot be and what cannot be cannot be thought. Thought, or mind, and being, or substance, are identical to him. All reality, he held, is endowed with mind, and mind is, in some way not quite clear to him, the cause of everything. Mind causes matter to be, creates matter. Although Parmenides does not see all the implications of this position, and although he does not hold to this point of view consistently, we find in his writings a foreshadowing of one of the major positions regarding mind and matter, the position that actually mind is all that exists and that which we call matter is a creation of mind for its own purposes.

By the time of ANAXAGORAS, during the fifth century B.C., we have a clear statement of the theory that all movement is caused by mind or "nous" which is distinct from the substance that moves. This mind is, for Anaxagoras, a free source of all movement. Further, it knows all things in the past, in the present, and in the future, and is the arranger and cause of all things.

Here Anaxagoras expressed fairly clearly what many philosophers before him had been striving to express, a vague dualism between matter and something else which causes matter to move and become. But, for him, mind is not an individual thing to be found in each object. Rather, it is a world mind which is free from the individual objects of the universe but which serves as the moving principle in them. This world mind rules all things and does not get itself mixed up or mingled with things. It started the world, and is, in some way, in the world and the immediate cause of the world.

Anaxagoras was anxious, as were most of the thinkers of his day, to explain the universe in purely mechanical terms. But he found instances in which this explanation did not seem to be adequate. Then he turned to the theory of the world mind. As Aristotle points out in commenting on this point: "Anaxagoras uses mind as a device by which to construct the universe, and when he is at a loss for an explanation of why anything necessarily is, then he drags it in; but in other cases he assigns any other cause rather than mind, for what comes into being." In other words, Anaxagoras was struggling to get away from the idea that matter is not a self-contained principle, but he was still held by the beliefs of the past.

The *Sophists* were not concerned with explanations of the nature of the universe. Indeed, most of them felt that all attempts to discover the origin of the universe or to locate the first substance or substances of which all else was created was nothing short of foolishness. They centered their attention upon man and especially upon the mind of man. They believed that this mind was the pivot about which all else revolved. All truth was, for them, measured by the mind of the individual man, so that what each man's mind told him was true was in fact true. Thus, the Sophists accepted the dualism between mind and matter and held that mind was the determiner of all things.

Plato, Aristotle, and the Later Greek Philosophers

The mind, which he also referred to as the soul, was for PLATO the seat of all knowledge. Ideas had been implanted in the mind before it became imbedded in the body. Birth clouded the mind, so that the individual forgot all that he knew. But, through a process of questioning it was possible, Plato believed, to cause the mind to remember what it had known before birth. All knowledge, he held, was located in the mind, knowledge gained from experiences before birth. When this knowledge was recalled or remembered, the individual knew.

Plato held firmly to the idea that the universe is composed of two principles: mind and matter. Mind is wholly distinct from matter. Matter is, for him, a dull weight that mind must carry because mind has become entangled with matter. Matter is the raw material upon which mind works. It has no form or reality except as mind works on it and forms it into being. Mind is the only true reality, the thing of most worth, the principle of law and order in the universe.

This matter, dead and thus a slave, is impressed by mind with the ideas which mind has experienced in the ideal world, ideas which are real and true. It takes the shape of these ideas, and holds this shape for some time. The tree which you and I see is not a real tree to Plato. It has come about because mind has taken some matter and impressed upon it the idea of tree. The true tree, the real tree exists only in the realm of ideas, and has been seen by mind before birth.

Plato resorts to a myth to explain how mind, pure and untarnished, originally got mixed up with matter. He says that it was existing on a star in its pure form but that it became possessed of a desire for the world of sense. Therefore it became imprisoned in a body. Here it seeks to free itself from the body and return to the star. This is, of course, not a satisfactory explanation; it is evidence of the fact that at this point Plato was not sure of himself. He was sensing what became later a most difficult problem: that of explaining the relationship between pure matter and pure mind. How could these very opposite things ever come into any relationship with each other? This problem has haunted philosophers even to the present. Plato could not solve it; and it remains unsolved.

ARISTOTLE could not solve it. But he sensed that the solution lay along the line of an intimate relationship between the two. Mind, for him, was in matter as its forma-

tive principle, as its form. He held that there could be no
matter without mind and no mind without matter. Even
the lowest forms of matter known have form and therefore
have mind. As we progress up the scale to man we find a
clearer mind. But mind is everywhere.

Mind, then, for Aristotle, is not outside of matter, as
Plato had held, but is within matter as the cause of all
that is. Matter has existence and offers resistance to mind
which attempts to form it into shapes. At the same time,
matter is the ground of beings and therefore must seek in
some way to be shaped. Mind, then, has both an antagonist
and a willing helper in matter.

The *Epicureans*, in their attempt to explain the relationship between the mind and the body, turned to the
writings of Democritus. This ancient philosopher had argued that all sense perception results from "idols" or images which objects throw off and which hit the sense
organs. For example, when I see a chair my eyes are being bombarded by little idols of the chair which it is constantly throwing off. These little images travel through
space to the eye, and I see a chair.

In the same way, the Epicureans argued, when I want
to run, an image of running presents itself to the mind.
Then the mind hits the soul with the image. Since the
soul is spread all over the body, it hits the body with this
image, and the body runs. This appears very crude and
unbelievable today, but it was an earnest attempt to explain how mind, which was so different from matter, could
influence matter so that when the mind has an idea the
body acts in accord with it.

The *Stoics* held that mind is material just as is matter,
but of a much finer texture. It is a spark of the divine fire.
The mind is, for them, the soul become rational or having
acquired the power of conceptual thought. Thus, mind is
distinct from matter only in degree, not in kind.

The *Skeptics*, such as PYRRHO, held that it was impossible to prove that matter existed, since all that we have
is our ideas or thoughts. To demonstrate that something
exists which corresponds to our thoughts is impossible.

Thus, all that we have is ideas in the mind. We must act upon these, hoping that we will get what we expect, but with no assurance. Mind exists, but there is no proof that matter exists.

The Positions of Philo and St. Augustine

As Greek thought came into contact with the Jewish religious thought of men like PHILO the attempt was made to find a basis for reconciling the ideas of both traditions of thought. Philo, being fundamentally interested in religion, thought of God as the world mind which shapes matter. Thus, the universe for him is composed of mind and matter. Likewise, man is a dualism of mind and matter. Pure thought, "nous," is the chief essence of man, and matter or the body is that upon which mind works. Thus mind in man controls his body or matter, just as the world mind, God, controls matter in the world. Pure intelligence is added to the soul from God, thus tying man on to the divine in the universe.

Christianity brought to the front the idea that matter is the source of all evil, a thing to be shunned. Matter holds the soul down and therefore must be denied by the soul if it is to attain salvation. Thus, throughout most of early Christian thinking we find a definite despising of matter. Although matter had been thought of by early philosophers as something less than mind, dead, or the material upon which mind worked, there was never that complete degradation of matter which characterized Christianity. Further, there was not the earnest desire to escape from matter, a desire born of fear of matter. Early Christianity taught man that matter was the source of all evil and that man's salvation lay in his turning away from matter to pure spirit or God.

AUGUSTINE recognized the difference between mind and matter in man, but held that truth is not something which the human mind creates. Rather, truth is, for him, something that exists independently of mind, and has its source in God. Mind may discover truth, just as the Platonic mind saw ideas in the ideal world. For Augustine, the mind of God is the abode of ideas and of truth.

According to the Medieval Christian Thinkers

Christianity emphasized another principle which had a telling effect upon man. Not only did it disparage matter by making it the source of evil, but it disparaged the human mind. This was done to elevate God to the place in the universe which Christian thinkers believed He should have.

The human mind, Christian philosophers taught, is a poor and inefficient instrument. It is full of mistakes and of error. Of course, man can use his mind to reason, but his conclusions must conform to the divine authority. No one could be permitted to reach a conclusion through use of his mind which in any way questioned the edicts of authority. The church and its doctrines were believed to be the ultimate in truth. Augustine had held that truth was independent of the human mind. Therefore, the function of the mind was not to create truth but to discover it.

When the Church ruled that a certain doctrine was true, the human mind had to accept it without question. ANSELM held to this position firmly. He argued that the human mind may try to understand the doctrines of the Church, but if it is unable to reach understanding, it must accept them just the same. This was the early position of Christian thinkers: the more contradictory to reason a thing is the more faith it takes to believe. But the human mind must never question. Belief must precede reason.

When ABELARD took the position that reason should precede faith, he was going against a long and honored tradition. But Abelard never for a moment doubted that reason would prove the Christian doctrines to be true. He was willing to give the human mind freedom to question doctrines, but he was certain that true reasoning would bring the mind to accept the doctrines as true and beyond question. Nevertheless, when once the human mind was permitted to question Christian doctrine the stability of this doctrine was in danger. Man was no longer beaten down by authority and began to venture out to challenge doctrine. The human mind, which had been held within a body of accepted doctrines for many centuries, began after Abelard to feel its way toward independence.

The result was nothing short of revolutionary. Once the restraint was eased, man began to think about many things and to question much that he had not dared to question previously. He began to exercise his mind and to wrestle with numerous problems which he had shunned or not even seen previously. A new and exciting world dawned.

THOMAS AQUINAS, though developing a position which was fundamentally religious, sought to champion the human mind by endeavoring to show that the universe as a revelation of God is rational. Recognizing the power of the mind, he sought to show that Christianity, as interpreted by the church, was logically consistent. In doing this, he fell within that tradition which was becoming so important, a tradition in which the human mind was fast becoming the court of final appeal. No longer was it possible for any institution, even the church, to disregard human reason or to insult it by proposing doctrines which were not consistent with the best that the mind knew.

It was clear to Aquinas that man was both mind and matter and that the two were intimately connected. However, he did not believe that mind was so tied to the body that it could not function in more or less complete freedom from the ills of matter. Indeed, even though matter was the seat of evil, mind was able to criticize matter and escape from it and its temptations.

Roger Bacon and Paracelsus

With the rise of natural science, the human mind began to assume a more important place in the scheme of things. ROGER BACON, a peculiar mixture of medieval monk and modern scientific scholar, stood midway between the old religious point of view and the more modern position of trust in the mind. He set about to use the mind to understand, and, in a small degree, to control matter. And he was startled to find that he could not only know, but could control matter. In him, then, we see the symbol of humanity feeling its wings, of the mind attacking the world of matter and realizing success which acted as a spur to further attacks and a growing confidence in the power of the mind.

It was inevitable that free thought should assume a more and more prominent place in the new world, which was coming into being. As man thought and found thinking good, he would think more, and gradually become impatient with any authority which denied him the right to think. Success bred courage, and courage resulted in more use of the mind and more success. There was no stopping this process once it was begun.

Of course, it was inevitable that the first blush of success should lead to extravagances, to an over-enthusiasm regarding the powers of the mind. In a man like PARACELSUS, for example, we see evidences of this over-enthusiasm. He visioned short cuts to mental mastery of the universe, and suggested many strange things which today appear little other than pure superstitions. Alchemy and magic appeared to him to be ways by which mind might master matter.

But these vagaries were soon to be corrected by men who saw further and saw clearer. The great scientists, among whom were GALILEO, KEPLER, NEWTON, and others, realized that the mastery of the understanding of matter by mind was a long and arduous task, requiring careful study and a growing keenness of understanding. They set man on this hard road with definiteness, and proved by their successes that this was the only road to success.

Francis Bacon and Hobbes

Then came FRANCIS BACON (not to be confused with Roger Bacon), a man who could take the modern spirit of confidence in the power of the human mind and the equally modern science and weave them together so as to suggest a method by which mind could master the universe. He showed how this new-found strength could be used and how it could lead to success.

Francis Bacon's method was fairly simple as we look at it today. He would first clear the mind of all "idols" or false ways of thinking. Then, as a free instrument, the mind could attack the world by careful observation, the collection of data, and the interpretation of these data. This was the method of "induction," the moving from numerous bits of evidence to a general principle which will explain the data collected. Here was a method which mind could employ, and which, Bacon believed, would lead inevitably to success. Thus, he set the pattern for thinking, and challenged men to think clearly and accurately.

But inevitably the question as to the relationship between mind and matter would arise. Though some earlier philosophers had attacked the problem, they were not in any position to do more than sketch in its bold outline. Then, during those early days of the Renaissance, when man was enchanted by the new-felt power which he was discovering, the question faded into the background. Man was more interested in using his mind than in asking questions about it. Nevertheless, sooner or later it was certain that the question would arise again and demand solution.

With THOMAS HOBBES we have an early modern attempt to explain the relationship between mind and matter. Being a materialist and believing that everything could be explained in material terms, Hobbes taught that mind is motion in the brain. In other places he refers to mind as an internal substance, a subtle body, in the head. When the mind has an idea, there is nothing more than motion of a material substance in the brain. Here Hobbes seems to solve the problem of the relationship between mind and matter by holding that mind is matter and that there is no difference. Mind is simply a more subtle matter than that of body. This was the ancient explanation.

But, though a materialist, Hobbes does not seem content with this explanation. In other passages we find him speaking of mental processes as appearances of motion, as the effects of motion rather than as motion itself. Consciousness comes after motion as its effect. This theory is known in modern philosophy as "epiphenomenalism."

Thus, though Hobbes attempts to account for mind in terms of matter, he is not quite satisfied with the results, and seems at times to drift in the direction of a dualism one side of which is motion and the other side the effect of motion.

Descartes and Spinoza

The same problem challenged DESCARTES. He did not try to dodge the issue, but stated clearly that the universe, for him, consisted of two substances, mind and body. And these two substances were fundamentally different. If, then, mind is wholly different from body or matter, how is it that mind can have an effect upon matter or move the body? How is it that when one wishes to walk, he walks?

The solution which he offers is vague and full of confusion. Determined to stick to his dualism, a complete and absolute dualism, he has difficulty in explaining interaction. Mind, he tells us, is troubled by matter, by the processes which go on in the body. At another place he offers an interesting but not wholly satisfying explanation of interaction. He suggests that the body and the mind make contact through the pineal gland, a small gland in the brain. The body, he says, moves the pineal gland or the mind moves it. In either case this movement is transmitted to the other which is itself moved: I wish to walk; I transmit motion to the pineal gland which transmits it to the body; and I walk.

The unsatisfactoriness of this theory is proof of the fact that Descartes, having once taken his stand as to the differences between mind and matter, could not find any explanation of the experienced fact of interaction. It seems that he must either deny interaction and leave the question unsolved, or take the position that mind and matter are enough alike to influence each other.

Descartes' successors rejected the idea of interaction and sought to explain the relationship between mind and matter by some other principle. ARNOLD GUELINCX taught that

God has so arranged the universe from the beginning that when the mind has an idea, matter moves as though it were affected, but actually there is no interaction. God created the world and in this creation he so determined everything that when my mind has an idea of walking my body walks. Guelincx writes that "God in his infinite wisdom has instituted laws of motion, so that a movement which is entirely independent of my will and power coincides with my free volition."

NICOLAS MALEBRANCHE held that we do not experience a world of matter and are not affected by that world. Rather, God is like mind, and influences our minds so that we think we experience a material world. Indeed, he tells us, "If God had destroyed the created world, and would continue to affect me as he now affects me, I should continue to see what I now see; and I should believe that this (created) world exists, since it is not this world that acts on my mind" but God himself.

Another point of view, held by many Cartesians, was that whenever something happens in matter, God affects us so that we think we are being affected by the happening in matter. This is known as the theory of "occasionalism": the happening in the material world is the occasion for God's action upon us.

These theories, as it should be clear, are not at all satisfactory. They make of God a sort of showman putting on a performance for us, fooling us by pulling the proper strings at the proper time. One is tempted to ask the question, if God created the world, why did he create such a situation? Would it not have been easier to have created a world in which mind and matter interacted?

But philosophers were not contented, and they struggled to reach a more acceptable theory of the relationship between mind and matter. SPINOZA taught that mind and matter were two attributes of one and the same substance, God. These two attributes were, for him, absolutely independent of each other and neither could influence the other. But, since they are attributes of God, we have thought and action moving along in parallel lines, both being the thought and action of God. This is the theory of "psychophysical parallelism." My mind, Spinoza would argue, is a mode of the thinking attribute of God, and my body is a mode of the extended attribute of God. My thought is paralleled by action in the body so that it appears that my mind influences my body. Actually there is no direct influence.

Locke, Berkeley, and Hume

JOHN LOCKE abandoned the attempt to make two unlike things influence each other. He begins his thinking with the thesis that the mind is a sort of blank tablet upon which the world of matter writes by means of sensations. This mind does not have innate or inborn ideas, but it does have the power to arrange impressions in such a way as to produce a consistent system of thoughts. Mind and body, for Locke, exist as real things, but they interact. Bodies act upon the mind and produce sensations. Locke spends a great deal of time developing this point of view, but, when he comes up against the question as to how these two unlike substances interact, he is confused, and even though he does not want to, he lapses into occasionalism.

Accepting the dualism of mind and body as his starting point, GEORGE BERKELEY draws the conclusion that the material cannot exist and that the only thing that we can prove as existing is mind. Matter, belief in which leads to atheism and materialism, as he argued, cannot exist. To exist means to be perceived, therefore bodies have no existence without mind. The mind creates the material world, and this world has existence only in mind. This is the idealistic position in modern philosophy.

DAVID HUME went a step further and showed that, on the basis of Locke's dualism, we cannot prove even the existence of mind. All that we can prove is that ideas, impressions, come one after the other. Whence they come cannot be proven. There is, for Hume, no material world and no mind; just a succession of impressions.

Philosophy could not stand this very logical position. Since it was logical, thinkers began to ask if the premises upon which it was based, those of a dualism between mind and matter, might not be false.

The Views of Leibnitz

LEIBNITZ attacked the problem by holding that body, or matter, is not something dead and static, but is composed of many monads or centers of force. These monads differ in clearness of their perceptions, and mind consists of these perceptions. Every monad or center of force has the power of perception. It perceives or represents and expresses in itself the entire universe. The higher the monad, the clearer are these perceptions.

For Leibnitz the human organism contains a central monad or "queen monad" which has before it the picture of the entire body. God, in creating the world, so arranged things that the monads composing the body and the "queen monad" are in perfect harmony. "Souls act," he writes, "according to the laws of final causes, by means of desire, ends, and means. Bodies act according to the laws of efficient causes or motions. And the two realms are in harmony with one another."

It is evident that here Leibnitz is attempting to erase to some extent the complete difference between mind and matter by holding that both are centers of force and that the "queen monad" is simply a clearer and more perfect monad than those composing matter or the body. Although no monad, whether it be "queen" or less clear monad, can influence another monad, there is a certain relationship among monads. The mind or soul monad holds its place because it is a better monad, not because it is something different from other monads.

Kant and Later German Philosophers

With KANT there emerged a fairly clear-cut theory of the mind as the only source of knowledge. While Kant admitted the existence of a world other than the mind, a world from which the mind received impressions, he held that the mind can know nothing of this world, this "thing-in-itself." The mind receives impressions according to its nature or its categories and shapes them into patterns which conform not to the world outside mind, but to the nature of mind.

We know, then, only what our mind shapes and moulds. We can, because of the necessities of the moral nature, believe in the existence of the "thing-in-itself," but mind can never prove it, nor can mind prove what it would be without mind. Indeed, we are shut up in our minds, and must interpret everything in terms of our minds. Space and time, for example, are not realities existing by themselves, but are ways our minds have of receiving and shaping sensations. "Take away the thinking subject," Kant argues, "and the entire corporeal world will vanish, for it is nothing but the appearance in the sensibility of our subject."

Kant's position gave rise to the great German Idealistic movement of the eighteenth century. Thinkers who followed him felt that the only solution of the problem of mind and matter lay in eliminating matter. This seemed the most logical approach. Mind seemed evident, but matter had to be interpreted as something other than and outside of mind, different from mind. But this gave rise to the problem of how these two so different things could interact. This problem and all its difficulties could be eliminated by doing away with matter. Such a solution, as we have seen, was not new, but it was greatly strengthened by the work which Kant had done. He had pointed the way and produced strong evidence that this way was right and true.

JOHANN GOTTLIEB FICHTE took his cue from Kant and argued that the mind, or ego, was everything, and that there was nothing outside of it. He held that Kant's "thing-in-itself" could not possibly exist outside of the mind. The material world is, for him, a creation of the mind and serves as a limiting principle for the mind. The material world is a projection into space of objects which exist only in the mind.

However, the mind which creates this world is not the mind of the individual, according to Fichte, but is a universal mind, an absolute ego. This universal mind is before and above all individual minds and is the creator of the material world which has existence only in the universal mind. The material world "is not a world of dead things, arranged in a spatial-temporal-causal order; the latter is the revelation in human consciousness of the absolute principle, and could not exist if it were not for the universal ego." Fichte seeks to solve the problem of mind and matter by making matter a creation of mind and denying it any existence other than that supplied it by mind.

FRIEDRICH WILHELM SCHELLING leaned heavily on Fichte in developing his theory of mind. For him, the absolute mind has limited itself in creating the material world. But, this material world is alive; it is mind at a lower level, a less clear level. Actually there is only a difference of degree between the material world and mind. They are both mind of a certain sort.

Although he approaches this question somewhat differently, HEGEL follows in this same idealistic tradition. For him, mind passes through three stages of evolution: subjective mind, objective mind, and absolute mind. The subjective mind is dependent upon nature as soul, is opposed to nature as consciousness, and is reconciled with nature as spirit. At its highest, mind is creative of the world which it knows.

Mind, for Hegel, is creative of the material world, therefore in both that world and in mind we discover the same dialectical principles. Throughout the universe Hegel finds mind creating and realizing itself in objects and institutions.

This idealistic tradition, developing out of Kant's thinking, held sway in Germany for a century. However, it was not satisfying to all philosophers. Many believed that the material world was too real to be explained merely as a creation of mind, whether it be individual mind or absolute mind. HERBART is representative of this position. He held that "things-in-themselves" do exist and the world is not merely our idea. He based his thinking upon the premise that experience is the only source of knowledge.

Every sensation is a sensation of something outside of the mind. Thus, there must be a real world which influences the mind. This world is composed, according to Herbart, of many simple principles or "reals." This world of reals is static and unchanging. The soul is a real which asserts itself against other reals and thus produces sensations in itself. These sensations, as they are organized, constitute the mind. Mental life is, for him, a most complicated fusion of ideas, a union and organization of sensations which become ideas or units of the mind. Mind, then, is material, of the same general nature as the material world.

Bradley, Royce, and Bergson

There are three principal answers to the question of the relationship between mind and the material universe. One answer is that of Idealism, which holds that mind is in some way the creator of that which appears as matter. The method by which mind creates matter may be thought of differently by various idealists, but in every case it is mind which is the real thing, and matter is a creation of mind, dependent upon mind for its existence. The more recent idealists, F. H. BRADLEY, JOSIAH ROYCE, HENRI BERGSON, and others, develop this position in one way or another.

Comte, James, Dewey, Santayana

Another approach is that of Realism. Here it is held that mind and the material world are actually both material. The realists hold that mind is another form of the material world, finer perhaps, but actually material. Recent representatives of Realism are the Positivist, AUGUSTE COMTE, and the Pragmatists, WILLIAM JAMES and JOHN DEWEY. Although these men differ in many respects, they agree that mind is a kind of behavior. We have, for example, acts which are of such a nature as to be held mind-less. Other acts have a different nature, and we can refer to them as minded or having the characteristic of mind. Thus, for these philosophers mind is not a thing but is rather a kind of behavior.

With the modern emphasis upon natural science and a moving away on the part of many philosophers from the more spiritual interpretation of the universe, the idealistic position has been in an eclipse. The materialistic point of view has seemed most logical in a world of natural science. BERTRAND RUSSELL has been more at home in this modern world than GEORGE SANTAYANA. John Dewey has expressed the thoughts of the man in the machine shop and on the street, the man of "common sense," more completely than did Fichte or Hegel.

But, with the coming of the present-day world, a world in which men are questioning the materialistic premises seriously, there are indications that some new form of Idealism is just over the horizon. Values, spiritual experiences, ideals and aspirations do not seem to be accounted for completely by materialism. There is a growing feeling among present-day thinkers that the next great step in philosophy will be a new Idealism.

Chapter X

IDEAS AND THINKING

HERACLITUS SOCRATES PLATO ARISTOTLE
GALILEO DESCARTES SPINOZA
LOCKE KANT HEGEL COMTE
MILL JAMES DEWEY

*Whence come our ideas? Are they born with us and
do they become conscious in time, or do we get them
from sense experiences? Or does some god reveal them
to us? What are the laws of thinking? How do the
thinkers of each age go about thinking?*

Everyone thinks. We all have "ideas" or thoughts, we
see the world about us, and remember what we see. We
make inferences from the facts which we experience, draw
conclusions, and make these the bases of our actions. Man,
we hold, is a thinking being.

Whether or not animals think has been a question of
interest for generations. Your dog sees, hears, and feels. He
receives impressions from his environment. Further, he appears to draw conclusions from these impressions and to
act upon them. He finds that an individual is friendly, and
he acts accordingly. He finds that another individual is not
friendly, and acts upon this fact. Does your dog think?
Does he have ideas?

The earliest philosophers struggled with the problems
which grouped themselves around the question of ideas
and thinking. How is it that ideas are formed? Where do

we get our ideas, and of what nature are they? How do we reach conclusions upon which we act? How do we come to know that one act will bring happiness and another misery? All these, and many other problems, have appeared upon the pages of philosophic writings from the very beginning of human thought, and they still fascinate philosophers.

When early man gave thought to these problems, he reached the only conclusion possible in his culture. He believed that his ideas came to him from the world of spirits which surrounded him at all times. Gods put good ideas in his mind, and demons put evil ideas there. He felt that his thoughts came from outside himself, from the forces and powers which governed and controlled every phase of his life.

In the history of philosophy, the explanation of ideas and thinking has tended steadily away from the supernatural. Man has struggled to explain thinking in natural terms and as a result of natural processes and subject to natural laws.

What Thinking Meant to the Early Greek Philosophers

The early Greek philosophers were interested primarily in the nature of substance and gave little attention to man and his thought processes. They centered their attention upon nature, the world in which man lived, and attempted to explain how it came to be and what was its essence. HERACLITUS was one of the few who gave some attention to the problem of thinking. He felt that reason was a more certain source of knowledge than sense perception and that the rational life was the best life. Reason, for him, was akin to divine reason, a sort of spark of the divine in man, which was able to see truth in ways not given to man devoid of reason. Most men, he said, live not by reason but by passion.

EMPEDOCLES believed that since man knew the elements of which the universe is created, he must be composed of these elements. Like is known by like, he argued. Therefore, if man knows the universe, he must be like the universe. Man knows water because particles of water pass from water to the eye and are there met by particles of water in the eye. This contact of water with water enables man to know water. He applied this same line of reasoning to man's knowledge of other things in the universe.

Sense experience, for DEMOCRITUS, was obscure knowledge. We really know, he argued, when we transcend sense perception. When sense perception can carry us no further, genuine knowledge begins. Here we are in a realm that deals with finer things than the senses can show us, the realm of true knowledge.

These early Greeks, though interested primarily in the problems of the nature of substance, recognized that man's ability to have ideas, to know the world about him, presented an equally difficult problem. But their suggested solutions of this problem were in line with their materialistic bent. In some way, they felt, ideas and the material world must be similar, though perhaps finer.

This interest of the early Greek thinkers in the nature of the universe seemed a great waste of time to the *Sophists*. They felt that the many theories suggested by different thinkers pointed to the fact that no real explanation was possible. Thus, they turned from such questions to concern themselves with man. And the conclusion of their study was that the knowing subject was the thing of most importance and therefore that which should be studied. Further, they concluded that knowledge depends wholly upon the individual knower. My ideas are true for me and yours for you, they would say. For them there could be no objective absolute truth which would be the same for all men. Rather, that which seems true to a man is true for him. "Man," PROTAGORAS held, "is the measure of all things," even truth.

This criticism of knowledge, this making of all knowledge dependent upon the individual knower, was a challenge to those who assumed without question man's ability to know truth. By denying the possibility of sure and universal knowledge, the Sophists made it necessary for philosophers to investigate thinking most carefully and thereby opened the door for a theory of knowledge. They hastened the discovery of the correct laws of thought and the development of "logic," which is the science of thought.

According to Socrates, Plato, and Aristotle

SOCRATES took up the challenge of the Sophists and asserted without hesitation that the problem of knowledge was the key to all other problems. He was interested particularly in discovering a method for reaching true knowledge as distinct from mere opinion. The method which he developed consisted of first clearing away all false notions and then proceeding with careful observation and thinking in order to reach universal judgments. Amid the diversity of thought Socrates attempted to discover that which was common to all, a ground which could not be disputed.

By constant questioning and careful examination of statements and opinions, Socrates proceeded to establish definitions which he later used as bases for further opinions and statements of fact. Having established a principle, he used it to define other principles.

It is customary to speak of logic as either inductive or deductive. Induction consists in starting with some particular fact and arriving at a general principle. Deduction starts with a general principle and shows its application to particular facts. Deduction is the more characteristic method of the early thinkers; and induction is the method of modern science. Socrates used something of both methods.

PLATO was among the first philosophers to offer a fairly complete theory of knowledge. He agreed with Socrates that sense perception could not give genuine knowledge. Man must pass beyond the senses to ideas which are not derived from experience and are not dependent upon experience. The soul, he taught, comes into the world carrying within itself true ideas. These have been planted in it in an existence previous to birth. True knowledge is reached when these ideas are remembered and take the front of consciousness. This is "conceptual knowledge" as distinguished from sense knowledge which is actually not knowledge. This reveals the essence of things rather than their mere accidental factors.

ARISTOTLE carried this line of reasoning further by holding that although our world of experience is the real world, genuine knowledge consists of knowing the reasons or causes of things. To reach these basic causes man must follow certain laws of logic or true processes of thought. The pattern of true thought is, he argued, the "syllogism," in which we move from a generally accepted principle to a particular.

A famous example of the syllogism is:

> All men are mortal.
> Socrates is a man.
> Therefore Socrates is mortal.

All men are mortal. This is a general principle which is evidenced through numerous experiences. We may look about us and, after observing a number of men and seeing that all sooner or later die, reach the general conclusion that all men are mortal. Since Socrates was a man, he can be classified under the general heading of "all men." What is true about all men must be true about Socrates. If all men are mortal, the particular man Socrates must also be mortal.

Aristotle worked out the science of deductive logic so completely that little or nothing has been added to it even to the present. He laid down all the laws and gave examples which men have been able to follow with success ever since.

The Views of the Later Greek Philosophers

EPICURUS turned to the senses as the criterion of truth. We must, he argued, trust our senses. All knowledge comes through the senses, and error is a mistake in judgment. If we observe correctly, we arrive at truth. When we make false interpretations of our sensations, or refer them to the wrong objects, we make mistakes and do not have true knowledge. We learn, then, by using our senses, and we must be very careful that we use them correctly.

We perceive copies of objects, and these are true copies since they come directly from the objects themselves. These copies strike the sense organs and produce ideas in us. If we do not get our ideas mixed up, we have the truth about the real world.

The *Stoics* agreed with the Epicureans in holding that all knowledge comes through sense perception. At birth, they maintained, the soul is an empty tablet which receives impressions from things. These impressions persist and form memory-images, and from these images ideas are formed. The mind organizes its impressions into general ideas. Thus, all knowledge which we have comes, they hold, from impressions and our organizing of these. If we have an immediate conviction that there is a real object corresponding to our idea, then that real object does exist.

It is evident that the Stoics disagreed completely with Plato. Ideas are not in the soul at birth, as Plato had argued. They come to the soul from the outside and through the senses. The mind does not have ideas until the senses give it impressions which it can organize into ideas. Plato was a "rationalist" in holding that the mind has ideas independently of experience. The Stoics were "empiricists" in holding that ideas come from experience.

Greek thought gave us these two great traditions in philosophy. The rationalists held that the ideas which man has are innate. Experience simply serves to stir them into consciousness. The empiricists held that the mind has no ideas of its own. It looks out upon the world through the windows of the senses. When these senses are stimulated by this outer world, they impress these experiences upon the mind, which in turn organizes them into ideas. The progress of philosophy is more or less a battle between various forms of these two major positions as regards ideas.

The Medieval Christian View

One phase of the conflict between the Nominalists and the Realists among the medieval Christian philosophers was concerned with thinking. The Realists held that ideas are general concepts or universals which have an existence independently of things or experiences. Ideas are real in the sense that they are not created by the individual's experiences. The Nominalists held that ideas are the results of experience and can have no existence except as they are supported by experience. We build general ideas, such as justice and goodness, out of experiences; and without experiences, individual and unique experiences, we could have no general ideas.

With AUGUSTINE we find ourselves in a period one of the chief characteristics of which was a distinction between ordinary ideas received through experience and revealed knowledge received from God. Augustine held that man has natural knowledge of the world about him. He knows physical nature, and can act on this knowledge. For the ordinary needs of living this knowledge is sufficient. But there is also a higher knowledge which comes not from experiencing nature, nor is it of the same kind as natural knowledge. This is revealed knowledge, which comes through faith.

In this way Augustine and the Christian scholars sought to protect the doctrines of the Church. Many of these doctrines were not in accord with the logic of human thinking. They seemed to contradict everything which man found in experience. But these thinkers held that they were true because of a knowledge different from and above natural knowledge. I know because God has revealed it to me, was the position taken by them.

This interpretation enabled the Church to extend the borders of knowledge far beyond that of natural experience. When man reached the limits of his ability to do logical thinking, to reason in line with the principles of Aristotle, he was able, by this method of divine knowledge, to go on to accept the doctrines of the Church.

This position became fundamental to the Church's philosophy, and developed into the doctrine of the "two-fold truth." One phase of truth is that which can be substantiated by logical reasoning. Another phase is that which is substantiated by faith and the authority of the Church. THOMAS AQUINAS made this basic to his general position. One phase of his thinking dealt with ideas received from sensations. He argued that genuine knowledge is conceptual knowledge and that concepts have their origin in sensations. But the mind is able to form universal notions from these sensations. External objects act on the soul. This raw material of knowledge is received and worked into conceptual knowledge by the higher faculties of the soul.

But there is also intuitive knowledge which is superior to knowledge gained through sensations, through reason, or through mere faith. This knowledge has its source in divine revelation and also gains its authority from the divine. We know about God, immortality, the divinity of Jesus, and other doctrines of the Church, not by reasoning, but by this higher type of knowledge.

JOHN DUNS SCOTUS goes further than Aquinas in limiting the sphere of reason. He did not believe that any of the Church's doctrines could be demonstrated by reason, and held that they all depended upon revelation. Reason, he held, could not prove these doctrines, but it was in perfect harmony with them. If, however, reason reached conclusions different from the doctrines of the Church, reason had to bow to superior authority and admit that it was wrong.

Thus, although Christian thinkers accepted the two-fold truth, it is evident that knowledge coming from divine revelation was thought to be superior to that coming from experience. The natural result was that human reason was constantly being corrected by the Church. Ideas which men gained by hard thinking were found to be opposed to the authority of religion, and the Church was powerful enough to suppress such conclusions in the interest of what it held to be revealed knowledge.

Galileo and the Beginning of the Scientific Attitude

This condition could not, of course, continue indefinitely. As man began to gain confidence in himself and to challenge the authority of the Church along other lines, it was inevitable that he would challenge the authority of revealed knowledge. As this developed strength, the fundamental bases of Scholastic thought began to crumble, and man stood more and more upon his own intellectual feet.

He saw the power of sense experience and the equal power of reasoning from premises such as Aristotle had established. The syllogism and sense experience gained in respect among men and the authority of the Church began to weaken. Man was demanding that all knowledge rest upon the ability of the human mind and not upon some revealed authority.

GALILEO, as representative of this movement, rejected authority and mystical speculation in matters of science, and held that all our ideas should rest upon observation or experimentation. But, he would add to experience, understanding. He would build ideas out of observation, experiment, and thought.

The scientists of the sixteenth and seventeenth centuries followed in this direction. They realized what could be done with observation and experimentation, and were unwilling that any other authority should determine man's thinking. As these men were more and more able to demonstrate the results of their position, the authority of extrarational processes came into question. This led to an increase of confidence in the human mind to build its own ideas and thought patterns. In other words, man was demanding the right to think for himself and reach conclus. is independently of authority.

Bacon, Descartes, Spinoza

This led inevitably to an interest in the processes by which man formulates his ideas and the grounds for their authority. FRANCIS BACON suggested a method for receiving true impressions and building them into true ideas. Having cleared the mind of all "idols" or prejudices and false points of view, he would have man observe his world carefully. As data was collected, man would be in a position to draw conclusions which would have the authority of the data upon which they were based.

To reach a justified conclusion, man must study all instances in which a certain factor appears, then those instances in which it does not appear, and then those instances in which it appears with variations of greater or less. For example, if one is seeking to discover whether or not drinking certain water causes a disease, he would study all cases of the disease in which the water was drunk and all cases in which water was not drunk. Then he would study the amount of the water drunk in each case. On the basis of data gathered from these studies, he will be in a position to conclude whether or not drinking the water is the cause of the disease.

DESCARTES sought a basis for establishing truth. He reasoned that one must start with premises which cannot be denied. Mathematics seemed to give him such premises. In mathematics he saw a model for correct thinking, the method of reasoning from self-evident truths. This appeared to him to be the method by which all true knowledge could be obtained. Thus he sought first for self-evident truths. The one truth which he was able to discover was: I think, therefore I am. With this as a basis, he reasoned to a body of ideas which he did not believe could be disputed. These ideas were, for him, clear and distinct, and therefore true beyond question.

Descartes established as a fundamental principle of all thinking that all true ideas must be clear and distinct. The mind has its norms of clearness and distinctness, norms given to the mind because of its nature. Thus, knowledge comes to man, Descartes argued, not by sense perception, but through careful reasoning from fundamental premises; and each idea can be accepted if, after it has been reasoned out, it is clear and distinct.

SPINOZA held that man can have three kinds of knowledge. Obscure and inadequate ideas, he argued, depend upon sense perception, and are the result of the imagination plus the failure of the individual to interpret correctly. Adequate knowledge, clear and distinct ideas, rational knowledge, is the result of reasoning from things already known. The third type of knowledge is intuitive knowledge, which is the finest kind of knowledge and gives a truth which cannot be disputed. Here no error is possible.

Locke, Berkeley, Hume, and Leibnitz

JOHN LOCKE made the "study of knowing" his chief occupation. His conclusion was that all ideas come to the individual through sense experience. The mind is, for him, a blank tablet with only the power to assimilate or organize impressions. As contact with the environment stimulates the senses and causes impressions, the mind receives and organizes these into ideas and concepts. Thus, there are no innate ideas in the mind; all its ideas come from without. The ideas which are received through sense impressions he called simple ideas. As such ideas are organized, complex ideas are built up by the mind.

Locke's writings are concerned in considerable part with the classifying of ideas and the study of the power of things to produce ideas.

GEORGE BERKELEY went further than Locke did in his emphasis on the mind, for he held that we cannot know anything beyond what is in the mind. We cannot know the material world since we do not have it in our minds. Indeed, we cannot prove that the ideas which we have are a result of contact with a material world. To account for the consistency among ideas, Berkeley held that God gives us our ideas. We receive them not from a material world, but from God who is mind on a higher level.

DAVID HUME went still further and held that all we have or can know is ideas. We cannot prove the existence of a material world or of God. There is just a stream of ideas. The mind is this stream of ideas, for him. We receive impressions, but do not know from whence they come. Then the impressions are organized into ideas. As we experience ideas we find that they bear certain relations with each other. Thus we get ideas of relations and come to the idea, for example, of cause and effect. But we cannot say that objects in a material universe are so related. All we can say is that ideas follow each other in a certain order, and this order we call cause and effect.

All the contents of the mind are ideas in certain relations. Beyond this we cannot go. We have ideas, and think in terms of them and their relations. Here we must stop. We cannot demonstrate anything beyond this.

LEIBNITZ disagreed with Locke, Berkeley, and Hume, by holding that the monad is self-contained and can in no way be affected or influenced from the outside. Thus, all ideas must be contained within the monad. Experience merely brings these ideas to the forefront. "The senses," he wrote, "can arouse, justify, and verify such truths, but not demonstrate their eternal and inevitable certitude." Ideas and truths are innate in the mind as tendencies. We do not receive ideas, but have them all the time.

Leibnitz held that Locke had not gone far enough. He said that Locke was right in holding that there is nothing in the intellect that did not exist before in sensation, but that he should add "except the intellect itself."

All these later philosophers were attempting to reach a satisfactory explanation of how the individual, living in and experiencing an environment, could have ideas, thoughts, could think. Some had reached the conclusion that the individual faced the environment pure and undefiled and received his ideas from the environment and through the senses. Others had argued that ideas were innate in the mind and needed only the stimulation of sensations to bring them to consciousness.

Kant, Fichte, Hegel

KANT sought to overcome the difficulties of both extremes by holding that we do receive impressions from the environment, from the "thing-in-itself," but that the mind is of such a nature that it shapes these impressions into ideas. The mind, for him, is like a bowl with many crevices and strange depressions in its contour. When one pours water into the bowl, it takes the shape of the bowl, filling all the crevices. In the same way the environment pours impressions into the mind and they are received by the mind and shaped in accord with the nature of this mind.

But knowledge is universal. This is due to the fact that all minds are fundamentally alike. They all have certain fundamental categories such as totality, unity, plurality, reality, and the like. Because all minds are of the same general nature, we all think very much alike. We organize impressions into ideas. But these are ideas of the mind and cannot be applied to a world outside the mind. This leads to the conclusion that we cannot know the world outside the mind. We can act as though it existed, and can correct our ideas in terms of the additional impressions which we receive. But beyond this we cannot go. Our ideas are a result of the kind of thinking organ which we have, and are determined by its nature.

We can, of course, bring ideas together into large, general ideas, and can act as though these generalizations were true. Indeed, to satisfy our moral natures, we must so act. But here we are dealing with judgments and not provable ideas.

Kant's masterful argument for the mind as the creator of ideas led FICHTE to the conclusion that one can understand only that which he can create freely in thought. The ideas which one has, the contents of one's consciousness, are results of an act of creation. The ego, active and free, creates everything that man knows, even the "non-ego" or that which seems not to be the ego.

By ego Fichte means universal reason or intelligence as such, not the individual self. Reason, the whole array of ideas which one has, is prior to the individual and is the creation of a reason which existed before the individual man. We know only our ideas. These are not the result of a material world which we experience but come from the universal ego.

HEGEL took the position that the processes of the human mind and those of nature are the same. In both he found what he termed a "dialectical process" operating. If one studies the mind, he will find it full of contradictions, full of disagreements, of opposites. But, a further study will reveal that there is a process in the mind by which each pair of opposites is reconciled in a synthesis which includes both but on a higher level.

This process is everywhere. First there is a thesis or affirmation, then we discover the antithesis to this thesis or its contradiction. The highest form of thought is the reconciling of both in a synthesis which lifts thinking one step higher. The human mind does not stop with contradictions, but strives to get rid of them by effecting a synthesis. This is not to be confused with a compromise. In a true synthesis the values of both the thesis and the antithesis are conserved and together they move toward new values.

The highest function of the mind, then, is that activity which enables one to see things whole, to see opposites unified. Here man rises to the true height of his nature. Thought moves from the simple ideas to more complex notions, from the individual to the rich and full.

Hegel saw what few philosophers had realized to his day. He recognized that thought is not a static thing, a mere receiving of impressions. Thought, for him, is a process, a moving from one point to another. The thinking being is a living logical process in which there is an unfolding and a progression. Study of thinking convinced Hegel that thinking moves from the simple to the complex not by discreet jumps but by a gradual development into syntheses which become theses for still higher syntheses.

But, since nature and thought follow the same process of evolution, Hegel reasoned that all reality is a logical process of evolution. The universe is a logical process of thought and not dead material upon which thought works.

This point of view, that everything is a logical process of thought obeying the laws of evolution from the simple to the more complex, held sway in Germany and influenced other countries until the middle of the nineteenth century. Indeed, even though it lost some of its popularity after that date, it continued to influence world thought for many years after.

A counter influence was the work of HERBART who looked upon thinking as the organization and integration of reals. Through experience the soul throws off reals which are organized in consciousness into ideas and points of view. Many of these are pushed into the subconscious, there to wait until the time is favorable for them to come back into consciousness and dominate it.

Comte, Mill, Spencer

COMTE took the position that the only knowledge worth while was knowledge which could be used. He was not concerned with theories of knowledge, with attempts to discover what knowledge is, but was interested in discovering knowledge which could be used in actual life situations. If one has knowledge, ideas, which work, which meet problems and solve them, that is all that is necessary. Their source or history is of little or no importance.

JOHN STUART MILL based his entire logical theory upon the laws of association. He sought to discover how and why one passes from the known to the unknown by the process of inferences. This became his theory of induction. As one collects data through experience, he draws certain conclusions. His data serves as a basis for his conclusions. When he goes beyond this data to generalizations he is acting upon a belief that nature is uniform. Mill believed that man had a right to so act.

Our ideas are a result, then, of experiences and of careful inferences from them. There are laws, Mill held, by which these inferences can be made. These laws have authority because experience has proved them valuable. Men have used them in the past and have arrived at conclusions which were successful. Therefore, the test of experience has been met, and we can afford to make use of them with a high degree of confidence.

HERBERT SPENCER held that all thought was founded upon the fact of relations. We think in terms of differences and likenesses. Our conclusions, our ideas are of these differences and likenesses among things. We know things in terms of their differences and likenesses and not directly. Here we have a theory of the relativity of knowledge. Ideas are expressions of the relationships between things.

James and Dewey

From the theory of knowledge many modern thinkers, under the influence of psychological advances of the last century, have turned to a study of thinking itself. WIL-

LIAM JAMES held that thinking is an instrument, and is no better than its service in a situation. We think for a purpose. Thus, James stresses the thinking process, interest in how it works and how it can be made more efficient.

JOHN DEWEY has given us one of the clearest analyses of reflective thinking ever worked out. He identifies reflective thinking with problem solving, and holds that man does not think unless he has a problem to solve. Mere passing fancy, daydreaming, and the like are not thinking in any real sense of the term. But, when one is faced with a situation for which he does not have a ready solution, he engages in thinking.

Now, the process through which he must go if he is to be successful in reaching a solution to his problem consists of several fairly well-defined steps. First, there must be a clearly defined problem. This is followed by a period during which data relative to the problem is collected. Then, on the basis of the data, a hypothesis or possible solution is arrived at. The fourth step is a mental trying out of the suggested solution or hypothesis to discover if there is any reason why it should not be the desired solution. If the hypothesis stands the test of this mental trial, it is put into action, and the results recorded. If this test is also satisfactory, the knowledge gained is generalized or applied to other similar situations, thus becoming a general principle which may then become a basis for future thought.

All reflective thinking takes place in this fashion, according to Dewey. If each step is carried through carefully and no mistakes are made, there is a high degree of probability that the thinker will arrive at an adequate solution of his problem. If, however, any step is neglected or the process is not carefully followed, the accepted hypothesis may prove false.

Other philosophers hold that Dewey is here considering only one type of thinking, and is neglecting the most important type, creative thinking. Studies seem to indicate that creative thinking proceeds by three stages. First, there is a period of preparation during which the thinker studies his problem carefully and collects data pertinent to it. Then there must be a period of incubation when this data and the problem are put aside, as it were, to become assimilated. This is, they say, a subconscious process which cannot be rushed and the outcome of which cannot be predicted. If it is successful, the third stage will reveal itself, a stage when the individual experiences illumination or the flash of a possible solution of hypothesis. This hypothesis is not necessarily the sought-for solution. It must be tested both mentally and practically to discover if it is adequate. If it fails, the problem must be returned to the subconscious and the process of incubation continued.

Modern philosophy seems to be moving more and more in the direction suggested by James and Dewey and other Pragmatists. While there are many philosophers who are struggling with the problem of knowledge and are seeking to discover how ideas are formed, the modern spirit of efficiency has so dominated many thinkers that they become impatient with such activity. They can see no real value in determining whether ideas are innate or whether they oome from the outer world. The problems with which Kant, Fichte, Schelling, Herbart, and others struggled, seem to them meaningless. Their interest is not in the genesis of ideas so much as in their working in actual life situations. The philosopher, they hold, is concerned with life and life situations. Here ideas are tools for solving problems. Thinking is a way one may go about meeting difficult situations. And its efficiency is to be measured by the success which the individual experiences in its use. If, by thinking, he solves his problem, the process has been satisfactory and his ideas true.

Chapter XI

SOME RECENT APPROACHES TO
PHILOSOPHY

KIERKEGAARD HEIDEGGER JASPERS SARTRE
WHITEHEAD RUSSELL MOORE CROCE UNAMUNO
TILLICH NIEBUHR MARITAIN BUBER

*Why re-examine old concepts and values? Is evil real
or an illusion? Is there a meaning to suffering? In the
face of inevitable death, what is the meaning of life?
Can the findings of science be reconciled with the concept of God? What is the function of moral laws in a
world explained by science?*

From the time of Plato and Aristotle, and even earlier,
philosophy has been largely concerned with helping man
to understand the basic, ordered pattern of the universe,
and man's relationship to man. These two large concerns
may be described as "metaphysical" and "ethical." In
some periods philosophers have sought to help men discover the meaning of God and in the light of this meaning
to live lives of goodness and rightness. At other times,
philosophers have concluded that men could live morally
without believing in God. All philosophies involve the critical analysis of concepts which many people accept in blind
faith.

In a changing world, however, old concepts and values
have to be re-examined. With the increasing importance
of scientific discovery, many of the traditional ideas about

the order of the universe began to change. With increasing economic progress and greater material comfort for individuals, both spiritual and ethical values have undergone subtle changes. In the middle of the nineteenth century, many keen thinkers sensed an inadequacy and inapplicability in much previous thought. The world, for these new philosophers, did not seem to be based on a neat and tidy absolute rule. The problem of man's existence had to be re-examined. New solutions were needed, new answers had to be found.

Kierkegaard and the Beginnings of Existentialism

SØREN KIERKEGAARD, a Danish philosopher and writer, took the position that religion was a personal experience. Using Kant's idea that the only thing we can "know" is experience as a stepping-off place, Kierkegaard evolved a philosophical system which divided existence into three categories; that is, he claimed that experience may be of three kinds: aesthetic, ethical, and religious. The child is an example of the individual who lives almost exclusively at the aesthetic level. For the child, all choices are made in terms of pleasure and pain, and experience is ephemeral, having no continuity, no meaning, but being merely a connection of isolated, non-related moments. The ethical level of experience involves choice; whenever conscious choice is made, one lives at the ethical level. At the religious level, one experiences a commitment to oneself, and an awareness of one's uniqueness and singleness. To live at the religious level means to make any sacrifice, any antisocial gesture that is required by being true to oneself. Clearly, these levels are not entirely separable, but may coexist: when one chooses the aesthetic level of existence, the very act of choice involved ethical experience; and when one makes choices at the ethical level, and these choices are true to one's own singleness, one lives at the religious level.

Kierkegaard believed that man, proceeding from one level of experience to another, would ultimately choose suffering and pain, and a constant awareness of the difference between ephemeral, temporal existence and ultimate truth. He concluded that only when man experiences the suffering of firm commitment to the religious level of experience can he be considered to be truly religious, and, further, that the suffering endured by God is greater than that endured by any man.

If religion, then, is a purely personal matter, truth is clearly subjective, quite separate from the "truth" of religious doctrine, for the truth of man's experience must emerge from his faithfulness to his own unique identity. Kierkegaard recognized this difference between the objective, universal truth, and the subjective, personal truth. Objective truth, such as that of geometry, is acquired by the intellect; subjective truth must be experienced by the total individual. One may *have* objective truth, but one must *be* religious truth.

The Views of Heidegger, Jaspers, and Sartre

MARTIN HEIDEGGER, a German, has perceived the meaningfulness of Kierkegaard's position that man is a tragic figure in a finite world. He agreed that man must become intensely aware of his own individuality, of the specialness of his own person. In that man is capable of questioning himself, existence precedes essence; that is, meaning can only be applied to what already *is* within an individual's experience. Man can define his existence by three traits: mood (or feeling), understanding, and speech. These traits Heidegger called *existentialia,* and the philosophic tradition derived from his theories is known as "existentialism." Only by questioning existence in terms of the existentialia can man become aware of his own true identity; and when he has found his identity, the essence of his existence, man is able to transcend the limits of the non-inquiring world and assert his destiny.

KARL JASPERS, a German psychologist and philosopher and a contemporary of Heidegger, has subscribed to many theories of the existential school. Jaspers' philosophy is also centered on the importance of the individual, and he has stressed the importance of the discrepancy between actual facts and the individual's interpretation of those facts. To Jaspers, truth is subjective, to a large extent non-rational, and constantly being reinterpreted by the individual. Freedom, according to Jaspers, is the ability of the individual to make spontaneous ethical decisions, and love is the highest level of existence.

Because of the importance of suffering in existentialism, and because of its concern with reconciling man with the necessity of death, it is not surprising that so many twentieth-century thinkers have been attracted by this philosophy. Because existentialism is intensely concerned with the individual, and with the concrete rather than the abstract, much of the keenest existential thought has come from writers and artists. JEAN-PAUL SARTRE, French playwright and novelist, has developed a philosophy which is, in many respects, negative. Yet much of his thought is founded on the optimistic principle that "Man is essentially a subjectively worthy being." Sartre recognized the pervasiveness of evil, holding that evil could not be redeemed, and that each individual man is responsible for the evil in the world. But he also credited man with the capacity for heroic action. The ultimate freedom, for Sartre, is the freedom to say "No." Man may not be able to overthrow evil, but he can—and must—refuse to co-operate with evil. The freedom to say "No," of course, can only be maintained by total consciousness; and man has, therefore, the responsibility to maintain his consciousness—both actual and spiritual—at all times. Man's existence precedes his essence, and from his existence man is free to make of himself what he chooses.

Three Philosophers of Science: Whitehead, Russell, and Moore

ALFRED NORTH WHITEHEAD, mathematician and scholar, was disturbed by the trend of twentieth-century scientists to "prove" with their science the non-existence of God. Deeply concerned by this non-religious current in philosophic thought, he sought to develop a philosophical system in which God and the findings of science would not be mutually exclusive or even unharmonious. The theory which

he evolved he called the "philosophy of organism." Whitehead perceived the relation of man to God in the fundamental processes of the world. He felt that philosophy
should not start with clear-cut items, but rather with a
sense of something going on, a process in an unending
continuum. Just as man's life is made up not of isolated
units strung together but of a connected series of minute
but interrelated moments, Whitehead felt that the world
is made up of essences and entities which, while undergo-
ing purely internal development, are nonetheless in active,
constant contact with each other. It is the interaction of
these essences throughout nature, and the effects of their
interrelation as they attempt to adjust to their environment,
that is the true world process. That the particular world
we know resulted from the combination of these forces
in a particular way, instead of the forces having interacted
differently to produce a different world, is the result of the
selection and ordering of God. For Whitehead, the ultimate good is the perception of God as this unifying force
behind the movement of the world process. Thus Whitehead constructed a metaphysical system which made room
for the incorporation of all scientific theory and discovery,
and which included as well all subjective experience.

BERTRAND RUSSELL, originally also a mathematician,
collaborated with Whitehead on many important early
projects, though they later disagreed philosophically. Russell's approach to mathematics was abstract and formal,
and he attempted to cast his philosophy in the same mould.
Russell has emphasized the importance of creativity for
man, as opposed to activity that is merely acquisitive and
possessive. Russell came to the conclusion that philosophy's
aim is to understand the world, and to isolate that which
may be considered knowledge from all that is merely spec-
ulative. To do this, man must rely on the scientific method.
In contrast with many other twentieth-century philosophers, both Whitehead and Russell agreed on the innate
dignity and value of man. It was this attitude that pro-
pelled Russell into the realms of social philosophy in his

later years, and his efforts on behalf of various social causes
have attracted wide attention.

GEORGE E. MOORE was a neo-realist whose position was
similar to that of Russell. Moore developed an ethical
theory which maintained that such words as "good" and
"right" have no objective meaning, and cannot be recognized as natural objects scientifically. "Goodness" and
"rightness" are states or conditions which are simple, un-
analyzable, and indefinable.

Logical Positivism

At the same time that existentialism gained importance
in world thought and Whitehead's approach to metaphysical philosophy was claiming wide attention, a philosophic
school was emerging which was to make radical charges
against the very nature of philosophy itself. This school
was "Logical Positivism." Among prominent thinkers in this
area were LUDWIG WITTGENSTEIN and the men who established the group known as the "Vienna Circle," MORITZ
SCHLICK and RUDOLF CARNAP. Instead of believing that
the province of philosophy is to understand the world, they
believed that its function is the analysis of the uses of language and the properties of sentences. To the logical positivists, all knowledge is empirical, and is derived from
sense experience; that is, all knowledge can be verified
either by personal experience or by knowing what observations would be required in order to verify by personal
experience. Because there may be an infinite number of
experiences relevant to the verification of any empirical
observation, the truth of such observations is at best probable, and may never be established absolutely. The most
radical charge of the logical positivists, though, is that the
statements of metaphysics, theology, and ethics are fac-
tually meaningless. For example, "Crime is wrong" as a
sentence makes only one factual, verifiable observation,
"Crime is." Wrongness, having no existence as an actual,
observable phenomenon, communicates only a feeling, not
a fact. Logical positivists claim that such "pseudo-proposi-
tions" of theology, ethics, and metaphysics are the result

of the misunderstanding and misuse of language. Because we use the word "God," they say, does not necessarily mean that there *is* a God; and yet, in error, we continue to make decisions concerning this non-verifiable concept. Inevitably, logical positivism, when carried to its extreme conclusion, becomes a matter of semantic interpretation rather than a creative philosophy. But its impact on twentieth-century philosophic thought has been profound, and its contribution to the clarification of thought and expression should not be minimized.

Two Philosophers of the Spirit

MIGUEL DE UNAMUNO was a Spanish poet, novelist, scholar, and philosopher of tremendous originality. His entire life was a struggle against the imposition of formalism upon the individual, and in his writing he constantly created new literary forms—novels, plays, and poetry—rather than submit to those established by tradition. Unamuno believed that only the internal will of an individual is real, and that the external world around him is merely mist; and, further, that the will of the individual person and the spiritual conflicts produced by its passions contain the final sense of all existence. The basic urge of life, thought Unamuno, is not simply to go on living, but to grow and to develop. Therefore the fundamental problem of life is the necessity of coping with the idea of death, which stops all growth. Each man lives in the agony of conflict between his will's need for a life after death, and his reason's denial of life after death. If one is to exist in meaningful terms, one must accept this frustration, and in spite of the awareness of death one must will passionate action; for even meaningless action, if it is profoundly motivated from the inner core of an individual's existence, will provide the necessary balance to the twentieth century's stifling, all-pervading dependence on impersonal reason.

BENEDETTO CROCE, an Italian critic and historian, concerned himself largely with problems of aesthetics. Croce took the position that the spirit is the only reality, though it manifests itself in various different guises in the external world, a concept similar to that developed by Whitehead. Croce extended this idea by maintaining that the physical does not exist at all, but is merely a construction of the mind. For example, a work of art is an image created in the mind of the artist and communicated to the minds of the audience. Only the image is a work of art; the physical object—painting, piece of sculpture, or other form—is merely a practical *act* to aid reproduction of the image. This concept is of great importance in the understanding of much modern art.

Some Current Philosophers in the Religious Tradition

Although much of contemporary philosophy has implied a negation of the concept of God, many twentieth-century philosophers have found themselves closer to the traditional religious points of view. They recognize the need for a new set of moral values as well as do the agnostics in the philosophical fraternity, but they believe that such values can be found by a re-examination and a redefinition of religious principles.

PAUL TILLICH, a German Protestant theologian, sees a true "God above the God of Theism." Man is beset by anxiety over the inevitability of physical death, but he has the responsibility to accept this anxiety, to take it upon himself. In so doing, he achieves transcendence. For Tillich, religion is man's striving for the ultimate, the absolute. There can be no atheistic society, since striving for any absolute is, by definition, religious activity, and the point of a society's existence is to strive toward a goal. In spite of a possible lack of meaning in existence, faith constitutes acceptance of what is given.

REINHOLD NIEBUHR, an American Protestant theologian, abjured the traditional liberal Protestant point of view that man is essentially good. On the contrary, according to Niebuhr, only God is good, and man is beset by sin. Man's only hope for salvation is to rely on the goodness of God.

JACQUES MARITAIN, a neo-Thomistic French Catholic, reconciled existential philosophy with the Thomistic tradition. To Maritain, all forms of knowledge—scientific, metaphysical, and mystical—are valid.

MARTIN BUBER, oriented in traditional Jewish values, has expressed the view that man was made less than human by the encroachments of science and mechanization. With the increase of dehumanization in the world, evil increases; and as men lose their identities, they lose their souls. To counteract this evil, Buber proposed his *Ich und Du* philosophy: *Ich,* the German word for "I," points out the importance of recognizing one's own individuality, one's own uniqueness; *Du,* the personal form of "you," emphasizes that the individuals one encounters must be loved and absorbed into one's own identity. But a generalized love of mankind is not enough; one must recognize the subjectivity of other people; and only when there is a harmonious balance within an individual of an awareness of his own self and an awareness of and love for the uniqueness of the selves of others can the individual find fulfillment and contentment.

As conditions change and man's environment becomes different, the mind of man must construct new philosophies for new times. What Plato and Aristotle did for their times, the thinkers of these recent days have done for theirs. And the mind of the philosopher, ever alert and sensitive to change, will continue to meet the challenges of the future as they arise.

CONCLUSION

One's experience, whether it be yours or mine or that of a Great Philosopher, may be thought of as many pieces of a jig-saw puzzle. The pieces are scattered everywhere in time and space. Some date back to earliest childhood while others are now in the process of being born. Some are the result of events far out near the horizon, while others are within one's own body. Often they have baffling shapes. Each one of us attempts to fit the pieces which are our experiences together so that they will form a picture that satisfies us.

You and I will often try to force pieces together when they are not made to fit in the way we desire. We will push and shove the pieces until the spaces between them are as small as possible. In doing this, we often force them out of shape. Thus, the final picture will be full of gaps which we may not be able to see but which are obvious to another of more experience and a keener insight and understanding. It will contain shocking contrasts of color. It will be small and incomplete.

Although the picture which you and I build may be adequate for most of the practical situations in which we find ourselves, there will come times of crisis when it will not prove adequate. A new experience may not fit into the picture at all. At such times we may try to rearrange the pieces so as to make a place for the new experience and thus fashion a very different picture, or we may throw the piece away, saying that it is an "unreal" experience, false, an illusion.

The experiences which a Great Philosopher employs to

weave his pattern, his philosophy, are far more numerous than ours. He attempts to include the entire universe, all that there is, in the picture which he constructs. Further, he is constantly on the alert to discover gaps, delicate shadings, fine cuts of the pieces with which he works. He trains his mind to a high degree of sensitivity to these differences. He can detect errors in the relationships between pieces which escape the less trained mind. Thus, the picture which he presents to the world is more accurate and complete than ours.

But even the Great Philosopher does not fashion a perfect picture. Only a God who knows all experiences of all men and can detect the finest relations can weave a perfect pattern. No philosopher, however great, is such a God. Thus the pattern of every Great Philosopher is imperfect and subject to improvement.

The history of philosophy is the story of how different philosophers have woven different patterns, proposed different solutions to the puzzle that is human experience. One philosopher will offer his solution and many will hail it as *the* answer. But it will not be long before another philosopher will discover and point to errors in his pattern, will reveal gaps and distortions, and will propose a somewhat different solution, one which seems to him more nearly perfect. He, in turn, will be followed by another who repeats the process.

In the pages which constitute this book we have seen how many Great Philosophers have attempted to piece together the world of human experience and have sought to answer some of the problems which have often interested us. We have seen how each has given a somewhat different answer and how later philosophers have corrected them and offered other solutions.

Thus, in a real sense, you and I can stand on the shoulders of all the Great Philosophers of the past. As we too look out upon the world, we can build our philosophies with the benefit of their experience and advice. We can learn from them, and by learning can make our picture more accurate and complete. Each philosopher says to us,

"Here is what the universe of human experience means to me, and here are the mistakes which I have found in the other philosophers who have preceded me. This is the best I know. Take it and begin your thinking from here."

You and I stand at the apex of centuries of struggling with the great problems of mankind. Behind us are great minds who offer us the service of their experience and thought. Indeed, we should be greater philosophers than any of the past since we have all the past to help us. Let us, then, consider what these of the past tell us. Let us ponder their advice carefully. And let us carry on from where they have had to stop. This is the way to progress and to a more perfect philosophy.

BIOGRAPHICAL NOTES

ABELARD, PETER: (1079–1142). Born at Palais, near Nantes, in Brittany. Opened a school in Paris in 1103 and became noted for his keen mind and theological penetration. Among his more important writings are *Ethics* and *Introduction to Theology*.

ALCUIN: (735–804). An English theologian and scholar. He was called from York to assist Charlemagne in establishing an educational system in the Frankish Empire. In his old age he retired to the monastery at Tours and devoted himself to theology.

ALTHUSIUS, JOHANNES: (1557–1638). A German thinker who is credited with founding the modern theory of natural law. He was born at Diedenshausen, studied at Basle and Geneva, and became Professor of Law at Herbon. Among his significant writings is *Political Method*.

AMBROSE, ST.: (340?–397). Born at Treves and became Bishop of Milan in 374. He often came into conflict with the highest authorities of his times. He wrote the great Christian hymn, "Te Deum Laudamus."

ANAXAGORAS: (500?–428 B.C.). Born at Clazomenae. After traveling widely he settled in Athens and opened a philosophic school there. Many famous thinkers studied with him. He was condemned to die for alleged impiety, but the sentence was changed to exile. He retired to Lampsacus and taught philosophy there until his death.

ANAXIMANDER: (611?–547? B.C.). Famous both as mathematician and as philosopher. He taught that the moon received her light from the sun and that the earth was round. He believed in the existence of many worlds.

ANAXIMENES OF MILETUS: (6th cent. B.C.). A Greek philosopher. He believed that the basic substance of the universe was air, from which everything else derives by rarefaction or condensation.

ANSELM, ST.: (1033–1109). He was Archbishop of Canterbury during the reigns of William Rufus and Henry I. He was a man of great piety and intellectual power and resisted efforts of the king to despoil the church of her dignity and revenue.

AQUINAS, THOMAS: (1225?–1274). Known as the "Angelic Doctor." He was descended from the counts of Aquino in Calabria. In 1323 Pope John XXII made him a saint. His writings form the basis for the Thomist sect. Several editions of his *Selected Writings* are available.

ARISTOTLE: (384–322 B.C.). Born at Stagira in Thrace. Began his study with Plato when he was 20 years of age. Philip of Macedon made him tutor to his son, Alexander the Great. He was accused of impiety and exiled to Chalcis where he died. Among his many important writings are *The Nicomachean Ethics* and *Politics*.

ATHANASIUS: (293?–373). Born in Egypt, entered the church at an early age, and became Bishop of Alexandria in 326. He was violently opposed to Arius and the Arian position and often came into conflict with the authorities.

AUGUSTINE, AURELIUS: (354–430). Born at Tagaste in Africa. He became Bishop of Hippo and wrote with great force against all he deemed as heretics. Among his most famous works are the *Confessions* and *City of God*.

BACON, FRANCIS: (1561–1626). Born in London. He rose to great heights in the English government and became lord chancellor. But his venality as a judge caused his downfall and imprisonment. After he was pardoned by the king, he retired to his studies. *The Advancement of Learning* is one of his more famous works.

BACON, ROGER: (1214?–1294). An English scientist and publicist. He is reputed to have invented gunpowder and to have manufactured magnifying glasses.

BASEDOW, JOHANN BERNHARD: (1724–1790). A German educator and teacher who attempted to work out the doctrines of Rousseau in an educational system. He wrote several books for children.

BAYLE, PIERRE: (1647–1706). Applied Descartes' method to the dogmatism of his day and effected reforms in thinking.

BENEDICT, ST.: (480?–543?). Born at Nursia, in the Duchy of Spoleto. He established the famous monastery of Monte Cassino near Naples in 529 and founded the first religious order in the West, the Benedictine order.

BENTHAM, JEREMY: (1748–1832). A distinguished English writer on political economy and jurisprudence. Among his writings is the well-known *Fragment on Government*.

BERGSON, HENRI: (1859–1941). Born in Paris. Was one of the great modern French philosophers and received many honors from the French government. He became a member of the French Academy in 1914. He held several important chairs of philosophy in France. Among his extensive writings are *Matter and Memory, Introduction to Metaphysics,* and *Creative Evolution*.

BERKELEY, GEORGE: (1685–1753). A famous English divine. Born in Ireland and educated at Trinity College,

Dublin. He conceived a plan for converting America to Christianity and set out for the Bermudas to erect a college there, but the project failed because the money which he expected did not come. In 1734 he was made Bishop of Cloyne. Prominent among his works are *A New Theory of Vision* and *Principles of Human Knowledge*.

BODIN, JEAN: (1530–1596). A French jurist. For a time he enjoyed the favor of Henry III, but later forfeited it by defending the rights of the classes and the masses against the king. He was closely allied with the group known as the "Politicians" in France.

BOEHME, JACOB: (1575–1624). An uneducated German cobbler who became famous because of his mystical experiences and his writings dealing with mysticism. One of his important works is *The Signature of All Things*.

BRADLEY, FRANCIS HERBERT: (1846–1924). Born in Glasbury in England and educated at Oxford. Made a fellow of Merton College where he lived for his entire life. He is the author of *Appearance and Reality*.

BRUNO, GIORDANO: (1548?–1600). A member of the Dominican order. He left the order and wandered throughout the world, at last returning to Italy where he was imprisoned by the Inquisition and burned at the stake.

BUBER, MARTIN: (1878–1965). Born in Vienna, Buber was raised in the Orthodox Jewish tradition. Intensely interested in Zionism, he escaped from Nazi Germany, where he had been teaching, to Palestine, in 1938. He was among the first of the former German citizens to resume cultural relations with Germany by accepting the Goethe Prize in 1951. One of his most important books is *I and Thou*.

CAMPANELLA, TOMMASO: (1568–1639). A Dominican monk who was persecuted by the Inquisition. He spent 27 years of his life in prison for ideas which he never attempted to put into practice. *City of the Sun* is one of his major works.

CARNAP, RUDOLF: (1891–1970). Born in Germany. While an instructor at the University of Vienna, he joined Schlick in founding logical positivism in the 1920's. In 1936, he came to the United States, where he was a professor of philosophy at the University of Chicago and at the University of California. His writings are particularly concerned with semantics. Published works include *Introduction to Semantics* and *Logical Foundations of Probability*.

CARNEADES: (213–129 B.C.). The greatest skeptic of the Academy established by Plato.

CICERO, MARCUS TULLIUS: (106–43 B.C.). Born in Arpinum. A Roman orator and statesman. He held many high offices in Rome, fought conspirators, and was eventually murdered by emissaries of Mark Antony. His philosophical works are available in several editions. One of his most important works is *On Orators and Oratory*.

CLEMENT OF ALEXANDRIA: (150?–220?). An early Christian theologian, he was one of the first to attempt to reconcile Platonic and Christian thought. With his famous pupil Origen, he helped make Alexandria a great center of learning. Among his surviving works are *Address to the Greeks* and *Who Is the Rich Man? Who Is Saved?*

COMENIUS, JOHN AMOS: (1592–1670). A great Moravian educator and leader of the religious life of the Moravians. He was persecuted violently but continued in his faith and his educational endeavors. He advocated the "method of nature" in teaching.

COMTE, AUGUSTE: (1798–1857). Born in Montpellier, France, and attended the polytechnic school at Paris. He was well versed in the exact sciences and in mathematics. Among his interesting writings is *Positive Philosophy*.

CROCE, BENEDETTO: (1866–1952). An Italian historian and critic, Croce devoted his life almost exclusively to studying and writing. He was a senator, and later became minister of education. Firmly opposed to Fascism, Croce emerged from retirement in 1943 to become the leader of Italy's Liberal Party. He is the author of *Philosophy of the Spirit*, which is the work presenting his system.

CUMBERLAND, RICHARD: (1631–1718). An English philosopher and churchman. His belief in the principle of universal benevolence opposed him to Hobbes's egoism and led to his being considered the founder of utilitarianism. Principal work: *On Natural Law*.

DEMOCRITUS: (460–370 B.C.). Born at Abdera in Thrace. He traveled widely and wrote many books on science, philosophy, and mathematics.

DESCARTES, RENÉ: (1596–1650). Born in the Touraine, France. Was a soldier and served the armies of the Dutch and the Bavarians. He settled in Holland and there wrote many books which had wide influence throughout the entire world. Among the most significant of these are *A Discourse on Method* and *Meditations on the First Philosophy*.

DEWEY, JOHN: (1859–1952). An outstanding American philosopher. Born in Vermont. He wrote widely on philosophy, education, psychology, political science. Through his writings and lectures he influenced the processes of thought throughout the world. Among his influential works are *Democracy and Education, Experience and Nature*, and *Logic: The Theory of Inquiry*.

ECKHART, MEISTER: (1260?–1327?). A German mystic. Member of the Dominican order. Taught and wrote widely and had great influence as a minister.

EMPEDOCLES: (495?–435? B.C.). Born in Agrigentum, Sicily, the son of a wealthy and public-spirited family. He was a leader of the democratic elements in his city, and is said to have refused the kingship. He was likewise a religious teacher, poet, and physician. He believed that he possessed powers of magic.

EPICURUS: (342?–270 B.C.). Born on the island of Samos of Athenian parents. He taught in many Greek cities and founded a school at Athens where he lived the remainder of his life. His complete *Extant Writings* are available.

ERIGENA, JOHN SCOTUS: (815?–877?). Born in Ireland and educated in Irish schools. Was called by Charles the Bald to head the Schola Palatina at Paris. One of his more important works is *On the Division of Nature*.

FICHTE, JOHANN GOTTLIEB: (1762–1814). Born in Saxony, the son of a poor weaver. Received his education through the generosity of a rich nobleman and rose to fame as a teacher of philosophy and a writer. Was one of the founders of the University of Berlin. Among his writings are *Science of Ethics* and *Science of Rights*.

FROEBEL, FRIEDRICH WILHELM AUGUST: (1782–1852). Born in a small village in the Thuringian forest. Attended the University of Jena and met and studied under some of the greatest minds of his times. Founded the first kindergarten.

GALILEO, G.: (1564–1642). Born in Pisa and educated at Florence. Studied medicine and mathematics. Became famous as an astronomer and invented the first telescope. He came into conflict with the Inquisition but was able to escape death when he promised not to teach that the sun was the center of the universe.

GREEN, THOMAS HILL: (1836–1882). Born in Birkin, Yorkshire. The son of the rector of the parish. Became student at Oxford where he spent the remainder of his life as student and teacher. Was widely interested in education. Had great faith in the common people and in democracy.

GROTIUS, HUGO: (1583–1645). Leader of the aristocratic party in Holland. Born at Delft. Spent most of his life in public office and was several times in conflict with the authorities. Became the Swedish ambassador to Paris in 1635 where he remained until shortly before his death. One of his chief works is *The Law of War and Peace.*

HAMILTON, SIR WILLIAM: (1788–1856). Scottish philosopher. Taught at the University of Edinburgh. He left his library to the University of Glasgow.

HARTLEY, DAVID: (1705–1757). An English physician and philosopher, he founded associational psychology, which holds that the whole mind does not represent a "soul" but is the result of the many different sensations impinging upon it. His principal work is *Observations on Man.*

HEGEL, GEORG WILHELM FRIEDRICH: (1770–1831). Born in Stuttgart and studied theology and philosophy at Tübingen. Served as professor at a number of the great seats of learning such as Jena, Heidelberg, and Berlin. Among his many literary works are *Phenomenology of Mind, Logic,* and *Philosophy of Right.*

HEIDEGGER, MARTIN: (1889–1976). A German philosopher, he was professor at the University of Marburg (1923–28) and at the University of Berlin (1928–33). He is generally regarded as the father of atheistic existentialism. Among his writings is *Existence and Being.*

HERACLITUS: (535?–475? B.C.). Born in Ephesus. Was an aristocrat and had no respect for democracy. He was called "The Obscure" because his writings were hard to understand.

HERBART, JOHANN FRIEDRICH: (1776–1841). A critical German thinker who opposed the entire Idealistic movement. He held many famous chairs of philosophy, including the one made famous by Kant at Königsberg.

HESIOD: (8th cent.? B.C.). Greek poet of whom virtually nothing is known. Possibly a Boeotian farmer, his works include *Works and Days*.

HOBBES, THOMAS: (1588–1679). Studied Scholasticism and the philosophy of Aristotle at Oxford and traveled widely on the continent where he met many of the great minds of his day. After the assembling of the Long Parliament he fled to France in November, 1640, and did not return until he made his peace with Cromwell in 1651. His writings include *Leviathan, Of Liberty and Necessity,* and *On Human Nature.*

HOLBACH, PAUL HENRI THIRY, BARON D': (1723–1789). A French philosopher, one of the Encyclopedists. An opponent of organized religion, he believed that man is innately moral though perverted by society. His principal work is *System of Nature.*

HUME, DAVID: (1711–1776). Born in Edinburgh. Studied law and became Under-Secretary of State in 1767. His fame during his lifetime rested upon his ability as an historian. Among his most important works are *Treatise of Human Nature, Philosophical Essays,* and *Inquiry Concerning Human Understanding.*

HUTCHESON, FRANCIS: (1694–1746). A professor of philosophy at the University of Glasgow from 1729. Hutcheson was an early utilitarian, believing that of man's many senses, the most important is the moral. He was also one of the first to write on the subject of aesthetics. Among his works is the *System of Moral Philosophy*.

JAMES, WILLIAM: (1842–1910). Born in New York City. He was educated in private schools and by tutors in New York, attended the Lawrence Scientific School and was graduated from the Harvard Medical School in 1869. His teaching career included anatomy, physiology, psychology, and philosophy. He taught at Harvard University, University of Edinburgh, and at Oxford. Among his many significant writings are *Pragmatism, The Meaning of Truth,* and *Essays in Radical Empiricism.*

JASPERS, KARL: (1883–1969). A German philosopher and psychologist, he taught philosophy at the University of Heidelberg. One of Germany's leading philosophers, he was associated with the existential movement. Two of his provocative books are *Man in the Modern Age* and *The Question of German Guilt.*

KANT, IMMANUEL: (1724–1804). Born at Königsberg, the son of a saddler. Nearly his entire life as student, teacher, and writer was spent in the town of his birth. His writings influenced the trends of thought as much as those of any philosopher who ever lived. The large body of his written works includes the *Critique of Pure Reason,* the *Critique of Practical Reason,* and the *Critique of Judgment.*

KIERKEGAARD, SØREN: (1813–1855). A Danish philosopher and writer on religious subjects. He had a profound effect on Danish literature as the result of his writings on aesthetics. Many of his ideas were incorporated into existentialism. His writings include *Stages on Life's Way* and *The Gospel of Suffering and The Lilies of the Field.*

LA METTRIE: (1709–1751). The founder of French materialism. For some time he was a military doctor but lost his position because of his materialistic views. He was hounded and persecuted and is believed to have died from poisoning.

LEIBNITZ, GOTTFRIED WILHELM: (1646–1716). Born in Leipzig and studied law, philosophy, and mathematics at Jena. He received his doctorate in law at the age of 20. He served as court councilor and librarian at Hanover until his death. Various editions of his *Philosophical Writings* are available.

LEUCIPPUS: (5th cent. B.C.). Little is known of his life. He is said to have come from Miletus and to have studied with Zeno at Elea. He possibly established the school at Abdera which Democritus made famous.

LOCKE, JOHN: (1632–1704). He studied philosophy, natural science, and medicine at Oxford. For many years he was in the service of the Earl of Shaftesbury as secretary and tutor to his son and grandson. He followed his patron in exile to Holland and returned to England with the rise of William of Orange. He is the author of *On Civil Government*.

LOTZE, RUDOLF HERMANN: (1817–1881). Studied medicine and philosophy at Leipzig and became a teacher of physiology and philosophy at that university. He also taught at Göttingen and at Berlin.

LUTHER, MARTIN: (1483–1546). The leader of the Reformation. While teaching at Wittenberg he challenged the church and was from then on the center of the rebellion against church authority. His written works have been collected several times.

MACHIAVELLI, NICCOLÒ: (1469–1527). An Italian diplomat. Secretary of the Council of Ten at Florence. In later years he was exiled by the Medici. His most famous book is *The Prince*.

MAISTRE, JOSEPH DE: (1753–1821). French writer and diplomat in the service of Sardinia. His great literary skill made his opposition to the French Revolution widely and effectively felt. He believed the world should be ruled entirely by the pope, with no separate civil authorities. His works include *On the Pope* and *Discussions in St. Petersburg*.

MALEBRANCHE, NICOLAS: (1638–1715). A member of the Oratory of Jesus. He sought to harmonize religion and philosophy, the position of Descartes and that of Augustine, but failed so that his works were put on the Index.

MARITAIN, JACQUES: (1882–1973). Raised a Protestant, he became dissatisfied with the values of his upbringing, and joined the Catholic Church in 1906 in his native France. Strongly interested in the writings of St. Thomas Aquinas, Maritain developed and integrated Thomistic principles with everyday life. From 1945 to 1948 he was French Ambassador to the Vatican. Among his important works are *An Introduction to Philosophy* and *Art and Scholasticism*.

MARX, KARL: (1818–1883). Born in Treves, Germany. Widely recognized as the foremost Socialist philosopher and founder of the international Socialist movement.

MILL, JOHN STUART: (1806–1873). Son of James Mill, secretary in the East India Company. His father gave him a special education consisting of much training in philosophy and political science. He also served with the East India Company, and later entered Parliament as a liberal. Some of his most significant books are *On Liberty, Representative Government,* and *Utilitarianism*.

MILTON, JOHN: (1608–1674). English poet and philosopher. He studied at St. Paul's School and at Cambridge. He was appointed foreign secretary to the Council of State in 1649 and later, because of much careful work, became blind. His writings are English classics. One of his most important philosophical works is *Tractate of Education*.

MOORE, GEORGE E.: (1873–1958). An English philosopher, he was professor at Cambridge University. He also was a guest lecturer at many colleges and universities in the United States from 1940 to 1944. A neorealist, his position is similar to that of Bertrand Russell. *Philosophical Studies* is one of his chief works.

NEWTON, SIR ISAAC: (1642–1727). Born at Woolsthorpe in Lincolnshire and educated at Cambridge where he studied mathematics. He made many scientific discoveries and was honored highly by the English government.

NICHOLAS OF CUSA: (1401?–1464). Though a Roman Catholic prelate and cardinal from 1448, Nicholas was a humanist and had an original and critical mind. In 1451, he was made papal legate and traveled widely, preaching and reforming monasteries. But his reforms were not carried through. He anticipated Copernicus in believing that the earth orbits the sun.

NIEBUHR, REINHOLD: (1892–1971). An American theologian, he spent the early years of his ministry as pastor of a church in Detroit, where many of his parishioners were automobile workers with whom he sided in their struggles for better working conditions. A liberal in politics, he adjured many of the liberal theological tenets. Among his many important writings are *Moral Man and Immoral Society*, *The Nature and Destiny of Man*, and *Beyond Tragedy*.

NIETZSCHE, FRIEDRICH WILHELM: (1844–1900). A distinguished German philosopher, born at Rocken near Leipzig. Became a professor of classical philology at Basle. Perhaps his most famous book is *Thus Spake Zarathustra*.

ORIGEN: (185?–254?). A Christian apologist, scholar, and theologian; born in Egypt. At age eighteen, Origen became head of the famous catechetical school of Alexandria, having previously studied under Clement of Alexandria. Later, Origen established his own school at Caesarea. He is reputed to have written 800 works, and he became famous for his exegesis of the scriptures. Among his surviving works are *Commentaries, Homilies,* and *Against Celsus.*

PARACELSUS: (1493?–1541). His real name was Theophrastus of Hohenheim. A leading figure among a group of "wonder men" of the period, men who worked miracles.

PARMENIDES: (5th cent. B.C.). The son of a wealthy Elean family who developed the philosophy of Xenophanes. He was probably a Pythagorean in his early days.

PASCAL, BLAISE: (1623–1662). A gifted mathematician and physicist. He was also influenced by mysticism and sought to combine a mystic religious point of view with the findings of mathematics and science.

PAULSEN, FRIEDRICH: (1846–1908). A German philosopher who presented an idealistic world-view similar to that of Lotze and Fechner. He was widely read in both Germany and the United States.

PELAGIUS: (360?–420?). A celebrated British monk and theologian. His opposition to Augustinian doctrines of predestination and total depravity led to his persecution and banishment from Rome in 418. A heretical sect (Pelagianism) grew from his teachings on the perfectibility of man. He is the author of *On the Trinity, On Free Will,* and *Commentary on Paul's Epistles.*

PESTALOZZI, JOHANN HEINRICH: (1746–1827). Born at Zurich. He was inspired to relieve the suffering of the peasantry about him and made many attempts to educate them and give them better methods of farming and living. His influence on modern education has been wide and deep.

PHILO: (20? B.C.–50? A.D.). Known as "the Jew" or "of Alexandria." He came of a priestly family and wrote widely on historical, political, and ethical matters. He held that Judaism was the sum-total of human wisdom.

PLATO: (427?–347? B.C.). Born the son of noble parents. The greatest pupil of Socrates. He traveled widely, had an independent income, and lived in the highest of style. He was intimate with Dionysius I, the tyrant of Syracuse, and is said to have hoped to establish an ideal state at Syracuse. He founded the Academy in a grove outside of Athens. His extant writings are almost all included in the famous *Dialogues* (of which the *Republic* is one).

PLOTINUS: (205?–270). Born in Lycopolis, Egypt. Studied philosophy under Ammonius Saccas in Alexandria for eleven years. He established a school in Rome soon after 243.

PRIESTLEY, JOSEPH: (1733–1804). A Unitarian natural philosopher. He made great discoveries concerning the properties of fixed air. His sympathies with the French Revolution resulted in his house being wrecked by a mob. After this he fled to the United States and remained here until his death.

PROTAGORAS: (5th cent. B.C.). A famous Sophist, he taught in Athens and was a friend of Pericles. His agnosticism caused his banishment from Athens. He was considered the first to systematize grammar, distinguishing parts of speech, tenses, and moods. One of his most noted works is *On the Gods*.

PYTHAGORAS: (580–500 B.C.). Born in Samos and emigrated to the Greek colonies in Southern Italy about 529. He founded the school of the Pythagoreans, a semi-religious and philosophic sect.

QUINTILIAN: (35?–95?). A Roman rhetorician whose work had great influence in antiquity and in the Renaissance. Among his more famous writings is *Institutes of Oratory*.

RAMUS, PETRUS: (1515–1572). His true French name was Pierre de la Ramee. He was influenced by Vives and attacked the Aristotelian logic as responsible for the barren dialectical methods used in the universities of his time. He attempted to establish a new logic. He was also influential as an educator.

REID, THOMAS: (1710–1796). Leader of the Scottish school in its reaction against the idealism of Berkeley and the skepticism of Hume. He attempted to return to "common sense" in philosophy.

ROSCELIN: (fl. 1092–1119). Scholastic philosopher. He was a canon at Loches and taught Abelard. Considered the founder of nominalism. He was forced to recant his doctrine of the Trinity by a council at Soissons.

ROUSSEAU, JEAN JACQUES: (1712–1778). French philosopher, political theorist, and writer whose colorful and scandalous life has led to many conflicting theories about his personality. Among his more important philosophical writings are *Emile* and *The Social Contract*.

ROYCE, JOSIAH: (1855–1916). Born in Grass Valley, California. Studied at the University of California and at Leipzig, Göttingen, and Johns Hopkins. Though he taught English for a while at the University of California, he spent most of his teaching years as professor of Philosophy at Harvard University. *The Spirit of Modern Philosophy* and *The World and the Individual* are among his major works.

RUSSELL, BERTRAND: (1872–1970). Born at Trelleck, Monmouth, England, and educated at Trinity College, Cambridge. He lectured widely and received many high honors for scholarship. In 1950 he received the Nobel

Prize for Literature. Among his extensive works are *History of Western Philosophy* and *Human Knowledge*. With Alfred North Whitehead he wrote the monumental *Principia Mathematica*.

SAINT-SIMON, CLAUDE HENRI DE ROUVROY, COMTE DE: (1760–1825). French political scientist who conceived the idea of a new society in which there would be equal distribution of property, power, culture, and happiness.

SANTAYANA, GEORGE: (1863–1952). Born in Madrid and graduated from Harvard University. He taught philosophy at Harvard for twenty-two years. Then, from 1912 on, he lived principally in Europe. In 1943 he was elected an honorary member of the American Academy of Arts and Letters. He was a poet and literary critic, as well as a philosopher. He died in Italy. His many important works include *The Realm of Essence* and *Scepticism and Animal Faith*.

SARTRE, JEAN-PAUL: (1905–1980). French novelist and playwright, he is considered the founder of French existentialism. He was imprisoned by the Germans during the early part of World War II, and upon his escape he joined the resistance movement in Paris. Both his philosophical writings and his plays and novels have received international attention and acclaim. Perhaps his philosophy is best stated in *Being and Nothingness*.

SCHELLING, FRIEDRICH WILHELM JOSEPH: (1775–1854). Studied theology at Tübingen and became professor of philosophy at Jena in 1798. He became one of the brilliant circle in which the Romantic movement centered. He was called to Berlin to stem the tide of Hegelian philosophy, but met with little success. Prominent among his major works are *Of Human Freedom* and *Transcendental Idealism*.

SCHLEIERMACHER, FRIEDRICH ERNST DANIEL: (1768–1834). Born in Breslau and received part of his education in the schools of the Moravian brotherhood. After a short stay as student and tutor at Halle, he went to Berlin as minister of Trinity Church. Later he became professor of theology at the University of Berlin.

SCHLICK, MORITZ: (1882–1936). Austrian philosopher. Strongly influenced by Wittgenstein, he joined a discussion group in 1923 called the Vienna Circle, out of which grew logical positivism. He developed a form of psychological hedonism in his book *Problems of Ethics*. Schlick called the principles of logical positivism "standpointlessness."

SCHOPENHAUER, ARTHUR: (1788–1860). Born in Danzig of a banker father and a novelist mother. He refused to enter his father's work, but chose philosophy. He lectured widely but met with little success since other philosophers held the popular ear. This made him bitter, a bitterness which was sweetened slightly in later life as his fame grew. He wrote several books, among them: *The World As Will and Idea* and *Fourfold Root of the Principle of Sufficient Reason*.

SCOTUS, JOHN DUNS: (1265?–1308?). A member of the Franciscan order. After studying at Oxford he became a teacher there and later taught both at Paris and at Cologne.

SHAFTESBURY, LORD: (1671–1713). Moral philosopher and pupil of John Locke. He believed in the essential harmony between egoism and altruism. In ethics, he was the first to apply the term "moral sense" to man's instinctual drive to promote both the general welfare and individual happiness. His collected essays are found in *Characteristics of Men, Manners, Opinions, Times*.

SMITH, ADAM: (1723–1790). Born at Kirkcaldy in Scotland. He studied at Glasgow and at Oxford, but was not at all happy at Oxford. He thought the professors there were narrow-minded. This was because they refused to let him read Hume. His writings in political science have had wide influence. His most famous book is *Wealth of Nations*.

SOCRATES: (469–399 B.C.). Born in Athens, the son of a poor sculptor and a midwife. He lived a most erratic life and never wanted more than the simple necessities. He often went barefoot and dressed in rags to stress simplicity. He married but never had a satisfactory home life. Because his views were considered dangerous by the powerful political leaders of his time, he was condemned to death by the court of Athens and forced to drink a cup of hemlock. These final events are recorded in Plato's *Dialogues*, especially the *Phaedo* and *Apology*.

SPENCER, HERBERT: (1820–1903). Utilitarian philosopher. He was for some time a civil engineer. In London he was intimate with a large circle of literary and philosophic geniuses and was greatly influenced in his work by them. His extensive writings include *Essays on Education, The Man versus the State,* and *A System of Synthetic Philosophy*.

SPINOZA, BARUCH: (1632–1677). He took the name Benedict. Born in Holland, the son of wealthy Portuguese-Jewish parents. Because of his views he was expelled from the synagogue and forced to wander about Europe. He gained a livelihood by grinding lenses. Among his major writings are *Ethics* and *Treatise on the Improvement of Understanding*.

TELESIO, BERNARDINO: (1509–1588). Italian philosopher, born in Milan of noble family. With Bruno and Campanella, Telesio attacked the Aristotelian basis of scholasticism and stressed the importance of knowledge based on empirical scientific inquiry. At Naples he established his Academia Cosentina to further scientific methods of study.

THALES: (640?–546? B.C.). Born in Miletus. Noted as a statesman, mathematician, and astronomer. He is said to have predicted the eclipse of May 28, 585. He is classified as one of the Seven Wise Men of Greece.

TILLICH, PAUL: (1886–1965). A Protestant theologian, Tillich was born in Germany. During World War I he served as field chaplain on the Western Front, and later taught theology and philosophy at Halle, Berlin, Breslau, Dresden, Leipzig, and Frankfort on the Main. After the rise of Hitler, Tillich came to the United States, becoming a citizen in 1940. He taught at Union Theological Seminary and at Harvard University. He is the author of *The Courage to Be* and other works.

UNAMUNO Y JUGA, MIGUEL DE: (1864–1936). A Spanish creative writer and scholar, Unamuno was rector of the University of Salamanca. His outspoken criticism of the monarch, and of the dictator, Primo de Rivera, caused his removal from his post, and later his expulsion from Spain. He remained in exile from 1924 to 1930; thereafter he resided in Spain again. His masterpiece is generally considered to be *The Tragic Sense of Life in Men and Peoples*.

VITTORINO DA FELTRE: (1378–1446). Founder of the famous court school at Mantua which set the pattern for many such schools throughout Europe.

VIVES, LUDOVICO: (1492–1540). Spanish scholar, born Juan Luis Vives at Valencia. After studying and teaching in France, Vives went to England and taught at Oxford. Later, having incurred the displeasure of Henry VIII, he went to Bruges where he wrote most of his major works. Rejecting the authority of Aristotle and scholasticism, Vives published pioneer works on psychology and was one of the first to urge scientific induction as a philosophical and psychological method. One of his major works is *De Anima et Vita*.

VOLTAIRE: (1694–1778). His original name was François Marie Arouet. Born in Paris. He was imprisoned several times for his writings, which include satirical romances and plays as well as philosophical treatises.

WHITEHEAD, ALFRED NORTH: (1861–1947). British mathematician and philosopher, resident in the United States for many years, he criticized positivistic antireligious science. The obscurity of his style and his coinage of new technical terms makes much of his work difficult to understand. He received the Order of Merit in 1945. His writings include *Science and the Modern World* and *Process and Reality*.

WILLIAM OF OCCAM: (1300?–1349). Known as "Doctor Invincibilis" and "Venerabilis Inceptor." An English scholastic philosopher and a member of the Franciscan order. He was first a pupil and then a rival of Duns Scotus. In his *Dialogues*, he laid the foundations for the modern theory of the independence of the secular government from the religious authorities. A vigorous and successful advocate of nominalism.

WITTGENSTEIN, LUDWIG: (1889–1951). Born in Austria, Wittgenstein studied at Cambridge University, England, and returned there to teach in 1929. He became a naturalized British subject in 1938. Although his major work *Tractatus Logico-Philosophicus* led to the founding of the Vienna Circle, and his teaching in the 1930's and 1940's at Cambridge inspired the logical positivists, Wittgenstein felt that his ideas were often misunderstood and distorted by those who claimed to be his disciples. He did not hold with the positivists that statements not verifiable through sense-experience are useless or meaningless. Other published works are *Philosophical Investigations* and *Remarks on the Foundations of Mathematics*.

XENOPHON: (430?–355? B.C.). A Greek historian and disciple of Socrates, his *Memorabilia of Socrates* gives a portrayal of that philosopher that differs markedly from the portrait given by Plato.

ZENO OF ELEA: (490?–430? B.C.). Greek philosopher of the Eleatic school. According to Aristotle, Zeno was the first to employ the dialectical method. He is famous for "Zeno's paradox"—the idea that a moving object could never cover a given distance completely because, after having gone half the way, it must cover half the remaining distance, then half again, and so on, ad infinitum.

ZENO THE STOIC: (336?–264? B.C.). Greek philosopher, founder of Stoicism. He integrated the views of Heraclitus, Plato, and Aristotle into a metaphysical and logical system which supported his ethical theories and program for living.

INDEX

ABOUT THE AUTHOR

S. E. Frost, Jr. (1899–1978) taught in the Department of Education, Brooklyn College, City University of New York. He received a Ph.D. from Columbia University and a Bachelor of Divinity degree from Yale University. He spent many years in the study and teaching of the history and philosophy of education and is the author of a number of books on philosophy, religion, and education.